Flint Faience Tiles A to Z

Margaret Carney, Ph.D.
and Ken Galvas

Schiffer Publishing Ltd
4880 Lower Valley Road, Atglen, PA 19310 USA

Library of Congress Cataloging-in-Publication Data:

Carney, Margaret, 1949-
Flint faience tiles A to Z / by Margaret Carney and Ken Galvas.
p. cm.
ISBN 0-7643-2040-8
1. Flint Faience & Tile Co.—Catalogs. 2. Tiles—Collectors and collecting—Michigan—Flint—Catalogs. 3. Decoration and ornament, Architectural—Michigan—Flint—Catalogs. I. Galvas, Ken. II. Title.
NK4670.7.U53F5832 2004
738.6'09774'37—dc22

2004002558

Designed by John P. Cheek
Cover design by Bruce Waters
Type set in University Roman Bd BT/Korinna BT

ISBN: 0-7643-2040-8
Printed in China
1 2 3 4

Published by Schiffer Publishing Ltd.
4880 Lower Valley Road
Atglen, PA 19310
Phone: (610) 593-1777; Fax: (610) 593-2002
E-mail: Info@schifferbooks.com

For the largest selection of fine reference books on this and related subjects, please visit our web site at
www.schifferbooks.com
We are always looking for people to write books on new and related subjects. If you have an idea for a book please contact us at the above address.

This book may be purchased from the publisher.
Include $3.95 for shipping.
Please try your bookstore first.
You may write for a free catalog.

In Europe, Schiffer books are distributed by
Bushwood Books
6 Marksbury Ave.
Kew Gardens
Surrey TW9 4JF England
Phone: 44 (0) 20 8392-8585; Fax: 44 (0) 20 8392-9876
E-mail: info@bushwoodbooks.co.uk
Free postage in the U.K., Europe; air mail at cost.

Contents

Acknowledgments

Flint Faience tile seems like a small niche in the big tile world, but upon closer examination this subsidiary of AC Spark Plug turns out to be a giant in terms of the variety of tiles produced between 1921-33, the versatility of the product, and the impact it has had on our daily lives. This can be proven by the sheer quantity of people and places who have been involved in making this research and book project a success.

It is difficult to determine who deserves the most credit for the inception of this project. Perhaps we should thank Ken Galvas's parents, because it could be Ken Galvas's genetic makeup that makes him an avid collector of Art Pottery and tiles. Or we could first thank the Tile Heritage Foundation, which not only provided more than one research grant to document Flint Faience tiles from its Doty Research Grant Fund, but whose founders Joseph Taylor and Sheila Menzies additionally serve as command central for anyone wanting to know anything about tile worldwide.

Kristine Burton, granddaughter of Flint Faience & Tile Company Art Director, Howard B. Burton, has been an inspiration during this project. She has shared not only ceramics, photographs, and information about her grandfather, but more importantly has offered valuable insights into sources that were vital to this research.

Mary Jo Bole, professor of ceramics, got me hooked on tiles and the Tile Heritage Foundation while working on documenting the collection at Baggs Memorial Library at the Ohio State University in Columbus.

The collectors, those people who pursue tile that they need to hold in their hands and spend their money for and own, they are special people. Some are dealers, others just collect, share, trade, and enjoy. This list is huge and would include alphabetically Dale and Doris Barrett, Gerard Burnash, Kristine Burton, Diane Dockery, Roger Ellingsworth, Rick Fusco, Jim Graham, Mark and Barb Harris, Phil Henius, Nick Hoffman, Ruth Hylen, Norman Karlson, Vance Koehler (also a curator), Dan Langdon, Andrew Pattison, Rick Reigle, Robert Rozycki, Bill Shesko, and Diane and Dan Veirs. Many thanks to the Estate Sale friends who contacted us when they found items of interest, including Ruth Hylen, Trudys' Antiques, Attic Treasures Liquidators, Kay Thompson, and Dean Bagnall. And special thanks to Jim Graham who loaned us one very precious copy of the 1929 booklet *Architectural Faience: An Introduction*. We breathed a sigh of relief when it was photographed and color copied and safely back to its owner. This is probably a good time to mention that when no specific collection is credited in the captions, the piece is owned by Ken Galvas.

The curators, museum registrars, archivists, historians, and librarians who assisted with access to collections and records and supported this project in every way include Carla Johnson, director of Scholes Library, Elizabeth Gulacsy, art librarian and archivist, Beverly Crowell, librarian, and Mandy Economos, Visual Resources librarian at Scholes Library of Ceramics at the New York State College of Ceramics at Alfred University in Alfred, New York, and Susan Kowalczyk, and Karen Enke, at the ceramics museum at the New York State College of Ceramics; Vance Koehler, curator at the Moravian Tile Works, who provided inspiration, scholarship, images and more; Susan Tunick, president of Friends of Terra Cotta in New York; Dave Larzelere, librarian at the *Flint Journal*; Mercedea Shriver, team librarian and local history expert at the Flint Public Library; Jim Johnson, associate director, Jeff Taylor, curator of collections, Pat Schierup and Andy Clark, both curatorial assistants at the Sloan Museum in Flint; Cynthia Altman, curator, Kykuit Collections and Michele Hiltzik, archivist at the Rockefeller Archive Center and Bertha Saunders and Patricia Higgins, also connected with the Rockefellers and the Playhouse at Kykuit, Poncantico Hills, New York; Betty Sanchez at the Archives at the Cenacle Retreat Center in Lake Ronkonkoma, New York; Josephine Shea, curator at the Edsel and Eleanor Ford House in Grosse Pointe Shores, Michigan; Bob Pence and Jean Bready at the Villa St. Elizabeth in Reading, Pennsylvania; Barbara Spaulding at the Genesee County Historical Society in Flint, Michigan; Lianne Hartman, graduate research assistant at the Bentley Historical Library in Ann Arbor; and Mike Flanagan at the Everson Museum of Art, who sent copies of documents pertaining to their handsome collection in Syracuse, New York.

Many other friends shared time and stories with us in our constant search for knowledge. They would include Charlie White, Jason Mickus, Mose Mesre, Andrew

Lopez, Wendy Harvey and Sandie Fowler, Betty Ward, Beth Starbuck, David Ellison, Richard Rademacher, Karen Guido, John Sekora, Bill Wolf, and Fred Kennard.

This project would not have been successful without the owners of property with Flint Faience tile installations or those who are in charge of these spaces, especially several realtors, who allowed us access to installations to document and photograph these tile wonders. They shared their special fireplaces, floors, bathrooms, kitchens, fountains, kindergarten sandboxes, theatres, swimming pools, and more with us. They allowed us to visit, phone, e-mail, and bother them on Sundays, nighttimes, and always via the Internet. Special thanks to realtors Grant Hamady and Maryanne Tremaine; Barry Copple who allowed access to the Warner Theatre in Erie, Pennsylvania; Father Fred Taggart who came to my rescue when I tripped the alarm at St. Matthew's Catholic Church in Flint; Linda Wallner, in charge of leasing at the Dryden East in New York City, who went to the trouble to find some remaining Flint Faience tiles in the basement after my first visit and Mario, the building super, who gave me access and left me alone with the magical tiles; Elaine R. Normile, historian with the Renaissance Vinoy Resort and Golf Club in St. Petersburg, Florida; Terry Bragg, historian with the McLean Hospital in Belmont, Massachusetts; Andrea M. Lynch, Director of Sales for the Hotel San Carlos in New York City, who let me wander through the renovation/construction site at my leisure; Janet Ryan, one of the Sisters of the Immaculate Heart of Mary who extended an invitation for us to visit and photograph their site in Monroe, Michigan; Marguerite Delacoma and Bob Shonk who live in the Park Gables Apartments in Chicago and rephotographed the stunning swimming pool; Stephen and Rosanne Heddy, Kevin and Cynthia Godin, Ken and Susan Kayser, Michael and Maryann Manley, Rex and Peggy Blackwell, J.D. and Ronee Winegarden, Jim Fitzell and Jessica Higgins, Mindy and Nate Kestenman, Drs. Srinkzas Mukkamula and Nita Kulkarnia, and Linda and Joseph Katrinic, Jr., who all graciously opened their homes to us, thus helping us to understand the diversity of the tile production; Bruce Zaretsky who owns the Warwick Masonic Lodge building in Warwick, New York, and sent photographs via the Internet; and Sue Gardner, local history librarian who researched the history of the Warwick Lodge. Others who opened the doors that allowed us to photograph the churches, universities, schools, hotels, factories, and homes include Maryann Dover and Micheal Pariza of Boxer Properties; Dorothy Muelman of Bank One; Laren Wood of the Birmingham Department of Public Works; Mark Coir and Brian Schiller of Cranbrook; Mena Cox of Delphi East; Larry Dokham, Pat Perna, and Al Kobisar of Dearborn Henry Ford Elementary School; Michelle Schuff of the Fox Theatre in Atlanta; Mary Thorson and Mona Austin of the Garfield Elementary School in Wyandotte, Michigan; Bill Thomas and Carolyn Harrison of Halo Burger in Flint, Michigan; Ramon Rangel of the U.S. Customs House in San Juan, Puerto Rico; Mary Ellen Brayton and Edward Rosas of St. Pauls Church in Grosse Pointe, Michigan; Elaine Normaile and Dennis Lesko of the Renaissance Vinoy Resort and Golf Club in St. Petersburg, Florida; Father Mark Henniger S.J. and Father Gary Wright S.J. of the University of Detroit Mercy; Janice Garrison of the Washington Elementary School in Wyandotte, Michigan; Victoria Brown of Strategic Security; Julie Truettner of the University of Michigan; Pat Kildea-Jones, who ran numerous errands; Adam Goldberg and Dr. Dan Goldberg; May Mulla, Community Relations Coordinator, Lakeshore Public Schools; and, of course, to all the rest of our helpful friends who wish to remain anonymous.

There were many others who assisted with this project – photographers, colleagues, and dear friends enlisted for various reasons, including photographers of the caliber of Brian Oglesbee who photographed the Alfred tiles, Theresa Johnson who used to occupy the office where the Alfred tiles were originally installed; Dave Hodgkin who photographed the mint set of Dryden tiles; my friend Ruth Pyne who, on very short notice, drove to Worcester, Massachusetts to photograph the Melville Shoe Corporation tile panel; Linda Huey and David Dronsick whose film and camera left blanks but fond memories of their photographic efforts, also of the Melville Shoe Corporation; Jeff Johnson, head of the physical plant at the New York State College of Ceramics at Alfred University who searched through architectural drawings to no avail; Philip Baker who tried to find where the tiles had gone in the Mayflower Hotel in Washington, D.C. and introduced me to Jim Graham; George Frankfield who gave us a lead on the old Durant Hotel in Flint;

A special thank you to Yvonne Galvas, who provided much support and encouragement along with countless behind-the-scenes errands. Lindsey and Jonathan Galvas deserve a big Thank You for sharing their computer time with dad.

Once again, heartfelt thanks to Bill Walker, life partner, creative force, and editor, who contributed his valuable time to keep the car headed in the right direction on road trips to document installations, photograph collections, and who kept his sense of humor in time to edit crud from this manuscript as well as invent computer programs to label photographic materials. Xima provided extra inspiration, while Libby provided a warm lap, and Luna provided diversion from computer monotony.

Thank you to Schiffer Publishing for allowing this project to move from research project and collector fanaticism to a finished book and for the good sense to allow us to work with Donna S. Baker, the best in her field.

Margaret Carney
Ken Galvas

Introduction

The use of hyperbole was evidently not discouraged in the promotion and marketing of the tile industry in the United States in the late 1920s. One manufacturer, Flint Faience & Tile Company, boasted that "Ordinarily one thinks of tiles only for bathrooms or floors, but there are more than 5,000 uses for Faience tile, including: Floors, sidewalls, vestibules, entrances of the home, automobile showrooms, hotel lobbies, store entrances, foyers, corridors, swimming pools, lavatories, sun porches, dens, kitchens, mantels, fireplaces, fountains, etc." (AC Spark Plug Company, 1929, 3) While listing less than twenty of the 5,000 uses for Faience tiles, this still remains a dramatic argument. Another tile protagonist wrote, "At the siege of Argos in the year 272 B.C., a tile fragment thrown from a housetop slew the battling King of Epirus. Thus tile played an important part in history." (McGinnis, 1930, 26) This proves there is tile history and then there is tile *history*.

2,193 years after the tile-induced demise of the king of Epirus and more than 80 years ago, Flint Faience Tile Company was founded as a subsidiary of AC Spark Plug. While the history of Flint Faience Tile Company was brief, 1921-1933, the emergence and evolution of the Company is a fascinating one, connected to such easily recognizable household names as Albert Champion, Amelia Earhart, Edsel Ford, John D. Rockefeller, and more. Literally, the story takes one from sparkplugs to palaces and back again.

While tile use began in ancient times, at least as early as the 14th century B.C. in Egypt, it was during the 1920s and '30s that there was a resurgence of interest in art tile in the United States. It is exactly during this time period that Flint Faience Tile Company came into existence and then vanished. Before that story unfolds, it is helpful to have an understanding of some of the pertinent terminology, such as "faience" (pronounced FAY-onse). The term is derived from the town of Faenza in Italy where faience is said to have originated in the 15th century. While the term faience historically describes tin-glazed earthenware, prior to the Great Depression the term "faience" was a popular buzzword in homes and industry. In the tile world, it described tiles with a handmade *look*, glazed and decorated with a rustic flavor.

Whatever one may think of the terms "faience" or "tile" today, through historic literature one knows exactly how the ceramic tile experts explained and promoted these materials during the time of peak ceramic tile production in the United States – in the late 1920s and early 1930s. "Tile is burned clay..." wrote one author, but "Certain materials called tiles are not tiles," including

Co-authors Ken Galvas and Margaret Carney seated in the University of Detroit Mercy Faculty Building large parlor in May 2003. Note the stunning Flint Faience tile floor. Photo by William J. Walker, Jr. *Courtesy of the Jesuit Community at the University of Detroit Mercy.*

substitute materials such as "rubber, cement, linoleum, painted sheet iron, and a score of building board compositions." (McGinnis, 1930, 26) The distinction between the "burned clay product" that is "as durable a building material as any produced by either natural or artificial means" (McGinnis, 1930, 26-27) and the resulting innuendo concerning the "substitutes" leaves little room for debate. Among these burned clay products or tiles, faience is given star billing. "Faience is the name for a unique group of tiles and represents the highest in grade and cost. It is the aristocrat of tiledom." (McGinnis, 1930, 26)

Many of the estimated seventy-five tile companies (Koehler, 1996/1997, 21, 24) operating during this time in the United States created tiles that were often recognizable and attributable to specific manufacturers without viewing back stamps. Flint Faience is an exception, producing several tile lines, all either hand-made or with a hand-made look, but some also subject to the whim or genius of the designer. It is this versatility of Flint Faience that will remind the avid tile collector why they have focused on this company and it is this same versatility that will attract the novice tile collector to seek out all the gems created in Flint, Michigan.

History of Flint Faience Tiles: The Automotive Connection

Albert Champion.

How many other tiles companies grew in the womb of a spark plug company? In 1921, the Flint Faience & Tile Company was organized as a subsidiary of the Champion Ignition Company, which later became the AC Spark Plug Co., located in Flint, Michigan, where it had been in operation since being incorporated on October 26, 1908. The history of the parent company – AC Spark Plug Division, General Motors Corporation, is well documented. The founder of the business was the European bicycle-racing competitor, Frenchman Albert Champion (April 2, 1878-October 28, 1927), who came to the United States in 1899. He formed the Champion Spark Plug Co. in 1905 in Boston, assembling the first spark plugs in this country using insulators imported from France. Disagreements with his financial backers caused Albert Champion to begin anew in Flint, Michigan, establishing on October 26, 1908 the Champion Ignition Company with the financial sponsorship of W.C. Durant. Durant was "famous for his financial promotions in the early automobile days" (McDougal, 1949, 445) and founded the General Motors Company earlier that year. Champion's associate in the business was Albert Schmidt, also a native of France. Albert Champion remained the general manager when Champion Ignition was purchased by Buick in 1910 and began to operate as a subsidiary of General Motors. The French insulator bodies were utilized until the 1914 invasion of France by Germany, when there was a threatened interruption of supply to Flint. Thus the Flint, Michigan plant began a dialogue with engineers at the Ohio State University and elsewhere (those consulted included Arthur W. Watts, Taine G. McDougal, and Karl Schwartzwalder) and began producing their own U.S. made insulator body.

Both history and legend tell the story of the tile company coming into existence because AC Spark Plug wanted to more fully utilize the spark plug kilns that were idle during part of the production process. The April 1929 issue of *AC Sparks* noted that "AC with its years of experience in making spark plugs was in an ideal position to sponsor manufacture of Faience tile. Its large staffs of ceramic experts, research engineers and other technicians fitted into the situation nicely, as did its modern machinery and tunnel kilns." (AC Spark Plug Company, 1929, 5) The history of Champion Ignition is intertwined with the creation of the Flint Faience Tile Company, in not only concept and ownership, but also from the composition of the tile body. It has been written that the tile company's origins can be credited to a casual visit by Belgian ceramic artist Carl Bergmans to Flint in 1925. (McDougal, 1949, 449) This same version of history notes that "...in consequence of an hour's conversation in French with Champion the Flint Faience and Tile Co. was launched as another AC enterprise." (McDougal, 1949, 449) While the date of inception of the tile company was actually four years earlier, in 1921 (AC Spark Plug Company, 1929, 5), the report by Taine McDougal (1889-1975), a ceramic engineer who worked at AC Spark Plug Division for forty years (retiring in 1954 as director of spark plug engineering at AC Spark Plug) accurately reports that the tile body was shipped from the Zanesville, Ohio area and mixed with grog from

The original sign above the entranceway of the Dort Highway plant.

crushed spent refractories of the spark plug manufacture. (McDougal, 1949, 449)

Carl Bergmans became the first head designer at Flint Faience Tile Company. He hired designer Julio Haro in 1921. More information about the Flint Faience designers, decorators, and other employees can be found in the A-Z guide under Employees as well as under individual names. Bergmans was associated with Flint Faience for five years.

In February 1922, Champion Ignition Co. changed its name to AC Spark Plug Co., with the AC standing for founder Albert Champion's initials. This name change was to assist in avoiding confusion with the company's competitor, the Champion Spark Plug Co., of Toledo, Ohio. In August 1926, *Ceramic Industry* reported that the Flint Faience & Tile Company on North Industrial Avenue was incorporated with capital stock of $10,000. (*Ceramic Industry*, 1926, 158) The tile plant was initiated in a building on Harriet Street adjacent to the main plant in Flint, Michigan. As it outgrew its quarters, a new and more spacious plant was erected on Davison Road and Dort Highway in 1928. In April 1929, in their publication *AC Sparks*, the company announced that "the increasing demand for Flint Faience recently made it necessary to virtually double the capacity" of their "tile plant and another modern tunnel kiln, and more loading dock space have been added together with other modern facilities." (AC Spark Plug Company, 1929, 7) Albert Champion died in 1927 and Basil W. deGuichard succeeded him as president until November 1929, when General Motors acquired the remaining stock from the Champion estate; with that twenty-five percent interest it became a Division of General Motors. Harlow H. Curtice, AC's comptroller and *Time Magazine's* 1955 "Man of the Year," then took over as general manager. He was among the leaders who in 1933 decided that since the tile business was foreign to the automotive field, it should be dropped. Other sources note that Flint Faience & Tile Company closed because the company now needed the kiln space to fire more spark plugs.

Tiles surrounding the old employees' entrance.

Detail of one of the accent tiles adorning the entrance wall. 9" x 9".

Detail of the raised line tiles that surround the employees' entrance.

At its peak, in addition to the main office and factory in Flint, the Flint Faience and Tile Co. had district offices on Park Avenue in New York City, in the Tribune Tower in Chicago, and in Detroit; Boston; Cleveland; Atlanta, Georgia; and Birmingham, Alabama. In 1932, through an agreement with the National Tile Company of Anderson, Indiana, Flint Faience expanded its sales facilities to include district offices in Los Angeles; St. Louis; San Francisco; Ardmore, Pennsylvania; West Roxbury, Massachusetts; Indianapolis; Philadelphia; Pittsburgh; Louisville; and Stamford, Connecticut. (*Flint Daily News/Flint Journal*, 1932, n.p.)

ENTRANCES, vestibules, lobbies, waiting rooms, corridors, even large display rooms—*spaces of utility and of show*—can be made charmingly attractive with Flint Faience and Vitrocraft (unglazed) tiles. At the same time the upkeep cost is established on a minimum basis.

Faience with its glass-like surface and Vitrocraft with its impervious vitrified body absorb no stains, while surface dirt can be easily brushed or wiped away, restoring the original brilliance of the installation.

The thick, heavy "bisque" or body of both Flint Faience and Vitrocraft withstands impact and the hand-roughened back enables the cement to grip the tiles strongly into the very structure of the building.

The Flint Faience Tile Company showroom from *Floor Flyer A-304. Courtesy of the Archives, New York State College of Ceramics at Alfred University.*

Identification and Marks

Collectors should not have many problems identifying the tiles produced by Flint Faience. The company was very diligent in signing its work. The majority of the tiles found in the marketplace today bear one of the many signatures used by this company. The most common of these signatures is the large 3" impressed, "Flint Faience Tile Co. Flint Michigan". This mark is used on all of the larger, 6" and above, tiles. On many of the tiles smaller than 6" a partial impression of this mark is found. This is the result of the stamps being impressed into the full size 15" tile sections that were later cut up into the smaller sizes needed for production. Other marks used would be a smaller 1.5" high mark, "Flint Tile Co Flint Mich." This was generally found on utilitarian items such as bookends, paperweights, and ashtrays. The third mark was common among the dry pressed ceramic tile that was made at Flint Faience. It was a raised arrowhead in the center of six raised lines. Many of the smaller, 3" and under tiles would have a "Flint F&T Co" mark. Also found on many of these smaller tiles was the word "Flintcraft." Some of the items produced, meant for utilitarian use, would be covered with a felt at the factory and then ink stamped with a "Flint Faience Tile Co" dye. A smaller ink stamp of "Flint Faience Tile Co" has been found marking the sides of tiles that were used in salesman sample boxes. These boxes would have samples of tiles mounted on a piece of wood with at least one tile removable, so that the salesman could explain the construction process to the potential customer.

Although not necessarily a mark, many Flint Faience tiles also bear a series of incised lines on the backs of the tiles. These appear to be made with a large comb like tool to give the tile additional grip in the installation process. Judging from the irregularity of direction of these lines it can be assumed that they were done by someone in the plant and not by machine.

Numbers are found on many of the Flint tile backs. Most of these are a series of four digits with a dash mark and another digit. These are the design numbers and would match those found in the catalogs that were used at the time. These numbers would be either impressed or painted on with a black material. Occasionally a 1" high number between one and five is found to be impressed into the clay. The significance of this is unknown at this time.

Other than the standard company marks, we find several examples of personal markings. Company materials do mention that workers could buy sample tiles for their own personal use. In order to help keep the tiles they wanted for themselves separate from those intended for installations, the workers would mark the tile. By doing this they could cull the tile they wanted to buy from the day's production. The cost of the tiles would then be deducted from their weekly pay. An example of such a tile is the 6" round trivet signed "E.I." on the back, which came from the estate of Eula Irish. Another example would be the cute Egyptian looking tile that came from the estate of Julio Haro, art director at Flint Faience. The last example shown here is a 4.25" tile on an "Arowa" blank of young girl in a sailor outfit. It is signed "E.I." and also came from the estate of Eula Irish. Other personalized tiles can be seen in the entry called "To My Mother" in the A to Z portion of this book.

3" Flint Faience backstamp on 6" tile.

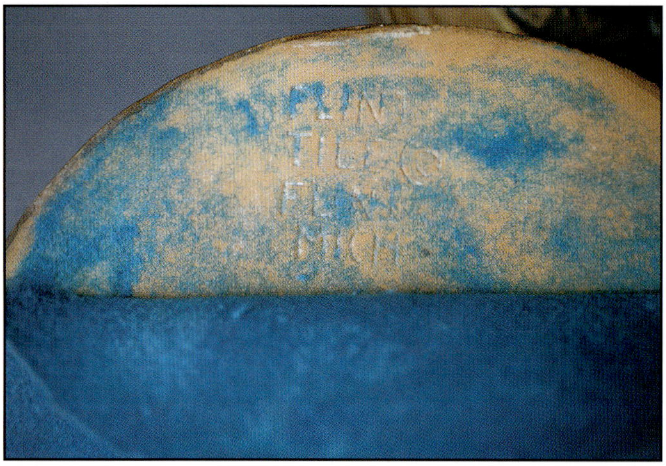

1.5" Flint Faience Tile Co. backstamp found on some bookends.

Arrowhead backstamp found on dry pressed tile.

"Flintcraft" back stamp.

Ink backstamp on protective felt backing found on paperweights.

Composition

The clay tile produced in Flint is similar in appearance to tiles produced at many of the Ohio factories working during this period. This is a direct result of the fact that Flint imported the raw clay from the Zanesville, Ohio area. The clay from the Zanesville area was plentiful, and Carl Bergmans, the chief ceramist, was very familiar with its composition. He had developed many glaze formulas that were compatible with it while working in the Zanesville area. It could be reasoned that starting a new company in an area not known for tile production would be much simpler for Bergmans if he were to start off with a clay body he was accustomed to. The one change that was somewhat unique to the Flint factory was that in Flint, spent spark plug refractories were ground up and mixed with the clay to act as a binder. This could have been one of General Motor's earliest recycling projects.

The result of this mixture gives Flint tile a somewhat coarse appearance. The light yellowish tan color is retained after the mixing with the ground up refractories. The vast majority of tiles produced in Flint have this yellowish tan color. The dry pressed tiles have a lighter tan, almost a white, clay body. While these colors of clay appear to be the norm, a couple of tiles have been found with a coarse red clay body. This variation was used with a cream colored over-glaze in both instances. This variation seems to be somewhat rare.

The size and thickness of the tiles is as varied as the many uses for which they were intended. Sizes have been found from one inch up to fifteen inches across. Shapes were only limited by the imagination. One installation found had as many as eighty different shapes making up the tile mosaic designs.

Large "Vitrocraft" tile. 12.25" in diameter.
Courtesy of the Alfred P. Sloan Museum.

Product Types

The Flint Faience Tile Company liked to advertise their ability to create whatever the customer wanted – your dream was their job to fulfill. This wish to please customers led to many unique and wonderful variations of tile, from intricate floor tile patterns with stock designed molded insert tile to carved one-of-a-kind tile for the family crest. Flint wanted to bring your dreams to life. Most of these works of art were created in their raised line process; Flint seemed to be most comfortable in the use of this technique and it is generally the most popular style with collectors of Flint Faience. Raised line process began with the creation of a watercolor of the intended subject, which was then placed over the tile while in its plastic, or unfired state. The artist or artisan would then take a pin and perforate the watercolor along the edges of the design. When the entire picture was

"Vitrocraft" backstamp. Note the impressed number 4. The significance of this number is unknown at this time.

perforated, the watercolor was removed to reveal the design underneath. The artist would then take a tube of the raised line material and proceed to outline the perforated lines by squeezing the material through the tube, similar to a tube of toothpaste. Colors of glaze were then applied to the areas between the raised lines. If more than one example of the tile were to be made, the artist would use the same watercolor with the perforations and lay it on the next tile. He would then sprinkle powdered graphite on the paper allowing it to fall through the perforations, thus leaving the design on the tile. The raised line material would then be applied to this tile. The fact that Flint used a fine nozzle for the raised line material gave it a distinctive look – the raised line tiles produced at Flint Faience have a much finer line than those produced by their competitors. The lines are lower in profile than most of those produced by others' manufacture. This difference in profile helps the artwork blend with the subject matter in a way that does not detract from the intended purpose. This subtle difference helps give Flint tiles a look of their own.

Flint Faience also used the services of artists skilled in the technique of carving tiles. Although they are not as plentiful as raised line tiles there are plenty around. Much rarer are sculpted figures. We know from previously printed articles that modelers such as Karla Lind were employed to create figures for churches and schools. To date, however, we have not found any signed examples. Modelers did create the molds used for the production of stock tiles. These production insert tiles seem to be varied and plentiful.

Raised line design trivet. 6". $125-150.

"E. I.," Eula Irish, signature on back of the raised line design trivet. 6".

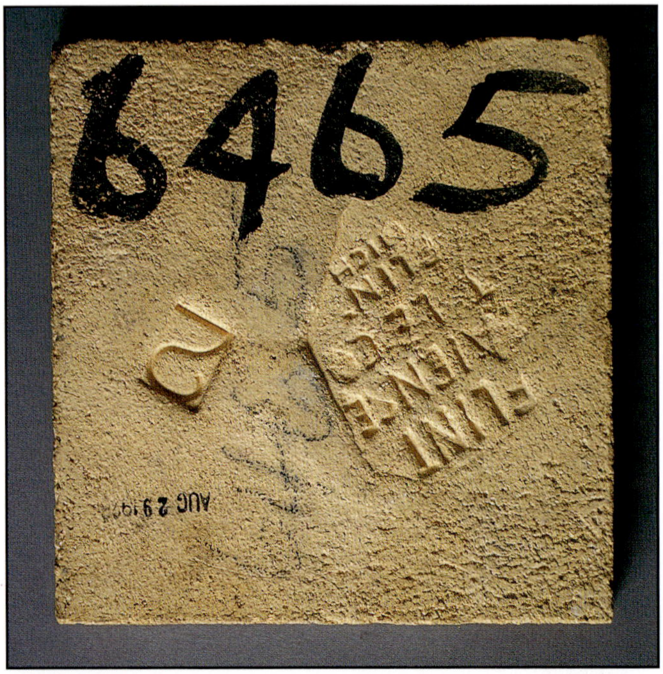

Factory design number in black. Note the impressed number 2. The significance of this impressed number is unknown at this time.

Pre-Columbian figure paperweight. 2.4" x 2.4". *Courtesy of Ruth Hylen.*

"Little Girl" tile in raised line design on an Arowa blank. 4.25" x 4.25". $250-300.

"Julio Haro" signature of the back of the Pre-Columbian paperweight. *Courtesy of Ruth Hylen.*

"E. I." (Eula Irish) signature on the back of the "Little Girl" tile.

Tables and Metalwork

Flint Faience produced a variety of wrought iron tables with tiled tops. These tables have not shown up in any of the catalogs that we have to date. It is also unclear if the tables were sold through the showrooms or made exclusively for specific installations. The question of identifying an original Flint Faience tile top table is further clouded by the fact that many wrought iron tables have been surfaced with vintage Flint tiles that were not original to the bases. To determine whether a table is original or a later creation, we must look at the characteristics that are consistent with the original factory table frames.

The first of these characteristic features is that the Flint tables were made with square rod for the legs. This rod was usually 3/8" or 1/2" square. Secondly, this rod was riveted to the bottom of the frame rather than welded. Next, the tile frame was made of an angle iron that is least 1" wide on top and bottom. The foot of the table is going to have a full turn of the square rod. Somewhere in the frame of all tables we have seen to date, there is twist of the square rod. The length of the twist has been consistent at 6" in length. Lastly, the finish on all original tables we have seen to date is a low sheen black. These features in the absence of signed examples are our best gauge as to what may have been made at the factory and what may have been made "after market."

Wrought iron fireplace screens have also shown up in the marketplace with many of the same identifying points.

Foot detail on wrought iron table.

Rivet detail on "Blue Vase" tile table.

Metal twist detail on "Blue Vase" tile table.

A to Z

Agriculture – Egypt

Agriculture in Egypt as seen in the 1929 Flint Faience publication *Architectural Faience: An Introduction. Courtesy of Jim Graham.*

Agriculture – Egypt is the title of one of a series of allegorical panels designed by Flint Faience & Tile Co. art director and architect, Howard B. Burton, and executed for the Wheatsworth Company in Hamburg, New Jersey. Two identical panels of this subject can still be seen today at the Wheatsworth Mill site. Another identical panel is currently on display on a deep stairwell wall in Plant 3 at the former AC Spark Plug (now Delphi) facility in Flint, Michigan. Either this same tile panel or still another identical one was in the possession of the American Ceramic Society at its headquarters in Columbus, Ohio circa 1930, as shown by a photograph published in the Vol. 9, No. 3, March, 1930, p. 63 issue of the *Bulletin of the American Ceramic Society*. It was illustrated more than any other Flint Faience mural, including in a black and white photograph on page 6 of their 1929 trade publication *Architectural Faience: An Introduction* and on page 7 of the April 1929 issue of *AC Sparks*.

A photograph showing the *Agriculture in Egypt* panel at the American Ceramic Society headquarters in Columbus, Ohio, c. 1930.

Agriculture in Egypt panel now on display in a stairwell of the Delphi East Plant 3.
Courtesy of the Delphi Corporation, Flint, Michigan.

Agriculture in Egypt mural as seen in the April 1929 issue of *AC Sparks. Photograph courtesy of the Archives, New York State College of Ceramics at Alfred University.*

Anadyomene

see Flintcraft

Animals

see also Bears and Fireplaces

Tiles with animal decorations, many with raised line designs and others modeled, were popular creations of Flint Faience Tile. These tiles depicting bears, cats, dogs, donkeys, elephants, foxes, giraffes, horses, llamas, pigs, pumas, rabbits, squirrels, wolverines, etc. can be found in groupings in many installations or as individual tiles in private collections. Unusual among these is a charming 2.875" square tile of a donkey, perhaps at a manger, with the name "Floyd Wilbur" underglazed on the bottom section of the face of the tile. Who Floyd Wilbur was remains a mystery.

"Floyd Wilbur" tile executed in raised line design. 2.875" x 2.875". $200-250.

Many of the animal tiles were standard and available through the company's catalogs. For instance, the 2.75" x 2.75" squirrel tile, no. 6671, illustrated on page 23 of *Catalog "G"* as raised line, can also be seen in the collection of Ken Galvas as embossed. The same stock design squirrel tile, intended to be used as an insert tile, can be seen installed in the façade of the E&B Brewery in Detroit, Michigan. The Brewery squirrel is unglazed bisque tile, somewhat worn and faded from outdoor conditions over decades.

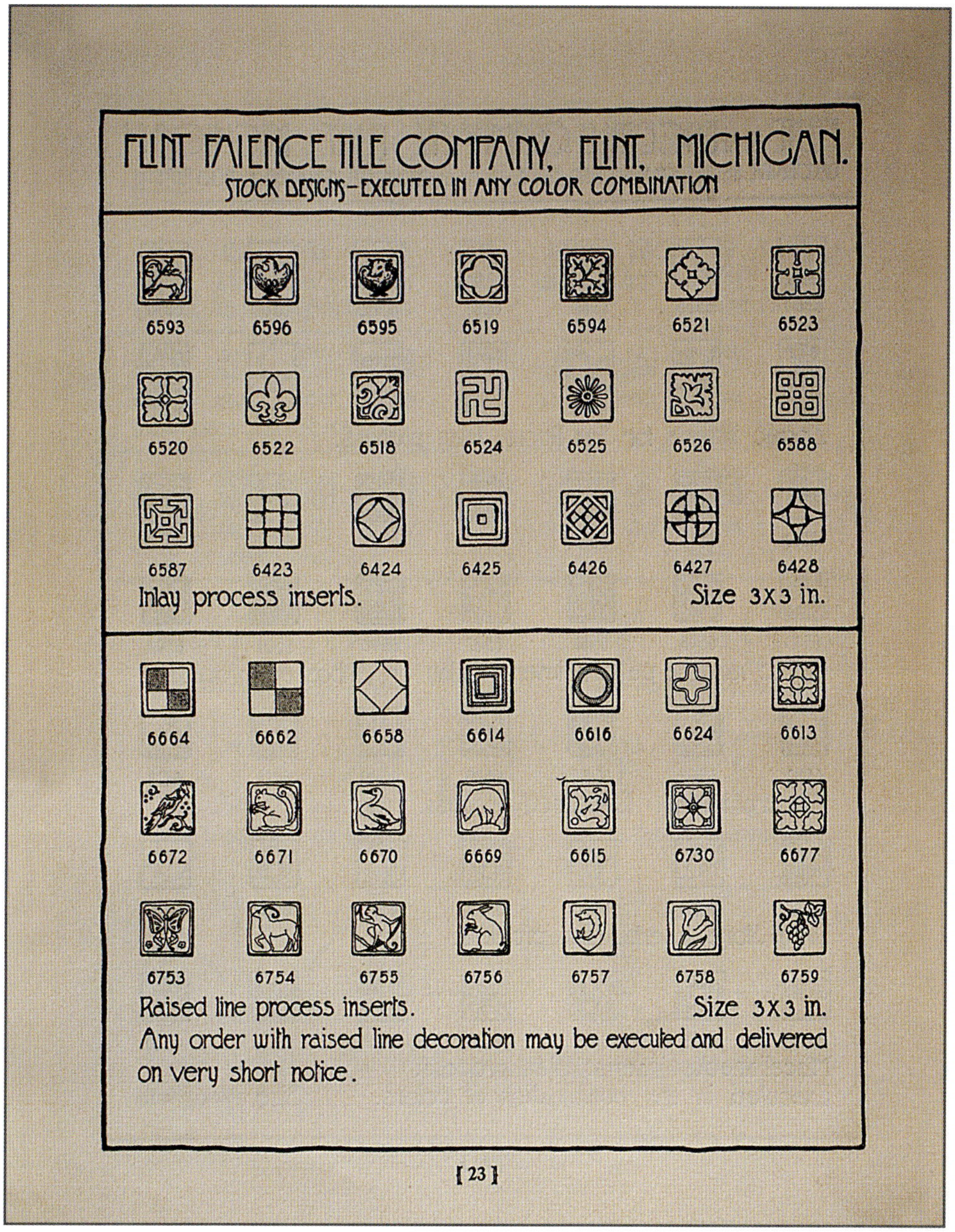

FLINT FAIENCE TILE COMPANY, FLINT, MICHIGAN.
STOCK DESIGNS—EXECUTED IN ANY COLOR COMBINATION

6593 6596 6595 6519 6594 6521 6523
6520 6522 6518 6524 6525 6526 6588
6587 6423 6424 6425 6426 6427 6428

Inlay process inserts. Size 3x3 in.

6664 6662 6658 6614 6616 6624 6613
6672 6671 6670 6669 6615 6730 6677
6753 6754 6755 6756 6757 6758 6759

Raised line process inserts. Size 3x3 in.
Any order with raised line decoration may be executed and delivered on very short notice.

[23]

Animal motif insert tiles illustrated on page 23 of *Catalog "G."*

Squirrel tile. 2.75" x 2.75". $50-75.

Bisque squirrel tile installed in the exterior of the E&B Brewery in Detroit, Michigan.

A few tiles did not follow standard geometric forms such as square, rectangular, hexagonal or round. One example that stands out from the rest is the cut-out form of a dog. One of these sweet puppies is a 3.25" x 4" cut-out dog tile in the collection of Roger Ellingsworth. It is similar to, but not an exact match with the one in the collection of Ken Galvas. Other puppies follow the standard square format, including a beige seated puppy design on the 3" square tile in the collection of Roger Ellingsworth. Another decorated tile depicts a charismatic pup with a collar and black eye, 4.25" square, from the Galvas collection.

Black-Eyed puppy. 4.25" x 4.25". $200-250.

Cut out of a dog figure executed in raised line design. 3.25" x 4". *Courtesy of Roger Ellingsworth*. $350-450.

The fireplace facing in room 103, the kindergarten room, at the Henry Ford Elementary School in Dearborn, Michigan contains 32 insert tiles, all 2.75" square. Each depicts some variety of animal or bird, including at least one wolverine, myna bird, snail, camel, ram, kangaroo, puma, tiger, porcupine, tiger, donkey, goat, fox, bear, vulture, woodpecker, parrot, hippopotamus, penguin, coyote, kingfisher, elephant, pigeon, and llama. For a complete view of the fireplace facing, see entry under Fireplaces.

Golden Retriever puppy executed in raised line design. 3" x 3". *Courtesy of Roger Ellingsworth*. $150-200.

Details of the Henry Ford Elementary School fireplace, showing various animal tiles.

There are so many charming Flint Faience tiles with animals of all sizes and shapes and species that the number of these tiles in installations and in private collections is too numerous to calculate. An alphabetical sampling would include a 3" x 3" black cat on a cream background in the Roger Ellingsworth collection, a 6" square elephant installed on the fountain/sink/sandbox area in the kindergarten room at the John Marshall School in Detroit, two similar stock design no. 6760, 6" x 6" elephant tiles in private collections, a 3" x 3" fox in the Roger Ellingsworth collection (similar to those in the Henry Ford School fireplace), a 6" square giraffe from the fountain/sink/sandbox installation in the kindergarten room at the John Marshall School in Detroit, as well as the same stock design no. 6718, 6" x 6" in an anonymous collection, a chocolate colored horse done in 3" square tile from the collection of Roger Ellingsworth, a magnificent 6" square amber lion on a black glazed background also at the John Marshall School, as well as another stock design no. 6721 green and brown lion on a lavender background in the Barrett collection, a 6" tile depicting a gentle llama (stock design no. 6719) on an eggshell background installed in the John Marshall School kindergarten room, a related stock design no. 6412 llama tile

Elephant tile. 6" x 6". Executed in raised line, stock design no. 6760. *Private collection.* $450-500.

Molded cat tile. 3" x 3". *Courtesy of Roger Ellingsworth.* $150-200.

6" Elephant tile mounted in the drinking fountain at the John Marshall School in Detroit, Michigan. no. 6760. *Courtesy of the John Marshall Elementary School.*

Elephant tile. Flint Faience stock design no. 6760, in raised line design. $450-500.

made by the embossing process and in bisque, a spotted pig on a 4.25" tile signed "I" for Eula Irish in the Ken Galvas collection, a seated brown 3" square pig from the Roger Ellingsworth collection, a crouching puma tile measuring 3" square in the Roger Ellingsworth collection, a 6" square pink-eyed rabbit tile with some greenery from the Galvas collection, another white rabbit with almond-shaped eyes measuring 3" x 3" from the Roger Ellingsworth collection, and finally, a 2.875" square tile depicting a swaggering wolverine from the Ken Galvas collection (originally inset into a Santa Monica, California fireplace but matching the tiles in the Henry Ford Elementary School kindergarten room fireplace in Dearborn, Michigan).

Wonderful fox tile executed in raised line design. 3" x 3". *Courtesy of Roger Ellingsworth.* $150-200.

Detail of a 6" giraffe tile mounted in the John Marshall Elementary School in Detroit Michigan. c. 1928. no. 6718. *Courtesy of the John Marshall Elementary School.*

A raised line brown horse tile on a burnt cream background. 3" x 3". *Courtesy of Roger Ellingsworth.* $150-200.

Flint Faience giraffe tile. 6". *Private collection.* $700-800.

Detail of a lion tile on the water fountain in the John Marshall Elementary School in Detroit Michigan. 6" x 6". c. 1928. *Courtesy of the John Marshall Elementary School.*

Lion tile executed in raised line design on a blue background. 6" x 6". Flint Faience stock design no. 6721. *Courtesy of the Dale and Doris Barrett Collection.* $500-600.

An unusual depiction of a llama on a tile in the John Marshall Elementary School in Detroit Michigan. 6" x 6". Stock design no. 6719. c. 1928. *Courtesy of the John Marshall Elementary School.*

A 3" x 3" molded tile, no. 6412, showing the same llama design in bisque tile as the previously illustrated tile that was executed in raised line design. $30-40.

A tile depicting a very happy pig executed in raised line design. 4.25" x 4.25". Signed "I" in the lower right corner. "I" was the signature for the decorator Eula Irish. $200-250.

This crouching puma tile executed in raised line design would certainly add some fun to a kindergarten fireplace. 3" x 3". *Courtesy of Roger Ellingsworth.* $200-250.

A very tired looking pig is depicted on this 3" x 3" tile. *Courtesy of Roger Ellingsworth.* $200-225.

A playful 6" x 6" rabbit tile is always a favorite of collectors. $550-650.

A 3" x 3" white rabbit on a blue background appears ready to run. *Courtesy of Roger Ellingsworth.* $150-200.

This fierce looking wolverine once adorned a Santa Monica, California fireplace. 2.875" x 2.875". $150-200.

In the early 1930s, an unusual pair of tile plaques was made for the Crapo farm, located near Flint, Michigan in Swartz Creek. Mounted on two stone pillars announcing the gateway to the historic farm were tile plaques depicting the heads of prize winning Hereford cattle, created in Flint Faience tile with glazes in a realistic color scheme. One of the tile plaques is now in the collection of the University of Michigan, Flint campus.

Gatepost tile salvaged from Crapo Farms. *Courtesy of University of Michigan, Flint Campus.*

Apartment Houses

While some apartment houses are known to have had Flint Faience field tiles in their lobbies and elevator entranceways, others utilized the tiles in stunning swimming pool areas. Primary among these examples would be the Park Gables Apartments, now the Park Gable Condominiums, located in the North Chicago Roger's Park area at 2438-84 W. Estes Avenue.

An advertisement in the March 1931 issue of *Keramic Tile Journal* illustrates the interior pool area with its tiles in an "interesting combination of beige, green and black" – "infinitely more than a cold, severe tiling job." (*Keramic Tile Journal*, March 1931, 3) The architect who designed the pool area (and apartment building) was James F. Denson of Chicago and the tiling contractor was Borden-Fitzgerald Co., also of Chicago. Constructed in 1927, the stunning pool area, located in the lower level of the Tudor-Revival-style apartment building, is a perfect fit for these luxury apartments. Still in mint condition, the pool reflects the exquisite taste of the residents of this 1920s-era neighborhood adjoining Indian Boundary Park, with beautiful gardens and fountains within the multi-unit complex.

Flint Handmade Faïence

Right—Swimming pool in an interesting combination of beige, green, and black. Park Gables Apartment Building, Chicago, Illinois.

Borden-Fitzgerald Co., Tiling Contractor
Chicago

Jas. F. Denson, Architect
Chicago

Center—Fountain in the residence of Mr. Francis Hunter, New Rochelle, N. Y. The effect of sunlight upon rippling cool water, brought indoors through the skillful use of Flint Handmade Faience. Special crystalline series, in foamy blue, silvery green, sunflecked brown.

Felleman & Farrell, Inc., Tiling Contractor
New Rochelle, New York

E. D. Parmelee, Architect
New Rochelle, New York

Below—Section of lunch counter, Minck Hotel, Tulsa, Oklahoma. Floor in unglazed non-slip Flint Vitrocraft, counter in blue Faience.

Consolvo Tile & Mantel Co., Tiling Contractor
Tulsa, Oklahoma

Alfred C. Fabry, Architect
Tulsa, Oklahoma

These three photographs clearly demonstrate the adaptability and distinctive character of Flint Handmade Faience. The swimming pool is infinitely more than a cold, severe tiling job. The fountain, though using tiles out of regular stock, is a unique and personal creation. The lunch counter is proof that Flint design brings distinction to the most utilitarian installations. . . . Write fo catalogs of Flint Handmade Faience, Flintcraft machine-made tiles, and Flint unglazed Vitrocraft, also details of our sketch service.

FLINT FAÏENCE AND TILE CO
FLINT MICHIGAN

3

The indoor swimming pool at the Park Gables Apartments, featuring Flint Faience tiles.

An ad as it appeared in the March, 1931 issue of *Keramic Tile Journal*, Volume 3, no. 3, Page 3, showing the swimming pool at the Park Gables Apartments in Chicago.

The exterior of the Park Gables Apartments. *Photograph by Margaret Carney.*

The pool has tiled columns, field tile floors, as well as molded and raised line tiles in an elaborate configuration beneath a striped fabric canopy. One design featuring large 9.25" square tiles in a Pennsylvania Dutch style motif with four hearts is repeated throughout the pool area. This same tile can be seen in the private collection of Bill Shesko. Even the border tiles, featuring stylized mums and tulips, are memorable. Some tiles depict wave motifs with even a visible pattern in the tiles located beneath the surface of the water in the pool. It is reminiscent of the exquisite Flint Faience tiled pool that the Rockefellers had installed at Kykuit in Pocantico Hills near Sleepy Hollow at about the same time.

This tile in the collection of Bill Shesko is of the same design as the accents in the Park Gables pool area. 9.25 x 9.25". *Courtesy of www.BungalowBill.com.* $900-1000.

Wainscoting surrounding the Park Gables swimming pool. *Photograph by Robert A. Shonk.*

Raised line border tiles featuring stylized mums and tulips adorn the top half of the tiled walls in the swimming pool area of the Park Gables Apartments.

Tiled columns line the Park Gables pool area. *Photograph by Robert A. Shonk.*

Corner detail of the Park Gables pool area. *Photograph by Robert A. Shonk.*

Park Gables floor detail showing the pattern X0497 featured in *Catalog "G,"* with insert tiles in the border. *Photo by Robert A. Shonk.*

Architectural Faience

Architectural Faience: An Introduction (also sometimes referred to as *Architectural Tile*) is the title of a fascinating full-color brochure published as a 16-page trade catalog in 1929 by Flint Faience & Tile Company. Copies are scarce. The copy reproduced here was loaned to the authors by Jim Graham. Although the precious booklet claims no specific author, Kristine Burton, granddaughter of Flint Faience art director and architect, Howard B. Burton, believes the writing style lends itself to authorship by her late grandfather. She further substantiates this claim based on a visual discovery she made while carefully studying this publication. Among the small tiles which adorn the title page, beautifully illuminated like a Medieval manuscript, is an almost subliminal tile never produced by Flint Faience bearing an artistic presentation of the initials "HBB" (Howard B. Burton).

An advertisement in Vol. I, No. 6 of *Keramic Tile Journal* referred to this publication as "Architectural Tile," Form A-318. It was being marketed specifically to architects and tile dealers, as it was Flint Faience and Tile Company's decision to not advertise to homeowners, but rather exclusively to these professionals. Another announcement, with illustrations from the new catalog, appeared in the December 1929 issue of *Ceramic Industry*. (*Ceramic Industry*, December 1929, 612)

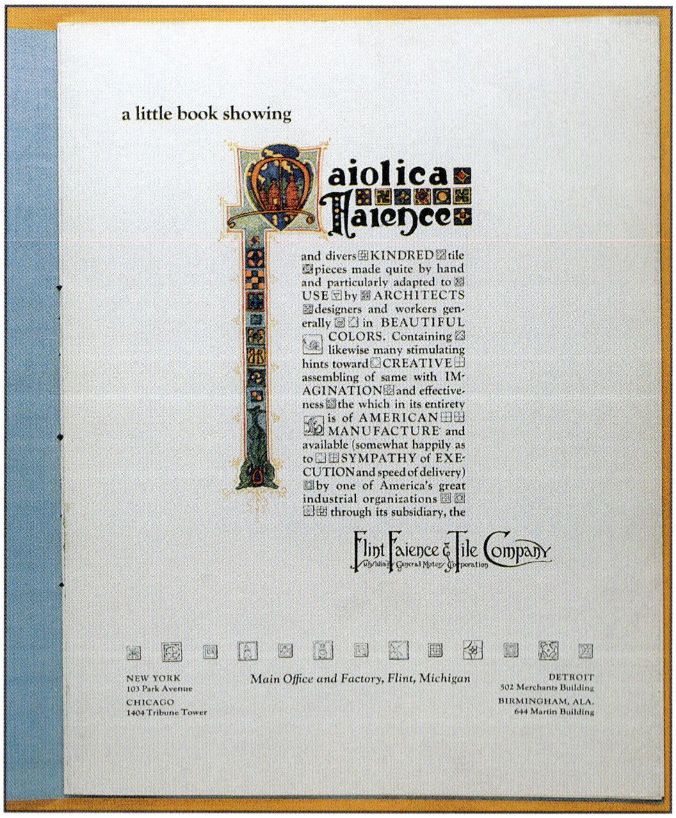

Title page of *Architectural Faience: An Introduction*, showing the almost hidden monogram of Howard Burton. *Collection of Jim Graham.*

Cover of *Architectural Faience: An Introduction*. c. 1929. 8.5" x 11". *Courtesy of Jim Graham.*

Arowa

The Arowa series tiles produced by Flint Faience Tile Company featured "rounded corners with undulating, glazed surface" and were illustrated on page 25 of the Flint Faience Tile Company's 1926 *Catalog "G."* Arowa series tiles can be seen in private collections. It is interesting to compare the same designs as they decorate Arowa blanks and standard Flint Faience tiles.

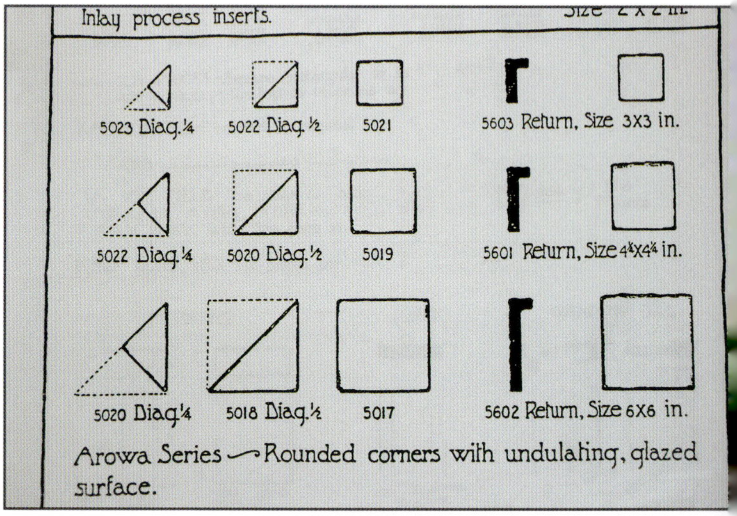

Page 25 of *Catalog "G"* showing the Arowa shape details.

A 6" Arowa blank in a monochrome blue. Arowa shaped tiles with their rounded edges generally sat higher than the grouted areas, thus giving a feeling of greater depth to the installation. $5-10.

These two charming tiles feature a little girl who may be the story character Pippi Longstocking. The one on the left is executed on an Arowa tile blank and is dated just below the girl, 9/27. The one on the right is on a typical flat blank tile. 6" x 6". $500-600 each.

Two more 6" x 6" tiles featuring the perky likeness of Pippi Longstocking. The tile on the left is an Arowa blank. Both tiles are executed in a raised line design. $500-600 each.

Arrowhead, Flint

The one easily recognizable logo for Flint Faience and Tile Company was the symbol of a flint arrowhead. This symbol was utilized on the company envelopes, signage, one of their tile backstamps, and on promotional products. Most of these items were produced in tile or other ceramic, although cast bronze signs bearing the arrowhead and company title are sometimes found.

An announcement concerning the adoption of a flint arrowhead as the Flint Faience tile trademark was made in the August 1929 issue of *Ceramic Industry.* (*Ceramic Industry*, August 1929, 194) The article noted that the trademark would be stamped on the back of every piece of Flint Faience tile and would easily differentiate its wares from that of other tile companies.

Large molded Arrowhead sign in the collection of the Sloan Museum, Flint Michigan. 15.25" x 11". *Courtesy of the Alfred P. Sloan Museum.*

Arrowheads used on Flint Faience Tile Company envelope. *Courtesy of Kristine Burton.*

Flint Faience arrowhead tile in a private collection. 8" x 8". *Courtesy of Dale and Doris Barrett* . $750-1000.

"Flint Faience Tiles" sign displayed today in the ceramics lab of Delphi East, Flint Michigan. 24" x 14". *Courtesy of the Delphi Corporation, Flint, Michigan.*

Bronze dealer sign featuring the Flint Faience arrowhead logo. 7.75" x 7.75". $650-850.

Arrowhead utilized as a back stamp on dry pressed Flint Faience tiles.

Blue change dish showing the Flint Faience arrowhead in the design. 4.25" x 4.25". Possibly a promotional gift. $50-75.

Later promotional materials continued to use the Flint Faience arrowhead motif. 2.25" x 1.25". $25-40.

Art Deco

Flint Faience tiles were designed and manufactured during a time period which overlapped several well-documented artistic styles, including the Arts & Crafts Movement as well as Art Deco. While Art Deco was fashionable between 1918-39, and Flint Faience tiles were manufactured between 1921-33, a relatively small number of Flint Faience ceramic tile installations fall into the artistic style easily recognized as Art Deco. These Deco motifs include streamlining, geometrical patterns of zigzags and circles, and vibrant color schemes.

Fisher Cafeteria from issue of *Keramic Tile Journal*. *Courtesy of John J. Sekora.*

Postcard showing the Fisher Building, Detroit, Michigan. c. 1930. *Courtesy of Margaret Carney.*

Art Deco design on a column of the employees' cafeteria in the Fisher Building, Detroit, Michigan. 123" x 36".

The Fisher Building, designed in 1928 by noted architect Albert Kahn and located on the northwest corner of West Grand Boulevard at Second Avenue, has been heralded as "Detroit's largest art object." The basement of the Fisher building housed what was once a glorious Art Deco design cafeteria. Part of the original 1928 building, the cafeteria met the same fashionable standards of the shops and theatre on the upper floors of the building. Apparently the Fisher Cafeteria closed to the public in the mid-1980s. Left in the basement today is what remains of an incomplete demolition of the cafeteria, complete with Art Deco patterns on columns and nearby wall surfaces.

Wall section showing Art Deco design in the area of the Fisher Building cafeteria undergoing a current remodel.

Art Deco designs in the bathroom of the E.T. Strong House in Flint, Michigan. *Courtesy of the Hamady Estate.*

The former E.T. Strong/Hamady house in Flint, Michigan has Flint Faience tiles in many areas of the home, which was built in 1929. The breakfast nook floor; the sunroom with a fountain, stair risers, and flooring; and three bathrooms are among the key features of this house that use Flint Faience tiles in stunning color selections and many in hexagonal shapes. The Art Deco bathroom, in shades of green and pinkish-lavender with black and gold accents, is quite unusual.

The wildly futuristic raised line tile designs created by Howard B. Burton for the Dryden Hotel also may be categorized as Art Deco style. See images and detailed descriptions under entry for Dryden Hotel.

Detail of the shower design in the home of E.T. Strong, Flint, Michigan. 27" x 32". *Courtesy of The Hamady Estate.*

Because of the era when Flint Faience tiles were being produced, some of them include stylistic elements reminiscent of Art Deco. A large 10.25" square tile in the Dale and Doris Barrett collection features a raised line decoration of a Japanese style house in a landscape. The color palette of blues and orange-rust and the lines suggest an Art Deco flavor, too. Another strong Art Deco style tile, 4.25" square, in olive, pink and black hues, is in the Ken Galvas collection.

A Japanese theme is evident on this Art Deco tile. 10.25" x 10.25". *Courtesy of the Dale and Doris Barrett Collection.* $1000-1250.

The fan design that adorns this Art Deco tile would be part of a larger overall design. 4.25" x 4.25". $40-60.

Arts & Crafts

While the Arts & Crafts Movement originated in late Victorian England and Europe, the ideas and ideals of William Morris and John Ruskin had profound influence in the United States between the 1870s and World War I. The goal of reviving handicrafts and improving the standards of decorative design is reflected in some of the tiles produced by Flint Faience & Tile Company. A 2-tile panel scene with a winding path in the foreground, trees in the middle ground with blue sky, and clouds in the background, all depicted in an Arts & Crafts style, can be seen in the built-in sink, drinking fountain, and sandbox at the John Marshall School, in Detroit, Michigan. Built in 1929, the two 9" x 9" tiles are located facing the sandbox side of the installation and are framed by twenty-eight smaller terra-cotta colored glazed tiles. This panel is based on stock design no. 6678, titled "Summer," on page 18 of *Catalog "G."*

Catalog "G" itself is produced in an Arts & Crafts style and Flint Faience tiles are often significant elements within Arts & Crafts style buildings, such as the large parlor in the University of Detroit Mercy Faculty Building.

A two-tile Arts and Crafts style pictorial titled "Summer," set into a sandbox at the John Marshall Elementary School in Detroit, Michigan. 9" x 18". Stock design no. 6678. *Courtesy of the John Marshall Elementary School.*

Detail of "Summer" pattern on page 18 of *Catalog "G."*

Detail of duck and chicken stock design no. 6778, on page 10 of *Catalog "G."*

Kindergarten fireplace in the Washington School in Wyandotte, Michigan. 53" x 85". *Courtesy of Washington Elementary School.*

Farm scene on the kindergarten fireplace in the Washington School. Stock design no. 6778. *Courtesy of Washington Elementary School.*

Another fireplace, this one at the Washington School kindergarten room in Wyandotte, Michigan, has several tiled panels that reflect the Arts & Crafts model of the idyllic, pastoral life with a scene of a duck and chicken near a quaint cottage, flanked on either side by a crowing rooster and an owl by the moon. All are stock designs shown in *Catalog "G."* Stock design no. 6778 can be seen in the fireplace, measuring 85" across and 53" high, with this central panel comprised of ten large tiles, each 6" square.

A few other Arts & Crafts motif tiles can be seen in private collections. Depicting landscapes featuring typical Arts & Crafts style trees with brilliant orange and yellow autumn leaf hues, two of these vintage tiles look charming when framed with era-appropriate sensitivity. In another private collection there are two 6" square tiles, nearly identical, in the Arts & Crafts style. From the Dale and Doris Barrett collection, one tile has a blue line (glazed) drawing of an Arts & Crafts style country bungalow, winding walkway, and trees against the sky. The second tile used the identical stencil, but is not glazed blue and white; rather more appropriate colors of nature (blue sky, green grass, brown walkway, green leaves, etc.) are seen. Both are exquisite and both reflect the ideal pastoral/rustic craftsman bungalow set harmoniously in nature. The second tile appears to have been decorated on an Arowa blank. A third 6" tile in the Barrett collection utilized the identical pattern, but with a slightly varied glaze palette.

Two framed Arts and Crafts landscape tiles in raised line design. 6" x 6". $1200-1500 each.

Blue and white glazed landscape shown on a 6" tile in raised line design. *Collection of Dale and Doris Barrett*. $250-300.

Farmhouse with winding walkway scene in an Arts and Crafts style in a raised line design on an Arowa blank. 6" x 6". *Courtesy of Dale and Doris Barrett.* $1000-1200.

Farmhouse with winding walkway scene in an Arts and Crafts design. 6" x 6". *Courtesy of Dale and Doris Barrett.* $1000-1200.

All of the series of allegorical tile panels created for the Wheatsworth Company in Hamburg, New Jersey could be classified stylistically as Arts & Crafts style. See additional illustrations under the entry for Wheatsworth Factory.

Narrative panel at the Wheatsworth Factory in Hamburg, New Jersey. *Courtesy of Joseph G. Catullo.*

Ashtrays

see Bookends, Paperweights, Ashtrays, Change Dishes, and Pen Holders

Athletics and Games

see also Swimming Pools, Apartment Houses, and Y.M.C.A.'s

Postcard showing the exterior of the Industrial Mutual Association Building in Flint, Michigan, c. 1940s. *Courtesy of Margaret Carney.*

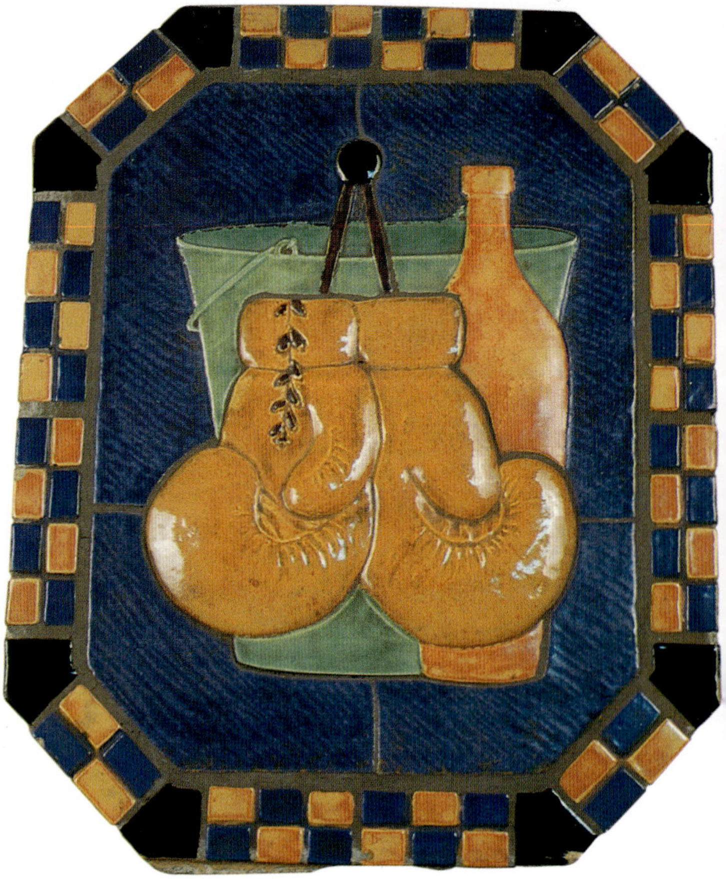

Boxing gloves and bucket plaque salvaged from the I.M.A. Building in Flint, Michigan. 19.75" x 25". *Courtesy of the Alfred P. Sloan Museum, Flint, Michigan.*

Although athletic or sports buildings might appear to be a potentially large application for decorative tiles, very few tiles with athletic motifs made of Flint Faience tile have been recorded. With the exception of swimming pools, covered separately, one notable example of tiles depicting sports themes would be the I.M.A. Building, once located in Flint, Michigan.

Basketball and net plaque salvaged from the I.M.A. Building in Flint, Michigan. 19.75" x 25". *Courtesy of the Alfred P. Sloan Museum, Flint, Michigan.*

The I.M.A. (Industrial Mutual Association) Auditorium, designed by architect Juan de Leonardi Hargove of Smith, Hinchman and Grylls and located at 815 East Second Avenue, was built in 1929. The building was a stylized Romanesque Revival Hall built for the Industrial Mutual Association, an association of factory workers. While it originally seated 6,200, it was later adapted for use as Autoworld, a theme park, before it was razed. Salvaged from the demolition site are two plaques depicting athletic themes which had been affixed to the exterior of the building. Now in the permanent collection of the Sloan Museum in Flint, Michigan, one ceramic tile plaque depicts basketball and the other a pair of boxing gloves. Each is modeled in high relief and measures 19.75" x 25". The series also included a tile with a music lyre decoration.

Individual tiles with sports themes can be seen in various collections, such as the 4.25" square tile depicting a football player in an almost cartoon-like style chasing a football, from the collection of Roger Ellingsworth. A similar tile, with nearly the same glaze color selection, can be seen in the collection on loan to the Western Reserve Historical Society in Cleveland. Two other sports-related tiles in this collection, probably designed by the same person, depict an aerial view of a football player "seeing stars" and a nervous-looking baseball player at bat. These three tiles, along with twenty-two others, were at one time installed in the Juvenile Court Building in downtown Cleveland. A handsome framed 2-tile panel (each 8" x 8") in the collection of Dan Langdon shows a very detailed and realistic design of a male shot putter as its subject matter. Shadows and motion are well illustrated in this exceptional tiled panel. Where it was originally installed is unknown. The series also included depictions of a hurdler and a discus thrower.

A rare tile portrayal of a football player in raised line design. 4.25" x 4.25". *Courtesy of Roger Ellingsworth.* $300-400.

Two 8" x 8" tiles comprise this shot putter panel from the *Dan Langdon Collection.* 8" x 16". $2000+.

Playing cards, or specifically poker, might not be considered a sport to some, but a royal flush with a 10, Jack, Queen, King, and Ace of hearts is crisply depicted on one 4.25" square Flint Faience tile with raised line decoration in the collection of Roger Ellingsworth. Perhaps it once served as a coaster for a beverage or as a paperweight for score tally sheets.

Poker hand featuring a Royal Flush. 4.25" x 4.25". *Courtesy of Roger Ellingsworth.* $250-300.

Automobile Showrooms

With Flint Faience's close ties to the automobile industry through AC Spark Plug, it is no surprise that their ceramic tiles were featured in some of the finest automobile showrooms of the day. An article in the May 1930 issue of *Keramic Tile Journal*, a popular trade publication, was titled "Making Your Salesroom Attractive." This article, which was illustrated with a handsome photograph of the Vesper Buick Salesroom in St. Louis, Missouri, touts the benefits of an attractive ceramic tiled showroom as "without a doubt one of the dealer's best advertisements and assets." (*Keramic Tile Journal*, May 1930, 33) The article continues, "One manufacturer, the Flint Faience & Tile Co., has a department that specializes in designing tile installations for automobile showrooms." It goes on to provide eight key pointers for the presentation of showrooms. An inset notes, "The modern home is clean, neat, attractive, and that is one reason an automobile salesroom should be the same. Besides, it builds business." Interesting facts for the article provided by Flint Faience included "the nerves of the human eyes are 22 times stronger and more active than the nerves of the human ears..." (*Keramic Tile Journal*, May 1930, 33, 35) They continued, "In this day of colorful cars, the showroom must possess a material having a wide range of color to effect harmony with whatever car displayed – whether it be a brilliant sport roadster or in delicate shades or conventional black." (*Keramic Tile Journal*, May 1930, 35) Other points favoring ceramic tile from Flint Faience were that they were economical and had easy upkeep, plus the "oil proof" nature of the tiles. Another sidebar on the same page as this article and photograph claimed that the same article was printed in *Automotive Merchandising* which had a readership of "some 100,000 dealers."

These elaborate automobile showrooms include the above mentioned Vesper Buick in St. Louis, the Packard Show Room in Philadelphia, and the Oakland-Pontiac, in Miami. All were illustrated in the April 1929 issue of *AC Sparks*. In the article in this issue, Howard B. Burton, the

Page 6 AC Sparks April, 1929

A Study in Automobile Show Rooms Extraordinary

Cars properly displayed sell better—A few who are profiting from this.

Left, Packard Show Room, Philadelphia; In Oval, Vesper Buick, St. Louis; Below, Oakland-Pontiac, Miami.

REMINISCENT of the familiar song: "I dreamt that I dwelt in marble halls," are these elaborate automobile show rooms in St. Louis, Philadelphia and Miami pictured here, and in which Flint Faience tile was used profusely.

The important effect of design and color in automobile show rooms is explained by Howard B. Burton, Flint Faience art director who says:

"A colorful floor in a quiet allover pattern, not panelled or otherwise interrupted at column, causes the columns decoratively to disappear, leaving in effect an unobstructed floor space.

"Absence of such divisions permits elasticity of display, as each car can be placed anywhere no matter whether a few are shown or the floor filled to capacity, and the exhibit appears neither bare nor crowded.

"In this day of colorful cars, the show room floor must be of a material possessing a wide range of color to effect harmony with whatever car displayed —whether it be a brilliant sport roadster or in delicate shades or conventional black.

"A good floor in color sets off a good car like a carved white gold setting triples the beauty of a diamond.

"From an economic point of view the floor is important to the dealer, not alone in enhancing the value of the displayed cars but in the very serious matter of upkeep.

"Upkeep can be referred to in terms of over a period of years, referring to wear and depreciation, or it can mean the daily, weekly or monthly cleaning in porter service. Actual installation of Faience floors have shown a saving over other material as great as one-eleventh of the former cost. Even one-fourth would be a desirable average.

"Scrubbing with water, kerosene and a little automobile soap once a month is all that is necessary for proper maintainence, besides that, little or nothing is to be done except wiping up foot marks in rainy weather and any oil drippings from time to time.

"The Faience floor under such simple cleaning appears not merely clean but new indefinitely.

"The thick, sturdy, rough-backed Faience tile stays in place indefinitely.

"The tile itself is positively oil proof, which is an invaluable asset in an automobile show room floor, as it eliminates the necessity of having a porter constantly on the job to mop up drippings.

"Another economic asset is in the color design selected, because certain combinations can become quite dusty and dirty and still not show it."

Three of the many outstanding show rooms equipped with Faience tile are the Packard in Philadelphia, Vesper Buick in St. Louis and Oakland-Pontiac in Miami.

Automobile showrooms from page 6 of *AC Sparks*, April, 1929 issue, illustrating article titled "A Study in Automobile Show Rooms Extraordinary." *Courtesy Archives, New York State College of Ceramics, Alfred, New York.*

Flint Faience art director noted, "A good floor in color sets off a good car like a carved white gold setting triples the beauty of a diamond." (AC Spark Plug Company, 1929, 6) The Packard Philadelphia showroom featured loggia risers with a Spanish effect, plus a reflecting pool with blue and green crystalline glazed tiles below the water level. In the Oakland-Pontiac showroom, "faience was used, but not in large masses of single colors or tones lest its beauty distract from the cars. The floor design called for some thirty colors although the field of the floor proper, as distinguished from borders and inserts, included only a dozen colors." (AC Spark Plug Company, 1929,7)

Various publications, such as the April 1929 issue of *AC Sparks*, listed additional automobile showrooms with Flint Faience tile installations. Others listed in the April 1929 *AC Sparks*, for example, included a Cadillac showroom and the Roberts-Nash showroom in Philadelphia, a Cadillac and Pontiac showroom in Detroit, and even a gas station and garage floor – Cadillac-LaSalle Sales in Flint, Michigan. None of these showrooms have been located at this time. In the company's 1929 publication, *Architectural Faience: An Introduction,* one automobile showroom "of over 10,000 square feet..." was illustrated and had Flint Faience tiling.

Automobile showroom illustrated on page 6 of *Architectural Faience: An Introduction. Catalog loaned from Jim Graham.*

Banks

At a time when bank lobbies were magnificent and imposing, several banks were documented to have had installations of Flint Faience tiles, including Central Savings Bank in New York and the floor of the First National Bank in Flint, Michigan. Although these bank floors seem to have long ago disappeared, one small image in an early *Sweet's Catalogue* illustrated a bank floor of Flint Faience in Flint, Michigan. In the March 29, 1930 issue of the *Flint Saturday Night* newspaper an announcement was made concerning the formal opening of the new quarters for the First National Bank and Trust Company. An illustration showing the tiled lobby was included.

B 1434

FLINT FAIENCE & TILE CO.
SUBSIDIARY OF GENERAL MOTORS CORPORATION
Hand-made Faience, Architectural and Wall Tile
MAIN OFFICE, SERVICE DEPARTMENT AND FACTORY
FLINT, MICH.
CHICAGO, ILL., 1404 Tribune Tower — DETROIT, MICH., 208 Barlum Building — BOSTON, MASS., 537 Little Building
ARCHITECTURAL DEPARTMENT AND NEW YORK SALES OFFICE, 103 PARK AVENUE

Products

FAIENCE TILE, genuine handmade, plain and ornamental.
FLOOR TILE, glazed, unglazed.
NON-SLIP TILE, floors, walkways, stairs, ramps.
WALL TILE, bathrooms, etc.
EXTERIOR FAIENCE, frost and sunproof.
SWIMMING POOLS, sanitary glazed faience combined with unglazed non-slip treatment.
MANTELS, stock and special.
FOUNTAINS, exterior, interior.
BATHROOM ACCESSORIES, matching faience quality and colors.

Description of Products

Made under supervision of A. C. Spark Plug Co., Subsidiary of General Motors Corp., using methods of precision, straight line production, exhaustive research and quality maintenance. Flint Faience products have in seven years taken their place among the leaders of high class faience and tile products.

Faience Tile

All our products are handmade exclusively.
Plain—Some one hundred and fifty colors, all equally available from clean, fresh stock, burned to order and immediately shipped.
Ornamented—Thousands of designs, also facilities for special design, and *all optional as to color combination.* Shipped with plain tile in same quick delivery.
Moulded—An extensive selection of architectural mouldings, trim, base, cap, stair-parts, etc., is available for immediate glazing and shipment.

Floor Tile

Glazed Faience—Suitable for residential, church, auto showroom and other uses.
Unglazed Tile—Known as Vitreous Grés for public buildings, corridors, stairs, etc. Will wear indefinitely.

Non-slip Tile

Vitreous Grés is also effectively and permanently non-slip as well as "steel hard" and therefore suitable for use in spaces where expensive abrasive grain would otherwise be required.
Colors—Buff to brown mixed regularly; or, for formal work, matched fairly uniformly.
Texture—Made by hand in faience moulds, rich and although non-slip can be readily cleaned. Individual, avoiding both hard mechanical lifelessness as well as the ultra-modern. When laid, has a surface architecturally interesting and with dignity to associate with highest type of interior or exterior treatment. Stands exterior exposure.
Wearproof—Six-year tests in store entrances and other public walkways, show substantially no wear.
Stairs—Steps, treads, risers, strings, cove and full sanitary trimmers available.
Designs—Numerous Stock patterns ready for immediate shipment. Made in all tile sizes, and special designs are readily made up.

Wall Tile

A new product in one quality only, thus easy to specify, inspect and superintend.

Exterior Faience

When specified "for exterior use" Flint Faience uses special frostproof bisque. The sunproof colors will stand every exposure. Six-year installational tests from Minnesota to Florida have proven both.

Swimming Pools

We have developed a standard scum gutter, curb, etc., but supplied in the full option of our entire palette of beautiful colors in genuine faience, decorated to order and deliverable in three to six weeks. Ambulatory nosing, steps or in non-slip Vitreous Grés.

A Bank Floor of Flint Faience Tile, Flint, Mich.

A Few Stock Floor Designs from Innumerable Patterns in Both Vitreous Gres and Genuine Handmade Faience

SWEET'S CATALOGUE

Continued on next page

Page from 1930 *Sweet's Architectural Catalogue* illustrating the floor of the First National Bank in Flint, Michigan, c. 1930s.

Detail of bank floor in First National Bank as shown in *Sweet's Architectural Catalogue.*

Bathrooms

A fascinating although now obscure article in a 1926 volume of *Ceramic Industry* (*Ceramic Industry*, January, 1926, 500), with the heading "Boom for Faience Seen," noted that, regarding faience tiles, the cost of a structure would not only "be gauged by the variety of contrasting high colors employed inside and out," but the "wealth of the prosperous American citizen may henceforth be approximated by the ornateness of his bathroom." This was the heyday for luxuriously and splendidly tiled bathrooms in America. While some homes had one Flint Faience tiled bathroom, others, such as the Edsel and Eleanor Ford home in Grosse Pointe Shores, Michigan, had more. The Ford home (constructed between 1926-29) contains twelve tiled bathrooms, all comprised of a pinkish-taupe monochrome tile, reflective of a quiet conservatism. Three of the twelve bathrooms are on the "official" home tour which is available to the public. These extremely understated, simple Flint Faience tiled bathroom installations were nonetheless featured in trade journal articles such as *Keramic Tile Journal*, Vol. III, No. 5, 1931, p. 3. Concerning the bathrooms, the monograph on the Edsel and Eleanor Ford house, written by James A. Bridenstine, notes that "Most of the bathrooms in the Ford House are modeled along similarly classic lines, with subtle, taupe tiling and little extraneous decoration..." (Bridenstine, 1988, 76)

Boys' bathroom in the home of Edsel and Eleanor Ford. Grosse Pointe Shores, Michigan. Photo by William J. Walker, Jr. *Courtesy of the Edsel and Eleanor Ford House.*

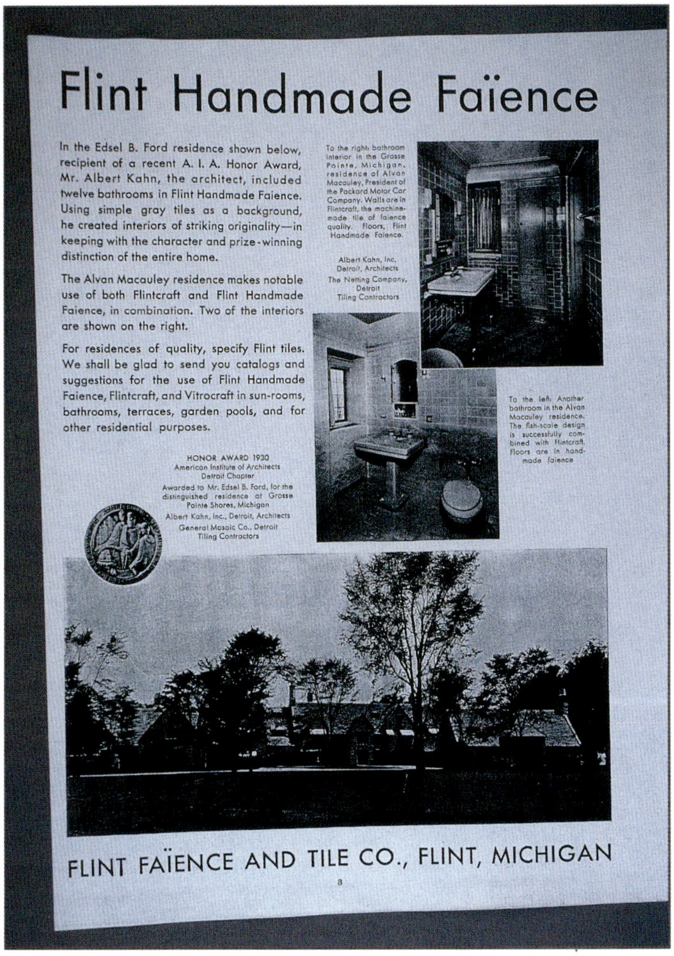

Keramic Tile Journal advertisement illustrating the exterior of the Edsel and Eleanor Ford home and several Flint Faience tiled bathrooms. Volume 3, no. 5, 1931, Page 3.

Other bathrooms which utilized Flint Faience tiles are much more exuberant, with glorious glazes and hexagonal shapes. A 1929 flyer produced by Flint Faience & Tile Co., No. A-303, illustrates several tiled bathrooms and touts the virtues of "The Colorful Individuality of Flint Faience Tile Bathrooms." The flyer notes the versatility of effects ranging from "delicate pastel shades of boudoir charm to brilliant – *even exotic* – color contrasts of individual preference," while it "always bespeaks the perfect taste of the owner."

The E.T. Strong/Hamady home, built in Flint, Michigan in 1929, has many striking uses of Flint Faience tiles in its five tiled bathrooms. In addition to the Art Deco motifs in one dramatic upstairs bathroom (see illustrations under entry for Art Deco), there are hexagons and diamond shaped tiles in a second bathroom, with base, trim, and cap molding in soft purple, walls in light orchid and darker orchid and a few decorative inserts for the floor. The tile installation pattern creates some optical illusion effects. Still another Flint Faience tiled bathroom, this one a salmon hue with colorful contrasting insert tiles, is located upstairs in the home. In addition, the E.T. Strong home solarium or breakfast room, conservatory, kitchen, and hallway were all spectacularly tiled in Flint Faience. An article in the April 1932 issue of *Keramic Tile Journal* noted, regarding the E.T. Strong home, that this was "regarded as one of the finest Faience installations in the country." (*Keramic Tile Journal,* April 1932, 27) These bathrooms, as well as the other tile installations in the E.T. Strong home, were designed by Julio Haro, who held the title of Art Director of Flint Faience & Tile Company at that time. The tiling contractor was Ernest Phelps. The architect chosen to design the Strong home was Joseph Savage. At the time, E.T. Strong was President of Buick Motor, Co., in Flint, Michigan.

There were Flint Faience bathrooms in palatial homes in the United States and there was at least one Flint Faience bathroom in a Presidential Palace. The Presidential Palace in Peru has a bathroom designed by Howard B. Burton, Flint Faience art director. This was proudly announced by the company in the April 1929 issue of *AC Sparks.* (AC Spark Plug Company, 1929, 7)

One might think that illustrating bathrooms would have been a no-no in the early 1930s, but the *Flint Journal* newspaper published two bathroom photographs with stunning Flint Faience tile installations during consecutive weeks in July 1930. One photograph featured the Eugene Zukor residence bathroom located on Park Avenue in New York City with a distinctive cat-tail design in raised line process on the recessed tiles by the bathtub. The second illustrated bathroom was also located in New York, and featured checkered tiles in peacock blue, deep red, and yellow.

An illustration from Flint Faience Tile flyer no. A-303. *Courtesy the Archives, New York State College of Ceramics at Alfred University.*

The Colorful Individuality of Flint Faience Tile Bathrooms

THE versatility of Flint Faience is well illustrated in its innumerable and appropriate uses throughout the home. It has an individuality all its own. It is always decorative and in perfect keeping, no matter what the style of furnishings may be.

Flint Faience exhibits a striking variety of tonal effects, from the delicate pastel shades of boudoir charm to brilliant—*even exotic*—color contrasts of individual preference. And it always bespeaks the perfect taste of the owner.

Centuries of artistic precedent are behind handmade Faience tile.

Like the old pieces which reach Museum importance, Flint Faience is similarly hand-made at every step. Fired at temperatures far above the melting point of metals, and with hand-dipped glaze of appreciable thickness, the colors, the textures, the eye-appealing variations of Flint Faience, mark it as one of the most luxurious decorative materials obtainable; yet at a price within reach of almost anyone.

A page from Flint Faience Tile flyer no. A-303 concerning bathrooms. *Courtesy the Archives, New York State College of Ceramics at Alfred University.*

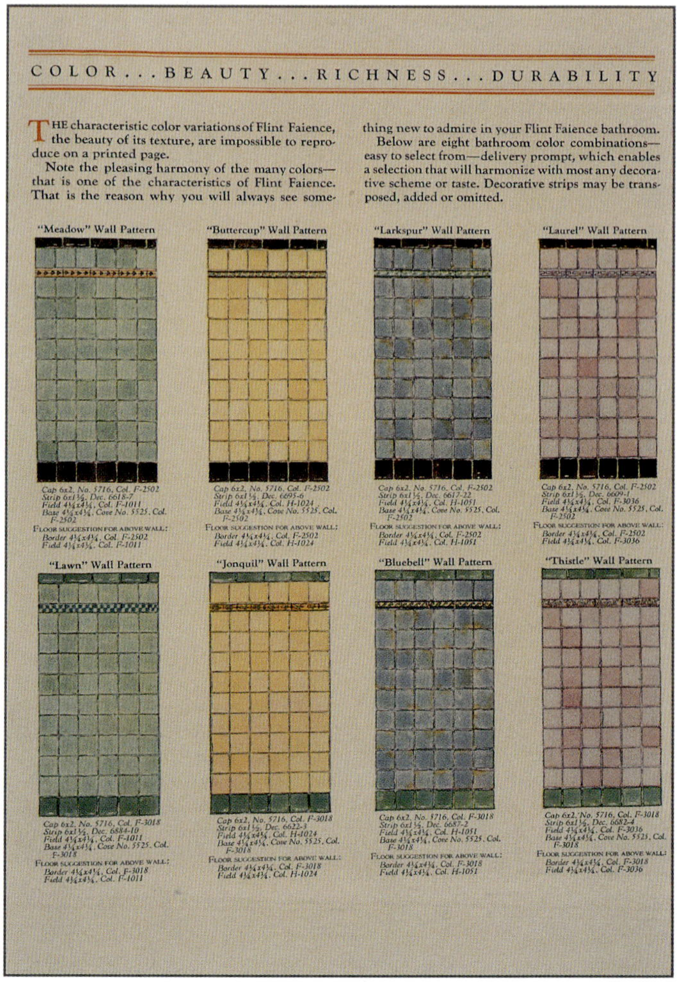

COLOR . . . BEAUTY . . . RICHNESS . . . DURABILITY

THE characteristic color variations of Flint Faience, the beauty of its texture, are impossible to reproduce on a printed page.

Note the pleasing harmony of the many colors—that is one of the characteristics of Flint Faience. That is the reason why you will always see something new to admire in your Flint Faience bathroom.

Below are eight bathroom color combinations—easy to select from—delivery prompt, which enables a selection that will harmonize with most any decorative scheme or taste. Decorative strips may be transposed, added or omitted.

"Meadow" Wall Pattern
Cap 6x2, No. 5716, Col. F-2502
Strip 6x1½, Dec. 6618-7
Field 4¼x4¼, Col. F-1011
Base 4¼x4¼, Cove No. 5525, Col. F-2502
FLOOR SUGGESTION FOR ABOVE WALL:
Border 4¼x4¼, Col. F-2502
Field 4¼x4¼, Col. F-1011

"Buttercup" Wall Pattern
Cap 6x2, No. 5716, Col. F-2502
Strip 6x1½, Dec. 6695-6
Field 4¼x4¼, Col. H-1024
Base 4¼x4¼, Cove No. 5525, Col. F-2502
FLOOR SUGGESTION FOR ABOVE WALL:
Border 4¼x4¼, Col. F-2502
Field 4¼x4¼, Col. H-1024

"Larkspur" Wall Pattern
Cap 6x2, No. 5716, Col. F-2502
Strip 6x1½, Dec. 6617-22
Field 4¼x4¼, Col. H-1051
Base 4¼x4¼, Cove No. 5525, Col. F-2502
FLOOR SUGGESTION FOR ABOVE WALL:
Border 4¼x4¼, Col. F-2502
Field 4¼x4¼, Col. H-1051

"Laurel" Wall Pattern
Cap 6x2, No. 5716, Col. F-2502
Strip 6x1½, Dec. 6609-1
Field 4¼x4¼, Col. F-3036
Base 4¼x4¼, Cove No. 5525, Col. F-2502
FLOOR SUGGESTION FOR ABOVE WALL:
Border 4¼x4¼, Col. F-2502
Field 4¼x4¼, Col. F-3036

"Lawn" Wall Pattern
Cap 6x2, No. 5716, Col. F-3018
Strip 6x1½, Dec. 6884-10
Field 4¼x4¼, Col. F-1011
Base 4¼x4¼, Cove No. 5525, Col. F-3018
FLOOR SUGGESTION FOR ABOVE WALL:
Border 4¼x4¼, Col. F-3018
Field 4¼x4¼, Col. F-1011

"Jonquil" Wall Pattern
Cap 6x2, No. 5716, Col. F-3018
Strip 6x1½, Dec. 6622-3
Field 4¼x4¼, Col. H-1024
Base 4¼x4¼, Cove No. 5525, Col. F-3018
FLOOR SUGGESTION FOR ABOVE WALL:
Border 4¼x4¼, Col. F-3018
Field 4¼x4¼, Col. H-1024

"Bluebell" Wall Pattern
Cap 6x2, No. 5716, Col. F-3018
Strip 6x1½, Dec. 6687-2
Field 4¼x4¼, Col. H-1051
Base 4¼x4¼, Cove No. 5525, Col. F-3018
FLOOR SUGGESTION FOR ABOVE WALL:
Border 4¼x4¼, Col. F-3018
Field 4¼x4¼, Col. H-1051

"Thistle" Wall Pattern
Cap 6x2, No. 5716, Col. F-3018
Strip 6x1½, Dec. 6682-4
Field 4¼x4¼, Col. F-3036
Base 4¼x4¼, Cove No. 5525, Col. F-3018
FLOOR SUGGESTION FOR ABOVE WALL:
Border 4¼x4¼, Col. F-3018
Field 4¼x4¼, Col. F-3036

Details of bathroom tile patterns from Flint Faience Tile flyer no. A-303. *Courtesy the Archives, New York State College of Ceramics at Alfred University.*

Overview of a bathroom in the former home of E. T. Strong. Flint, Michigan. *Courtesy of The Hamady Estate.*

Optical illusion pattern in a bathroom of the former E.T. Strong home. Flint, Michigan. *Courtesy of The Hamady Estate.*

Hexagonal insert tile in one of the bathrooms in the former E.T. Strong home in Flint, Michigan. It is unusual to see hexagonal insert tiles. *Courtesy of the Hamady Estate.*

Salmon-colored bathroom in the former E. T. Strong home, Flint, Michigan. *Courtesy of the Hamady Estate.*

Insert tile detail in a bathroom of the former E. T. Strong home. 2" x 2". *Courtesy of the Hamady Estate.*

Bathroom accessories glazed in colors to match their Faience walls were also available in stock designs as listed and illustrated on page 36 of the Flint Faience Tile Company 1926 publication *Catalog "G."* These included a combination grab bar and soap holder, a projecting tumbler holder, towel bar posts, a recessed soap holder, and shelf supports, among other useful accessories. An overview of the upstairs pinkish-lavender bathroom in the former Prosper Champion home in Flint, Michigan, reveals built-in bathroom accessories such as towel racks and soap holders.

Today it might seem strange that people thought about conservative versus exuberantly colored bathrooms, but publication of a little article titled "Prescribes

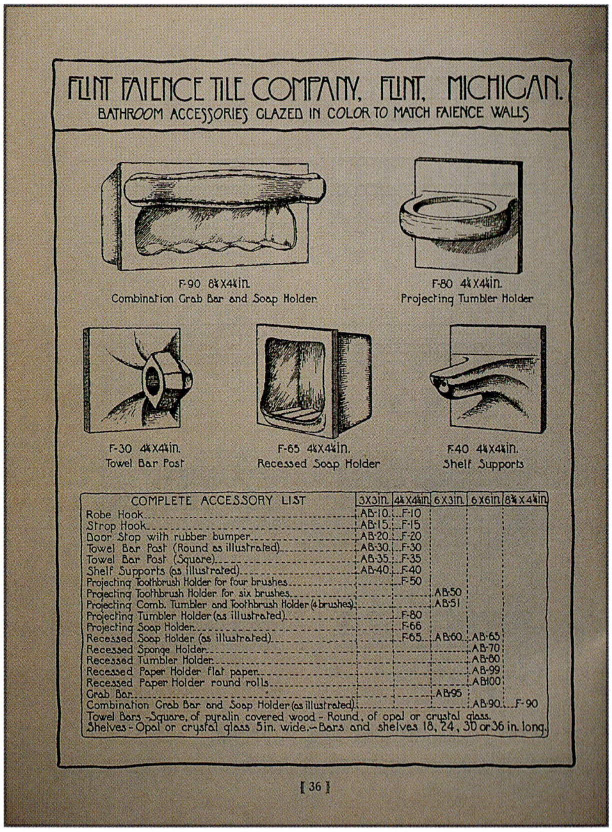

FLINT FAIENCE TILE COMPANY, FLINT, MICHIGAN.
BATHROOM ACCESSORIES GLAZED IN COLOR TO MATCH FAIENCE WALLS

F-90 8¼X4¼in.
Combination Grab Bar and Soap Holder

F-80 4¼X4¼in.
Projecting Tumbler Holder

F-30 4¼X4¼in.
Towel Bar Post

F-65 4¼X4¼in.
Recessed Soap Holder

F-40 4¼X4¼in.
Shelf Supports

COMPLETE ACCESSORY LIST	3X3in.	4¼X4¼in.	6X3in.	6X6in.	8¼X4¼in.
Robe Hook	AB-10	F-10			
Strop Hook	AB-15	F-15			
Door Stop with rubber bumper	AB-20	F-20			
Towel Bar Post (Round as illustrated)	AB-30	F-30			
Towel Bar Post (Square)	AB-35	F-35			
Shelf Supports (as illustrated)	AB-40	F-40			
Projecting Toothbrush Holder for four brushes		F-50			
Projecting Toothbrush Holder for six brushes			AB-50		
Projecting Comb. Tumbler and Toothbrush Holder (4 brushes)			AB-51		
Projecting Tumbler Holder (as illustrated)		F-80			
Projecting Soap Holder		F-66			
Recessed Soap Holder (as illustrated)		F-65	AB-60	AB-65	
Recessed Sponge Holder				AB-70	
Recessed Tumbler Holder				AB-80	
Recessed Paper Holder flat paper				AB-99	
Recessed Paper Holder round rolls				AB100	
Grab Bar			AB-95		
Combination Grab Bar and Soap Holder (as illustrated)				AB-90	F-90

Towel Bars – Square, of pyralin covered wood – Round, of opal or crystal glass.
Shelves – Opal or crystal glass 5in. wide. – Bars and shelves 18, 24, 30 or 36 in. long.

[36]

Bathroom accessories illustrated on page 36 of *Catalog "G."*

Overview of one bathroom in the former Prosper Champion home in Flint, Michigan, showing an array of tile fixtures. *Courtesy of Jim Fitzell and Jessica Higgins.*

Rainbow Tiles Only for Bathrooms of Rich" in the November 1, 1925 *New York Times* made front page business news. The article elaborated on the theory that "the more money a man has, the more colors he should have in his bathroom." It also suggested that "Bathing in a rainbow atmosphere, would be only for the very wealthy. A $10,000 home...should not aspire beyond a plain white tile bathroom, while only a blue or pink tint would be permissible in one costing $20,000. Not until the $40,000 stage was reached...would the bathroom colors begin really to warm up, with purple, yellow or green tiles." (*New York Times*, November 1, 1925, 1) Lest one needed still another argument in favor of installing tile in the bathroom, the April 1929 issue of *AC Sparks* noted "...floors are uninjured even when the forgetful member of the family sometimes lets the tub overflow." (AC Spark Plug Company, 1929, 3)

Bears

Flint Faience designers, and evidently the consumers as well, simply couldn't get enough bear tiles. There are so many types that they warrant their own heading separate from "Animals." They include polar bears, 6" x 6", stock design no. 6720 in *Catalog "G"* page 20; or smaller ones, no. 6669, 3" square, illustrated on page 23; or even smaller 2.75" square size inserts for wall and floor, no. 6582 in *Catalog "G"*, page 24; polar bears on ice such as the 3" square tile in the Roger Ellingsworth collection; and cuddly bears such as the 3" square tile also in the Roger Ellingsworth collection, which is identical in every way to the one installed along with thirty-one other 2.75" inserts in the fireplace facing in the kindergarten room at the Henry Ford Elementary School in Dearborn, Michigan.

Detail of animal stock design patterns from page 20 of *Catalog "G."*

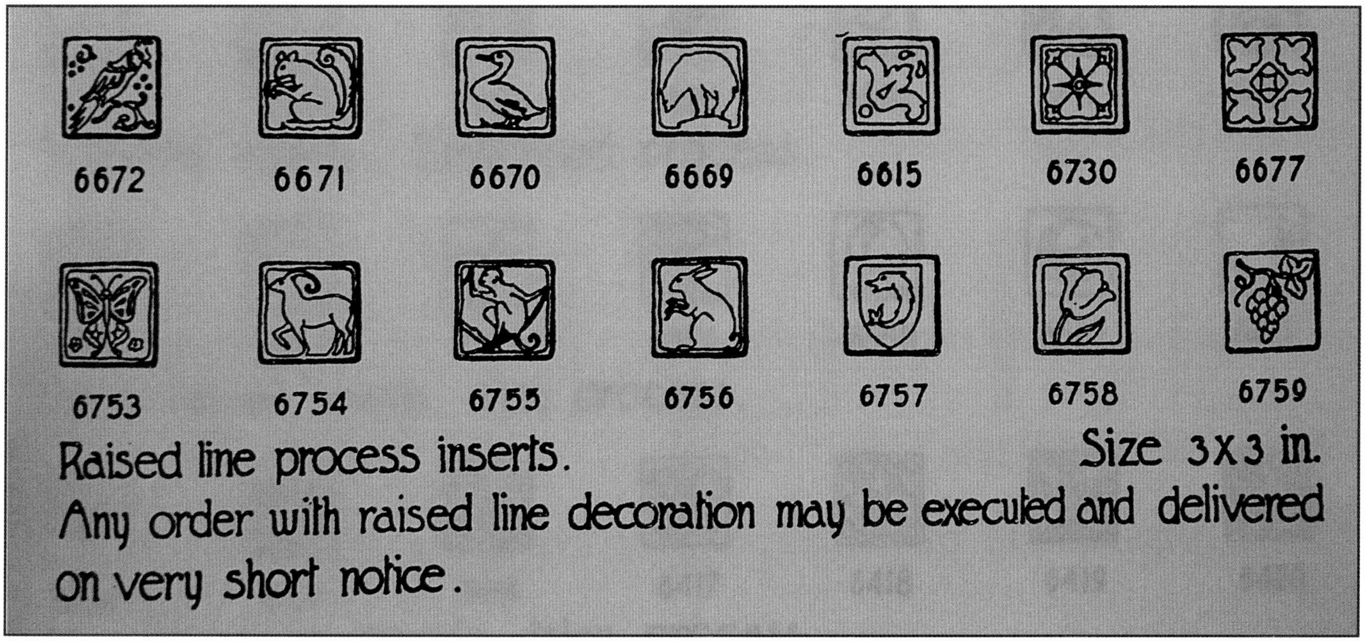

Detail of animal stock design patterns from page 23 of *Catalog "G."*

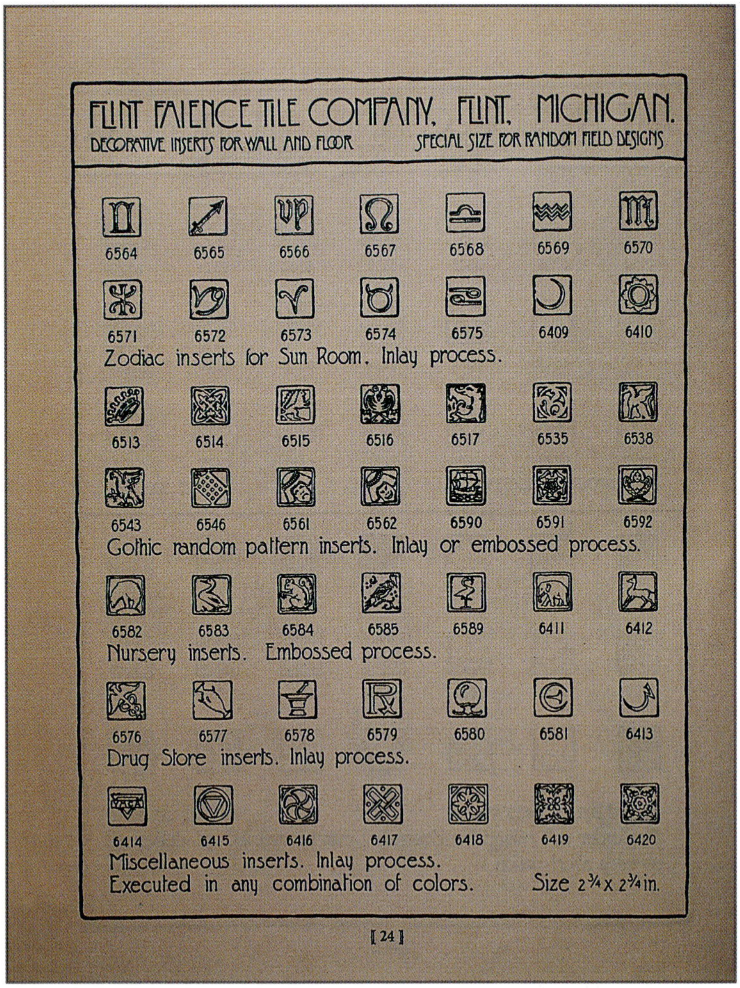

FLINT FAIENCE TILE COMPANY. FLINT. MICHIGAN.

DECORATIVE INSERTS FOR WALL AND FLOOR SPECIAL SIZE FOR RANDOM FIELD DESIGNS

6564 6565 6566 6567 6568 6569 6570

6571 6572 6573 6574 6575 6409 6410

Zodiac inserts for Sun Room. Inlay process.

6513 6514 6515 6516 6517 6535 6538

6543 6546 6561 6562 6590 6591 6592

Gothic random pattern inserts. Inlay or embossed process.

6582 6583 6584 6585 6589 6411 6412

Nursery inserts. Embossed process.

6576 6577 6578 6579 6580 6581 6413

Drug Store inserts. Inlay process.

6414 6415 6416 6417 6418 6419 6420

Miscellaneous inserts. Inlay process.

Executed in any combination of colors. Size 2¾ x 2¾ in.

[24]

Page 24 of *Catalog "G,"* illustrating 2.75" x 2.75" tile inserts with animal motifs in stock designs for nurseries.

Cuddly seated bear tile in raised line design. 3" x 3". *Courtesy of Roger Ellingsworth.* $150-200.

Tile depicting polar bear on an ice flow. 3" x 3". Executed in raised line design. *Courtesy of Roger Ellingsworth.* $150-200.

Cuddly seated bear tile installed in the fireplace of the Henry Ford Elementary School in Dearborn, Michigan.

There were additional cuddly and cute bear images among the tiles created by Flint Faience. Another obvious choice would be the 4.25" tile decorated with a teddy bear and flowers in the collection of Ken Galvas. This charming tile design is identical except in size, orientation, and glaze color choices with one installed in the sandbox at the Garfield School in Wyandotte, Michigan. That larger 6" square tile at the school was installed on point next to an equally charming tile of a rabbit in fancy clothes.

When installed with giraffes, lions, and elephants, the polar bears are striking; they are usually depicted in stark white on sky blue backgrounds and often shown perched on an ice float. A wonderful 6" square example, circa 1928, can be seen today at the John Marshall Elementary School in the Kindergarten room, located in Detroit. An identical polar bear on ice can be seen in the collection of Ken Galvas.

Tile featuring a teddy bear with flowers executed in raised line design. 4.25" x 4.25". $200-250.

Teddy bear tile installed on point in a sandbox in the Garfield Elementary School in Wyandotte, Michigan. 6" x 6". *Courtesy of Mary Wharton Thorson.*

Polar bear tile installed in a sandbox of the John Marshall Elementary School. 6" x 6". Detroit, Michigan. *Courtesy of the John Marshall Elementary School.*

Polar bear tile in raised line, stock design no. 6720. 6" x 6". $500-600.

Bergmans, Carl

(variously spelled Karl, and Bergmann, Bergman, or Bergmanns)

Carl Virgil Bergmans was born on October 27, 1889 in Brussels, Belgium and died in 1955. He graduated from the Royal Academy of Brussels. Legend has it that he was instrumental in establishing the Flint Faience Tile Company, working there as an artist and designer for approximately five years (1921-1925). He had earlier worked for Mosaic Tile Company (1914-15) and later as a designer for American Encaustic Tiling Company until around 1919. He designed the *Tree of Life* mural now in the permanent collection of the Sloan Museum in Flint, Michigan. It is the only signed mural of Flint Faience tiles, signed on the lower right corner "C. Bergmans." See the Tree of Life entry for illustrations and detailed descriptions.

Carl Bergmans was a gifted watercolorist as well as ceramic designer. An exquisite pair of peacocks shown on blossoming branches with the moon behind, within a lunette format, executed by Bergmans in watercolors (33.5" x 18") and signed in the bottom right hand corner is in a private collection in the United States. Two known versions of this sketch were executed in tile, one for the American Encaustic Tiling Company, measuring 30" x 14.5" (illustrated) and the other for Flint Faience and Tile Company. The Flint Faience version was confiscated after the owner was arrested on drug charges in the 1990s; its whereabouts are not currently known.

Watercolor painting of a peacock lunette executed by Carl Bergmans. 33.5" x 18". *Private Collection.*

Tiled peacock panel executed by the American Encaustic Tiling Company. c. 1920. 30" x 14.5". *Private Collection.*

Little has been published about Carl Bergmans, but a few early tile tomes, including the Evan and Louise Purviance book titled *Zanesville Art Tile in Color*, provide a glimpse into his importance to the tile industry. Illustrations in the Purviance book include Chinese form ginger jar covered vases, low bowls with handles in the form of ancient ritual bronzes, Buddha figure incense burners replicating the famous Chinese De Hua ware, small animal sculpture, and much more, which Bergmans apparently created while at American Encaustic Tiling Company. Authors Evan and Louise Purviance had purchased all pieces from Mrs. Bergmans. In one photo in this fascinating small book, Carl Bergmans is seen seated at a drawing table in front of a watercolor of a peacock which is identical to no. 6784 stock design peacock panel illustrated on page 7 of the Flint Faience *Catalog "G."* The watercolor painting of the pair of peacocks is also illustrated in the Purviance book. The watercolor painting and Mr. Bergmans can be seen in a photograph with Julio Haro, at work at Flint Faience.

By 1927, Carl Bergmans was president and general manager of the Continental Faience & Tile Co. in Milwaukee, Wisconsin.

Binns, Charles Fergus

Charles Fergus Binns was born in Worcester, England on October 4, 1857 and died in Alfred, New York on December 4, 1934. His father was co-managing director of the Royal Worcester Porcelain Works in Worcester, England and he was apprenticed there beginning at an early age. He first came to the United States in 1894, accompanying the Royal Worcester exhibition to the World's Columbian Exposition in Chicago. In the late 1890s, he emigrated with his family to the U.S., working at the Ceramic Art Co. (later Lenox China) in Trenton, New Jersey, before being selected in 1900 as the founding director of the New York State School of Clay-Working and Ceramics (now the New York State College of Ceramics) in Alfred, New York. Often referred to as the Father of American Studio Ceramics, Binns created classical stoneware jars and vases with rich monochrome glazes, taught summer school as well as regular courses, and lectured and wrote prolifically. His book *The Potter's Craft*, first published in 1910, taught many students who could never attend formal classes about clay bodies, making pottery, and glazes.

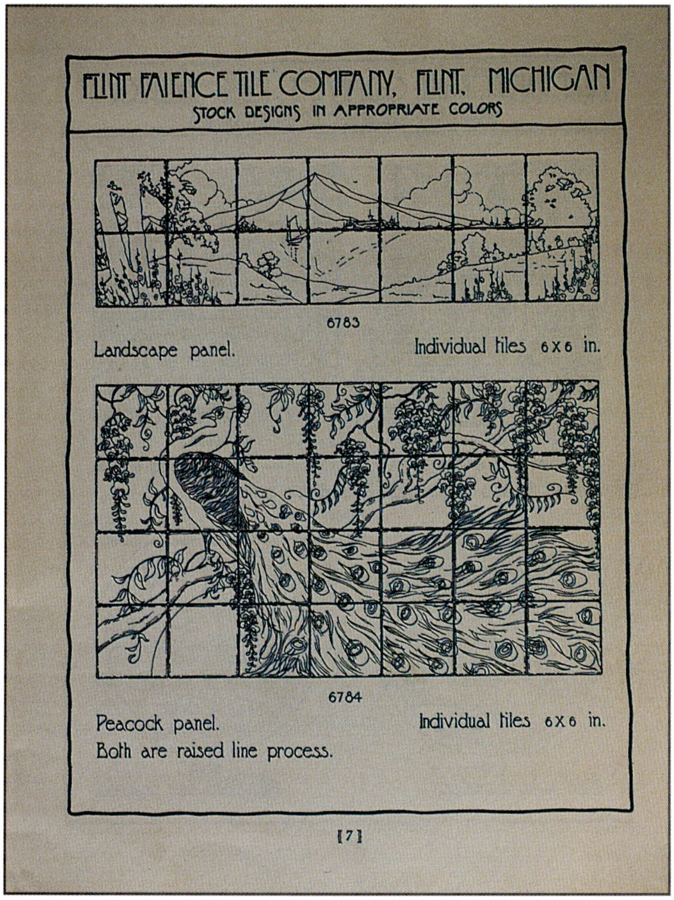

FLINT FAIENCE TILE COMPANY, FLINT, MICHIGAN
STOCK DESIGNS IN APPROPRIATE COLORS

6783
Landscape panel. Individual tiles 6 x 6 in.

6784
Peacock panel. Individual tiles 6 x 6 in.
Both are raised line process.

[7]

Page 7 of *Catalog "G,"* illustrating a drawing of a design for a Flint Faience tiled peacock panel based on the Carl Bergmans watercolor painting.

Charles Fergus Binns. *Courtesy of the Archives, New York State College of Ceramics at Alfred University.*

Ceramics Building at Alfred. c. 1930. *Courtesy of the Archives, New York State College of Ceramics at Alfred University.*

Binns's connection with Flint Faience Tile Company is an interesting one. When plans were underway for a new Ceramics Building in Alfred, Binns conceived of a design for some special decorative tiles to be installed in the foyer of the new building. Through correspondence between Binns and other parties, as well as the existence of original watercolor sketches prepared by Flint Faience & Tile Company and a number of signed Flint Faience tiles, it is known that Binns and Flint Faience Tile Company collaborated on the design of eight tiles with four designs, which honor the tradition of pottery making. The tiles were removed from the walls of the building during two separate renovations, and are part of the permanent collection of the Schein-Joseph International Museum of Ceramic Art in Alfred, New York. They depict a classical potter forming, decorating a jar, trimming a pot, and loading a kiln.

Looking back, it is easy to say that these eight Flint Faience custom designed tiles for Alfred were important. However, it is more interesting to note that the December 1931 issue of *Ceramic Industry* included the entry "New Building for Ceramic Department of Alfred University," in which it was noted that "...The entrance hall or lobby on the main floor is to be the keynote of the building. The walls are to be marble with polychrome tile inserts..." (*Ceramic Industry*, December 1931, 498)

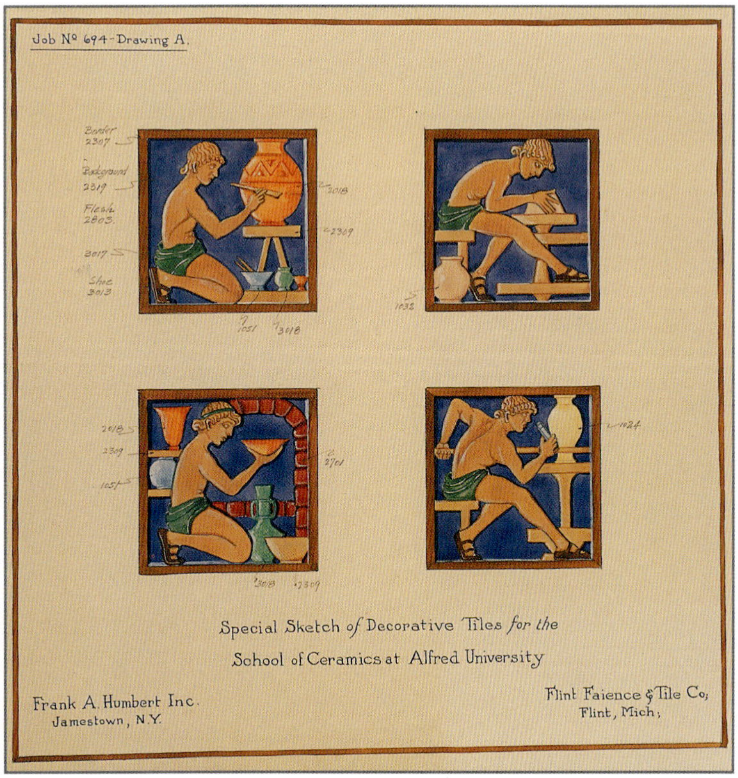

An original watercolor sketch of four Flint Faience tiles to be installed in the Ceramics Building at Alfred. *Courtesy of the Archives, New York State College of Ceramics at Alfred University.*

These are three of the remaining Binns/Flint Faience tiles from the collection of the Schein-Joesph International Museum of Ceramic Art. *Courtesy of the Schein-Joseph International Museum of Ceramic Art, Alfred New York. Photograph courtesy of Brian Oglesbee.*

Birds & Bees

Birds were such popular motifs for Flint Faience that they were found in elementary schools, building facades, hotel interiors; in raised line design, high relief, and molded bisque; in classical poses, Arts & Crafts style, and "futuristic all over." The Washington School, in Wyandotte, Michigan, has a kindergarten room with a fireplace featuring many large tiles depicting animals and birds. *Catalog "G"* has stock designs on page 10 illustrating a large 2-tile panel of a rooster, no. 6779, comprised of two 8" inch square tiles, as well as no. 6780, another 2-tile panel (also 16" x 8") depicting an owl flying among the moon and stars. These stock designs became a reality on the front of the fireplace in the Washington School kindergarten room. Another 4.25" square design of an owl and moon was created and signed by Flint Faience & Tile Co. decorator, Eula Irish, and is now in the collection of Ken Galvas.

Tiled rooster panel in the kindergarten fireplace in the Washington Elementary School, Wynadotte, Michigan. 8" x 16". Flint Faience stock design no. 6779. *Courtesy of Washington Elementary School.*

Flint Faience stock design of rooster no. 6779, illustrated on page 10 of *Catalog "G."*

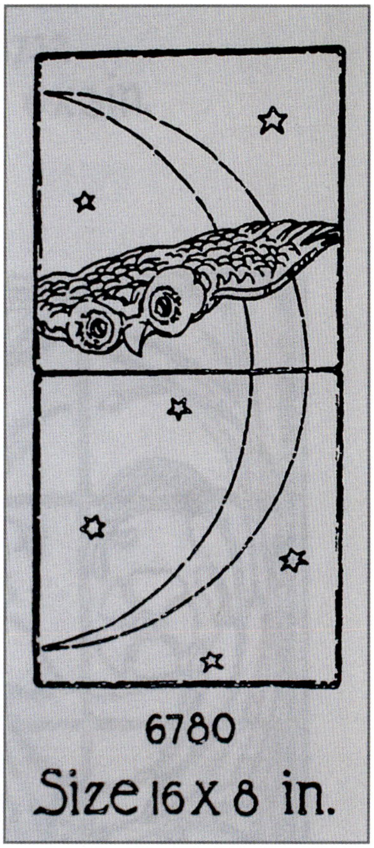

Detail of owl and moon panel illustrated on page 10 of *Catalog "G"* as Flint Faience stock design no. 6780.

Tiled owl and moon panel in the kindergarten fireplace facing in the Washington Elementary School, Wyandotte, Michigan. 8" x 16". Flint Faience stock design no. 6780. *Courtesy of Washington Elementary School.*

Owl and moon tile. 4.25" x 4.25". $200-250.

Detail of stock design no. 6630, birds in a basket, illustrated on page 19 of *Catalog "G."*

Other bird designs are portrayed with much character, such as the prancing chicken seen on the 4.25" square tile from the collection of Roger Ellingsworth or the pair of highly ornate birds shown with a basket on a 12" x 12" tile, no. 6630 in *Catalog "G"* page 19 (also in the Ellingsworth collection). Another stock design from *Catalog "G,"* no. 6752, depicts 8" square double birds in brilliant glazes. Parrots, puffins, and kingfishers are also creatively portrayed on 3" square tiles in the Ellingsworth collection. These three small bird decorated tiles are identical to those found among the thirty-two bird and animal designs installed in the fireplace facing at the Henry Ford Elementary School in Dearborn, Michigan. See other related illustrations under the entry for Animals.

Two birds on a basket tile. Flint Faience stock design no. 6630. 12" x 12". *Courtesy of Roger Ellingsworth.* $1500+.

Chicken tile. 4.25" x 4.25". *Collection of Roger Ellingsworth.* $200-250.

Double lovebirds on an 8" x 8" tile executed in raised line design. Flint Faience stock design no. 6752. $800-1100.

Puffin bird tile. 3" x 3". *Courtesy of Roger Ellingsworth*. $150-200.

Tile depicting a parrot on a branch. 3" x 3". *Courtesy of Roger Ellingsworth*. $150-200.

Kingfisher tile. 3" x 3". *Courtesy of Roger Ellingsworth*. $150-200.

Detail of animal tiles, each 2.75" x 2.75", on the fireplace in the Henry Ford Elementary School. Dearborn, Michigan.

Additional detail of animal tiles on the fireplace facing in the Henry Ford Elementary School.

Bees and moths are occasionally the subjects of Flint Faience tiles, and when they are depicted it is always with a carefree design style. Prime examples would be individual 4.25" tiles from the Roger Ellingsworth collection depicting a bee in a vivid pink flower and a moth on a sky blue background. An unusual butterfly insert tile is installed in the aisle of the Grosse Pointe Memorial Church in Grosse Pointe, Michigan.

Unusual tile decoration of a bee on a flower. 4.25" x 4.25". *Courtesy of Roger Ellingsworth*. $200-250.

A friendly-looking moth. 4.25" x 4.25". *Courtesy of Roger Ellingsworth*. $200-250.

For a rather fantastic combination Art Deco and futuristic interpretation of a bird design, the premiere example in Flint Faience tile would be found in the tiles created by Howard B. Burton for the Dryden Hotel in New York City. These designs were so successful that they were utilized in many promotional materials, including the 16-page *Architectural Faience: An Introduction* booklet published by Flint Faience & Tile Co. in 1929.

Futuristic birds and cats from the tile installation at the Dryden Hotel in New York City as illustrated on page 15 of *Architectural Faience: an Introduction. Courtesy of Jim Graham.*

More birds with varying personalities can be seen in the sweet images of ducks in private collections, such as the duck with three flowers decoration utilizing the raised line process in 4.25" tile format from the collection of Ken Galvas, or the molded duck, quite classically presented in 2.75" format, also in the Galvas collection. Slightly less warm and fuzzy bird portrayals would be the 5" x 5" tile depicting a raven in flight among the pines in the Barrett collection or the vulture depicted in raised line process on a 2.875" fireplace tile that was once in a Santa Monica home, now in the collection of Ken Galvas. The vulture tile is identical to those installed on the fireplace at the Henry Ford Elementary School in Dearborn, Michigan.

White duck tile with stylized flowers. 4.25" x 4.25". $200-250.

Molded duck tile, Flint Faience stock design no. 6670. 2.75" x 2.75". $50-75.

Vulture tile. 2.875" x 2.875". $150-200.

Several other images of birds appeared as stock designs in *Catalog "G"* and can be found as insert tiles in wall and floor installations as well as in private collections. These would include stock design no. 6589, a 2.75" tile depicting a bird holding a snake, and a rather heraldic portrayal of a black bird on a gold background, intended to be used as an insert tile, 2.75" square, stock design no. 6543 in *Catalog "G."*

Raised line tile featuring a raven gliding through the pine trees. 5" x 5". *Collection of Dale and Doris Barrett*. $600-800.

Molded tile of a crane with a snake. Flint Faience stock design no. 6589. 2.75" x 2.75" $50-75.

Molded tile depicting a black bird. 2.75" x 2.75". Flint Faience stock design no. 6543. $50-75.

Bisque tile with a representation of St. John. Flint Faience stock design no. 6465. 6" x 6". *Collection of Norman Karlson.* $100-125.

Tiles with bird designs also appear in bisque (unglazed but fired tile) both in installations and as individual tiles in private collections. The E&B Brewery in Detroit has many worn, faded tiles on its façade, including quite a few bisque examples such as the small tile depicting a pair of entwined birds shown beak-to-beak. Another example would be the bisque tile bird stock design no. 6465, representing St. John and inscribed "August 29, 1928," in the collection of Norman Karlson. A powerful image of a bird in bisque tile would be the carved bird image in 4.25" square format in the collection of Ken Galvas.

Bisque lovebirds tile mounted in the wall of the E&B Brewery in Detroit, Michigan. 2.75".

Bisque bird with a strong Art Deco flavor. 4.25" x 4.25". $100-125.

Bisque

Bisque tile can best be explained as unglazed, but completely fired tile. Both private collections and installations contain a considerable quantity of quality bisque tile, making it clear that both glazed and unglazed tiles could be utilized in installations. The E&B Brewery in Detroit is one example of an exterior wall installation where glazed and unglazed bisque tiles were installed side-by-side. This installation alone could be seen as proof that the Flint Faience bisque tiles found in private collections were not merely tiles that had been bisqued and were waiting for the next glazing phase of decoration and refiring in the tunnel kiln.

3" insert tiles on the exterior of the E&B Brewery. Detroit, Michigan.

Detail of the exterior of the E&B Brewery in Detroit, Michigan, illustrating many patterns of insert tiles.

A striking bisque relief tile, carved or modeled, in 6" x 6" format, which resembles stock design no. 6660 (a raised line decorated tile), but has the number 6220 in pencil on the face of the border is in the Dale and Doris Barrett collection. The design in high relief depicts an unglazed basket of fruit, featuring grapes and pears, with vines and other fruit. From the estate of Josephine Ellis, one of the key decorators at Flint Faience, this could be a model for making molds or a product sample or standard. Bisque could be finished tiles, or could be samples used in the factory or by the designers.

3" glazed and bisque tile inserts in exterior panels at the E&B Brewery. Detroit, Michigan.

Bisque tile fruit basket, measuring 6" x 6". Flint Faience stock design no. 6220. *Courtesy of Dale and Doris Barrett.* $100-125.

Three bisque tiles. 4.25" x 4.25". *Courtesy of Nick Hoffman.* $75-100 each.

Clown tile in bisque. 4.25" x 4.25". $75-100.

A grouping of three bisque tiles in the Nick Hoffmann collection, all 4.25" square, demonstrates the crispness of the tiles used in the "inlay" decoration process. Illustrated right to left they are stock design nos. 6432, 6435, and 6553. Other 4.25" square bisque tiles in the private collection of Ken Galvas match those found in the kindergarten room sandbox at the Washington School in Wyandotte, Michigan. They are depictions of a spooky clown, a mask, and a small pirate's ship that looks like the Jolly Roger, complete with a skull and cross bones. These are all decorated with the inlay process.

Jolly Roger tile in bisque. 4.25" x 4.25". $75-100.

Mask tile in bisque. 4.25" x 4.25". $75-100.

One final interesting bisque piece – and this one is in process, rather than a finished tile – is a 6" diameter bisque trivet with pencil decorations by Josephine Ellis, one of the important decorators at Flint Faience & Tile Co. as noted above. The trivet is now owned by her relatives, Dale and Doris Barrett. Pie-shaped demarcations are on the top in pencil while some greater detail has been drawn on one of the "slices."

Bisque trivet with pencil sketches by Josephine Ellis. 6". *Courtesy of Dale and Doris Barrett.*

Bookends, Paperweights, Ashtrays, Change Dishes, and Penholders

Not much is known about the other types of ceramic products produced by Flint Faience Tile Company, which include bookends, paperweights, ashtrays, change dishes, penholders, vases and flower pots. Some appear to be individualized creations of various designers and decorators at the company and others seem to be more related to the general tile product line of Flint Faience. None is advertised in any of their promotional materials.

Bookends are one small niche, and those that exist are rare. A pair of bisque bookends in the design known as "Solitude" were created by Flint Faience Tile Company designer Carl Bergmans, and have a "1930" date attached. The pair is 6.5" high and from the collection of Dale and Doris Barrett. These may have been unglazed samples retained by the company for quality control. Since this pair of bisque bookends came from the estate of the decorator who modeled them, she may have wished to keep a copy that was not obscured by a glaze. A pair of bookends in the same "Solitude" design, but with a black lustre or gunmetal glaze and measuring 6.75" x 4.75" x 2.5", are in the Ken Galvas collection.

"Solitude" bookends in bisque, dated 1930. 6.5". *Courtesy of Dale and Doris Barrett.* $100-150 pair.

Black-glazed "Solitude" bookends. 6.75". $150-200 pair.

Another unusual pair of bookends, with an Art Deco style and glaze palette, are in the Ruth Hylen collection. The stylized figure on each bookend wears a purple headdress and purple cloak. In addition, a pair of "Man & Candle" bookends in the Ken Galvas collection are semicircle shaped and depict a balding man with a beard, perhaps a monk, pouring over a book by candlelight. His left arm rests on a short stack of books. His clothing is very defined in deep relief carving. The backstamp is a stamped "Flint Faience Tile Co Flint Michigan." See the chapter on Identification and Marks for an illustration and further information.

Side view of unusual "Madam Butterfly" bookends. 9". *Courtesy of Ruth Hylen.*

Fine and rare pair of "Madam Butterfly" bookends. 9" x 4.25" x 2.375" *Courtesy of Ruth Hylen.* $700-900.

Pair of "Man & Candle" bookends. 8.65" x 5.25" x 2.375". $700-800 pair.

Paperweights were (and are) another use for Flint Faience tiles. Some tiles appear as though they were originally produced to be used as paperweights, while many of the 2" x 2" or 3" x 3" tiles lend themselves to this responsibility whether or not that was the original intention. One paperweight design could be described as a face portrait with turban, and can be seen in one private collection with three different glaze effects. The red-turbaned paperweight has an ink backstamp on the felt protector covering the base, which reads, "From Flint Faience Tile Co. Flint, Michigan." Each of these tiles measures 4.5" x 3.5" and all are in the Ken Galvas collection.

Grouping of Flint Faience paperweights. 4.5" x 3.5". $250-350each.

Several change dishes with arrowhead motifs were produced by Flint Faience & Tile Co. They are hexagonal in shape, measuring 4.5" across. A scroll border and a flint arrowhead in relief design form the border, while the compartment that would hold the coins has a concave apple shape. Another example can be seen under the entry for Arrowheads, Flint. One example has a glossy black border glaze and a rich yellow bowl interior.

Change dish with arrowhead design. 4.5". $100-125.

A few Flint Faience pen holders have been identified. They may be seen as novelty products or items used in hotels or banks, but are handsome and make one wish more had been produced. The one in the Ken Galvas collection is from the estate of Ralph Stoneburner, General Foreman of Flint Faience & Tile Company, and has a black lustre or gunmetal glaze. It is hexagonal shaped, measuring 3.5" across.

Fountain pen holder with hexagonal base. 3.5". Possibly for use in hotels or banks. $75-100.

Although ashtrays are no longer politically correct, all ceramics companies manufactured ashtrays at the time that Flint Faience & Tile Co. was in business (1921-33). Only a few examples exist today. The Flint Faience example in the Ken Galvas collection has an amber glaze and a 4" diameter with indentations for four cigarettes.

Circular ashtray with an amber glaze and measuring 4" in diameter. $40-60.

Border Tiles

Border tiles are so important in tile installations that they rated a full five pages in the 1926 Flint Faience Tile Company's *Catalog "G,"* including pages 13-17. In general, Flint Faience border tiles are 6" x 6", 4.25" x 2.125", 6" x 3", 6" x 2", 6" x 1", or 6" x 1.5". Some are decorated with the raised line process, others utilize inlay or embossing. Exquisite examples exist, such as the raised line border tiles no. 6735, with green leaves motifs on a pinkish-lavender background, measuring 2.75" x 6", found in the upstairs bathroom of the Prosper Champion home built in 1928 in Flint, Michigan. Nearby, in the same bathroom, is border tile no. 6675, waves created with the raised line process, executed in green with a pinkish-lavender background. This border tile is illustrated within the entry for Waves.

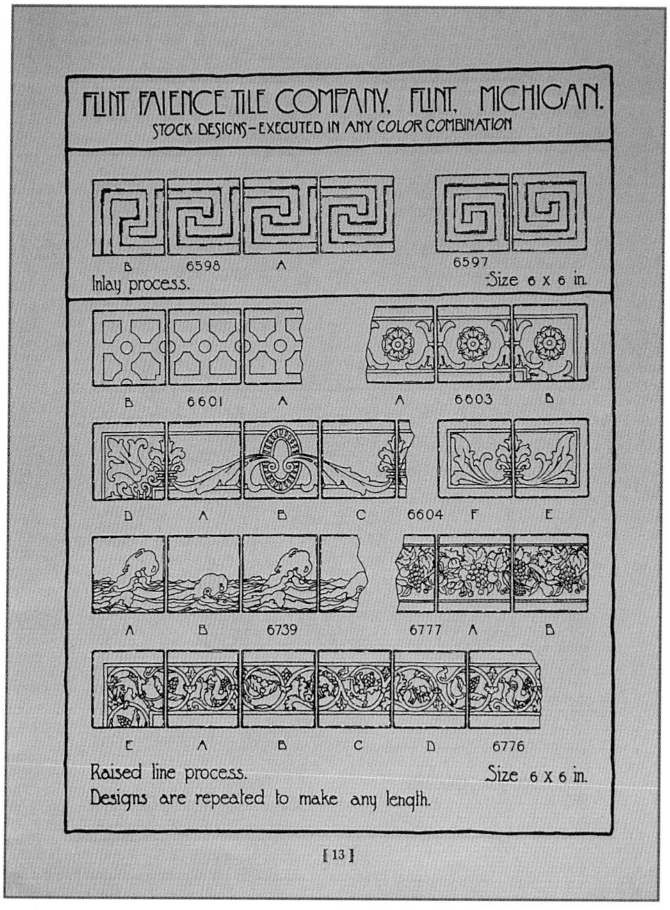
FLINT FAIENCE TILE COMPANY, FLINT, MICHIGAN.
STOCK DESIGNS—EXECUTED IN ANY COLOR COMBINATION

B 6598 A 6597
Inlay process. Size 6 x 6 in.

B 6601 A A 6603 B

D A B C 6604 F E

A B 6739 6777 A B

E A B C D 6776

Raised line process. Size 6 x 6 in.
Designs are repeated to make any length.

[13]

Border tiles depicted on page 13 of *Catalog "G."*

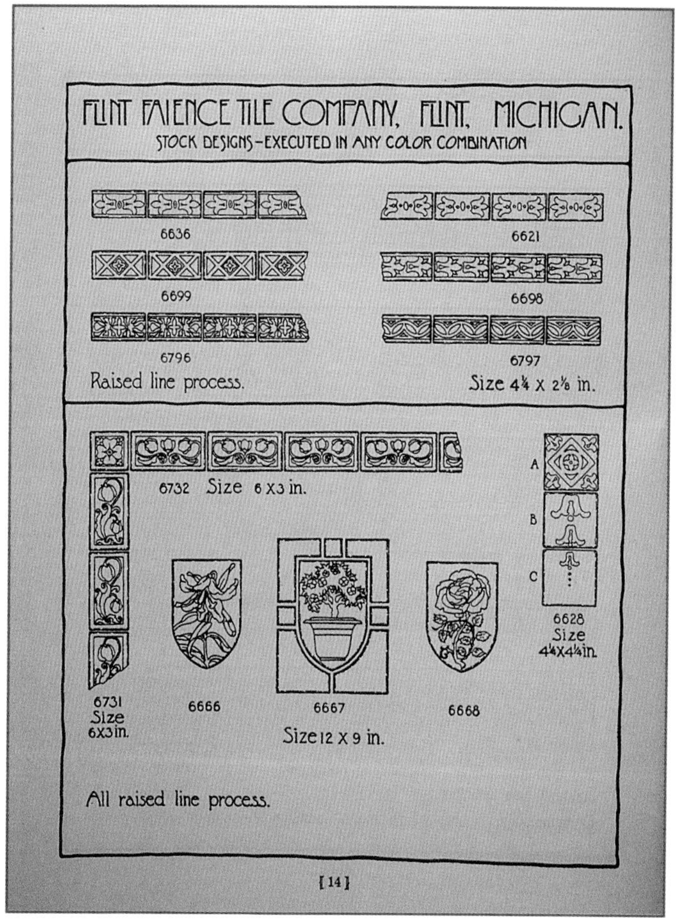
FLINT FAIENCE TILE COMPANY, FLINT, MICHIGAN.
STOCK DESIGNS—EXECUTED IN ANY COLOR COMBINATION

6636 6621
6699 6698
6796 6797
Raised line process. Size 4¼ x 2⅛ in.

6732 Size 6 x 3 in.
A B C
6628 Size 4¼x4¼ in.
6731 Size 6x3 in. 6666 6667 6668
Size 12 x 9 in.

All raised line process.

[14]

Border tiles depicted on page 14 of *Catalog "G."*

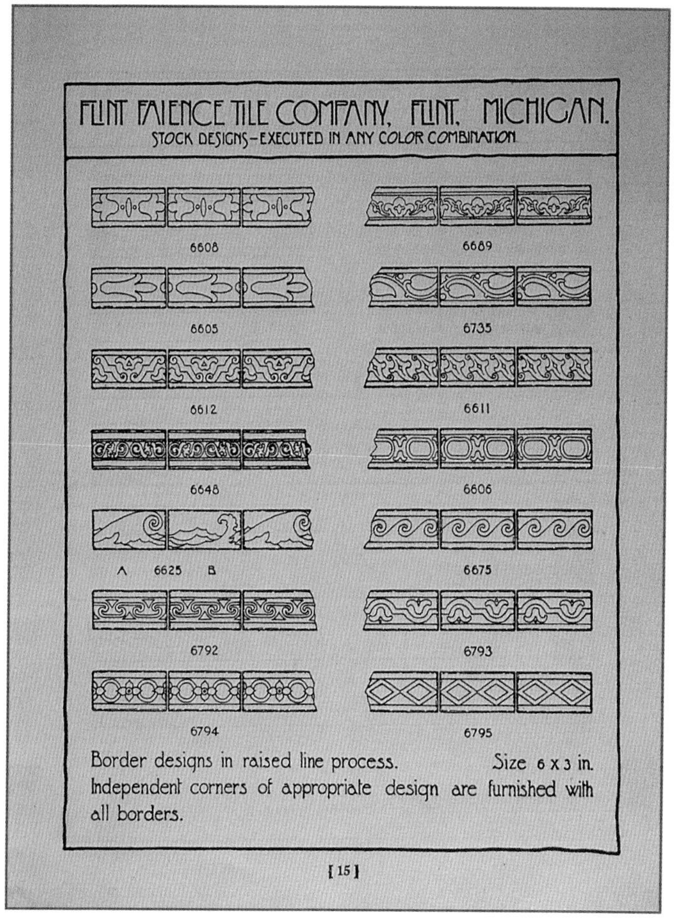
FLINT FAIENCE TILE COMPANY, FLINT, MICHIGAN.
STOCK DESIGNS—EXECUTED IN ANY COLOR COMBINATION

6608 6689
6605 6735
6612 6611
6648 6606
A 6625 B 6675
6792 6793
6794 6795

Border designs in raised line process. Size 6 x 3 in.
Independent corners of appropriate design are furnished with all borders.

[15]

Border tiles depicted on page 15 of *Catalog "G."*

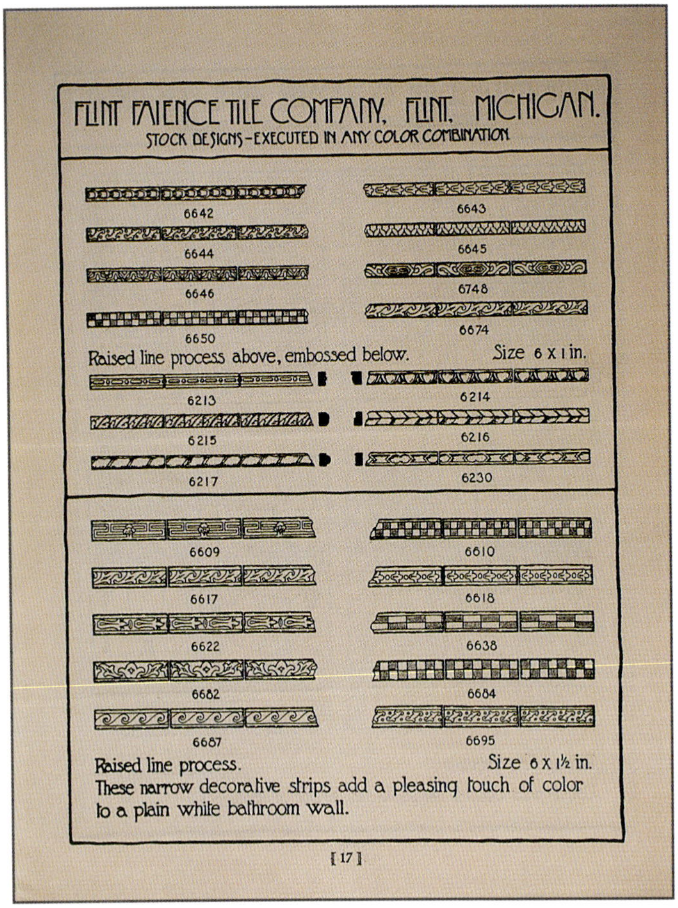
FLINT FAIENCE TILE COMPANY, FLINT, MICHIGAN.
STOCK DESIGNS—EXECUTED IN ANY COLOR COMBINATION

6642 6643
6644 6645
6646 6748
6650 6674

Raised line process above, embossed below. Size 6 x 1 in.

6213 6214
6215 6216
6217 6230

6609 6610
6617 6618
6622 6638
6682 6684
6687 6695

Raised line process. Size 6 x 1½ in.
These narrow decorative strips add a pleasing touch of color to a plain white bathroom wall.

[17]

Border tiles in stock designs as depicted on page 16 of *Catalog "G."*

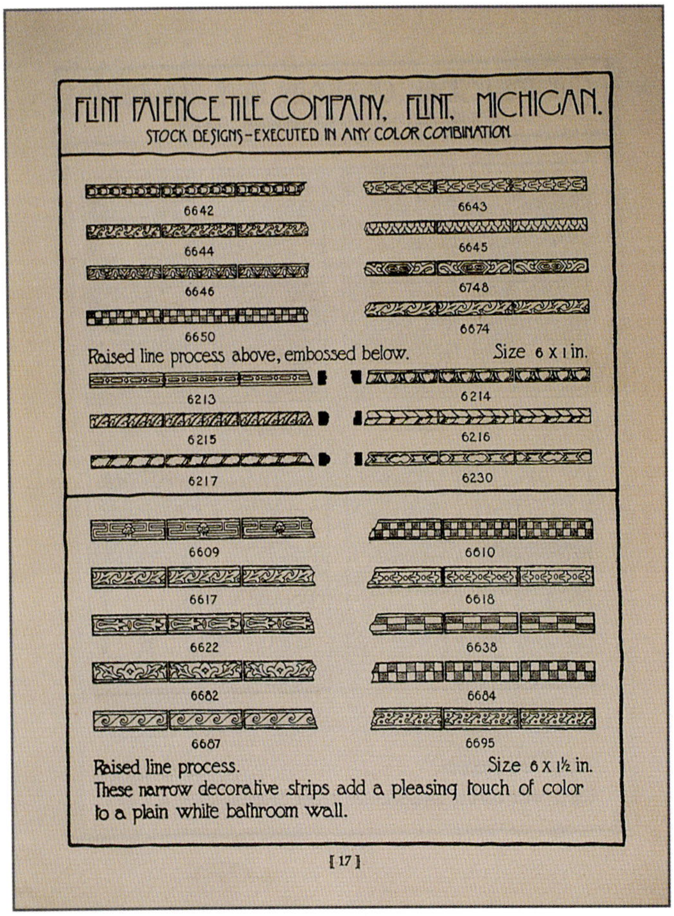
FLINT FAIENCE TILE COMPANY, FLINT, MICHIGAN.
STOCK DESIGNS—EXECUTED IN ANY COLOR COMBINATION

6642 6643
6644 6645
6646 6748
6650 6674

Raised line process above, embossed below. Size 6 x 1 in.

6213 6214
6215 6216
6217 6230

6609 6610
6617 6618
6622 6638
6682 6684
6687 6695

Raised line process. Size 6 x 1½ in.
These narrow decorative strips add a pleasing touch of color to a plain white bathroom wall.

[17]

Depictions of border tile stock designs, page 17 of *Catalog "G."*

Leaf border tiles in one of the bathrooms in the former home of Prosper Champion in Flint, Michigan. Flint Faience stock design no. 6735. *Courtesy of Jim Fitzell and Jessica Higgins.*

A comparison of the same stock design no. 6611 with the same 6" x 3" dimensions but different glaze choices, one a border tile and the other a panel, can be seen in the Ken Galvas collection. A beautiful border design with a rich glaze palette in amber, moss green, and brown is stock design no. 6403, 6" x 3", also in the Ken Galvas collection. Border trim, 6" x 1", also comes in intriguing patterns such as stock design no. 6642, with several examples found in the Galvas collection. More borders in the raised line decorating process utilize bright colors and a wide variety of design motifs, including 6" x 1.5" borders featuring stock designs (top to bottom) no. 6638, 6617, 6610, and a checkerboard pattern, all in the Ken Galvas collection.

Border tile in stock design no. 6611. 3" x 6". $30-40.

Border tile executed in raised line design. 3" x 6". $40-60.

Amber and olive glazed border tile measuring 3" x 6" in stock design no. 6403. $30-40.

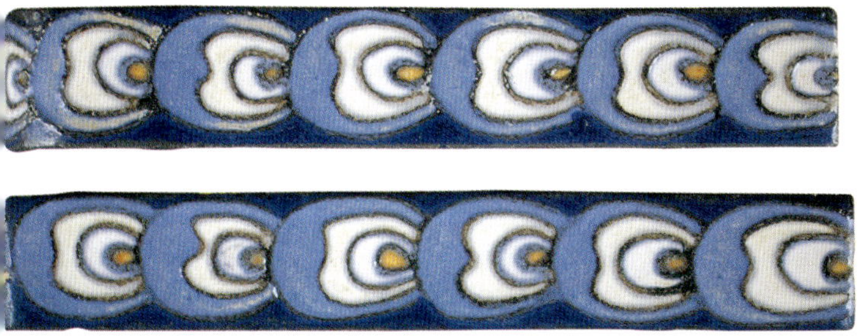

Border tiles 1" x 6" in raised line design no. 6642. The top tile is rounded for a wall return and this shape is referred to as a "bullnose" tile. $20-30 each.

Grouping of border tiles, illustrated top to bottom, stock designs no. 6638, no. 6617, no. 6610 and a checkerboard pattern. Each 1.5" x 6". $30-40 each.

Some border designs are recognizable from *Catalog "G"* illustrations and others are not. Recognizable are four stock design patterns in 6" x 1" border tile, all with raised line decorations, nos. (top to bottom) 6674, 6643, 6644, and 6645, which looks like bunnies when flipped upside down as in the photograph. Another stunning design when coupled with contrasting glazes is stock design no. 6458, a 6" x 3" border tile with blue diamond patterns within an amber, black, and beige setting.

Grouping of border tiles, illustrated top to bottom, stock designs no. 6674, no. 6643, no. 6644, and no. 6645. All executed in raised line design and measuring 1" x 6". $ 30-40 each.

Border tile stock design no. 6458. 3" x 6". $40-50.

There are border tiles that do not have stock design numbers but their purpose is known, such as the church window border set measuring 9" x 4.25" from the Ken Galvas collection. Similarly, a 6" x 4.25" border tile in the Galvas collection matches those in St. Paul's School in Grosse Pointe Farms, Michigan. Still others are simply beautiful, such as the four 6" x 1" border tiles that have an Art Deco flavor perhaps mixed with some Southwestern accents. Blue clover and diamonds are featured on a 5.875" x 3" border tile in the Galvas collection. If it was a stock design, that number is now lost. Diamonds and circles in amber and white present a memorable design pattern in a 3.125" x 1.5" border fragment, also in the Galvas collection.

Four border tiles with a Southwest flavor. Each 1" x 6". $20-30 each.

Church window border set. Executed in raised line design. 4.25" x 9". $75-100.

"Clover and Diamond" border tile. 3" x 5.875". $40-60.

Large 4.25" x 6" raised line border tile. $200-250.

Diamond and circle pattern. 3.125" x 1.5".

Botanicals

Flowers, trees, and plants of all types adorn Flint Faience tiles, regardless of the style of the tile installation. These popular motifs range from traditional raised line designs to carved relief depictions of iris, bluebells, tulips, and more. Some are stylized while others are shown more or less realistically portrayed in their natural setting or in vases, baskets, and compotes. Many were stock designs that can be seen in *Catalog "G."* Often the design pattern is seen over and over again, in different tiles and installations but with different glaze treatments.

Bluebells decorate this 4.25" x 4.25" tile. Stock design no. 6724. *Courtesy of Mark and Barb Harris*. $275-325.

Iris pattern stock design no. 6711 in raised line. 6" x 6". *Courtesy of Kristine Burton*. $450-550.

Raised line design iris tile. 6" x 6". *Courtesy of Mark and Barb Harris*. $450-550.

Bluebell tile in raised line design. 4" x 4". $275-325.

Stock design no. 6758. Tulip tiles in raised line design. 3" x 3". $75-125.

Catalog "G," page 11, illustrates an iris carved in relief, no. 6204 of the modeled stock designs, with dimensions of 8.75" x 4.25". The same modeled stock design can be seen in the green and amber glazed iris tile, measuring 8.5" x 4.125" in the Roger Ellingsworth collection. Many similar iris tiles were salvaged from the Winchester Hospital in Flint, Michigan. An example is illustrated under the Hospitals entry.

From page 11 of *Catalog "G,"* detail illustrating stock design no. 6204 relief iris.

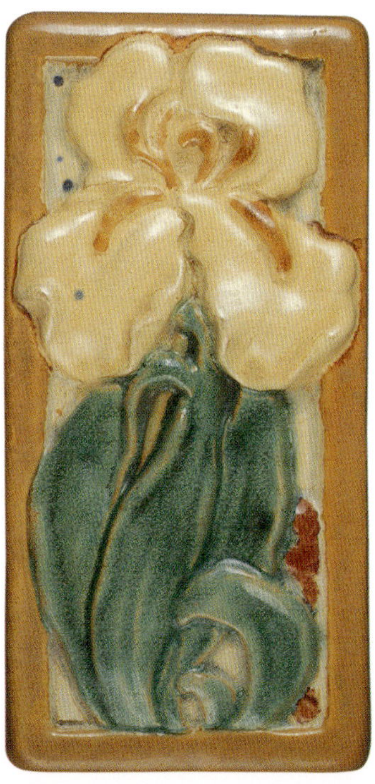

Iris tile in high relief. Stock design no. 6204, measuring 8.5" x 4.125". *Courtesy of Roger Ellingsworth.* $750-1000.

Traditional bouquets of flowers (or sometimes fruit) are seen displayed in vases, baskets, or compotes, often with a black or brown background which gives an almost glowing effect to the sharply contrasting, brilliantly colored glazes comprising the design. This is certainly the case in a pair of tiles, each depicting an urn with stylized flowers including a daisy. The one on the right is an Arowa blank and the one on the left is the standard Flint Faience 6" tile. The shape of the Arowa tile adds a three-dimensional effect because the tile was installed 0.375" higher than the grout line. The same wonderful contrast can be seen in the jewel-like quality of a similar floral arrangement with a daisy, but designed with a different vase, 6.25" square, in the Galvas collection. Another grouping of flowers on a 6" square tile, with the bouquet shown in a fancy urn, stock design no. 6715 in *Catalog "G,"* is in the collection of Rob Rozycki. Another no. 6715, with a variation of glaze hues, is in the collection of Ken Galvas. A 6" x 6" variation on the flowers in urn theme, decorated by Josephine Ellis and signed "JE", is now in the Dale and Doris Barrett collection. A wonderful abstract bouquet form, stock design no. 6656 in *Catalog "G,"* with the bouquet tied with a ribbon and rick-rack decoration serving as the border of this charming 12" square tile, is in the Galvas collection.

Tiles depicting colorful flower urns. 6" x 6". On the right an Arowa blank. $400-450 each.

Flower basket tile. 6.25". $400-450.

Flower basket tile, stock design no. 6715. 6" x 6". *Courtesy of Robert Rozycki*. $400-450.

Basket of flowers tile, measuring 6" x 6". Signed "JE," for the decorator, Josephine Ellis. *Courtesy of Dale and Doris Barrett*. $400-450.

Detail of flowers stock design no. 6656, from page 19 of *Catalog "G."*

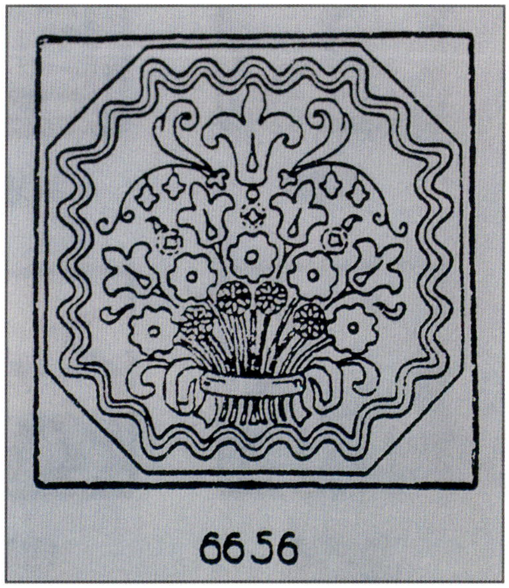

Flower basket tile, stock design no. 6715. 6" x 6". $400-450.

Large floral tile, stock design no. 6656-1. Executed in raised line design. 12" x 12". $1200-1500.

There is no shortage of tiles with abstract floral designs, some available as stock designs, many geometric in character. Stock design no. 6722, is a 4.25" tile whose design of three flowers and vines was created using the raised line process and was intended to be used as an insert tile in an installation. Stock design no. 6769 is an abstract flower shape with blue and peach petals, also raised line design and 4.25" square. Very striking is the design of the 4.25" insert tile, stock design no. 6761, with five daisies, four depicted in an unexpected profile. A pair of stock design no. 6723 4.25" insert tiles can be seen with contrasting glazes providing dramatically different overall effects on the tile.

Floral tile, stock design no. 6769. 4.25" x 4.25". $250-300.

Floral tile, stock design no. 6722, measuring 4.25" x 4.25". $250-300.

Floral design, stock design no. 6761. 4.25" x 4.25". $250-300.

Floral tiles in contrasting glaze color combinations, stock design no. 6723. 4.25" x 4.25". $250-300 each.

An assortment of ingenious abstract, geometric floral patterns can be seen in other tiles in private collections, including stock design no. 6444, depicting four tulips on a 6" x 6" tile in the Ken Galvas collection; an almost wild orange, blue, and yellow decorated 6" square tile in the Norman Karlson collection; another 6" square tile in stock design no. 6528, with a lustre glaze on a tulip form in the Galvas collection; a subtle but beguilingly modeled four-petaled 5.75" tile in the Galvas collection with muted lavender and pink glazes; stock design no. 6535, a 2.625" decorative insert tile described as one of the "Gothic" patterns created by the embossing process, glazed pale blue giving it a lyrical quality; and finally, a sweet 1.5" insert tile, no. 6509, which can either be interpreted as a white "X" on a blue background or a small four-petaled white flower on blue.

Circus flower in raised line design. 6" x 6". $125-175. *Courtesy Norman Karlson.*

Molded tulips grace this tile. Stock design no. 6444. 6" x 6". $125-150.

Molded floral tile with lustre glaze, stock design no. 6528. 6" x 6" $125-175.

Four large petals form this 5.75" x 5.75" tile with pastel glazes. $125-175.

A petite floral tile. Stock design no. 6509, measuring 1.5" x 1.5". $15-20.

Blue floral pattern, stock design no. 6535. 2.625" x 2.625". $40-50.

Not all floral motifs found their way onto square or rectangular tiles. An unusual abstract design which has been described as Native American in flavor is an almost circular tile, approximately 7.25" diameter except where it bulges at the edge where each petal or leaf protrudes, decorated in stunning red, blue and orange glazes and located in the Ken Galvas collection. Another circular tile, 4.25" in diameter, has a striking design of two 5-petaled white flowers shown against a dark blue glazed background, also in the Galvas collection. A hexagonal tile with a vivid flower in pink, turquoise, yellow, and black is also in the Galvas collection. Executed in raised line design, it has a flint arrowhead backstamp which indicates that the tile was probably manufactured by dry pressing. Quite a number of hexagonal tiles were installed as inserts in important residential installations in Flint, Michigan. These would include many 3.5" hexagonal floral patterns among bold lavender bathroom floor tiles in the former E.T. Strong/Hamady home and larger 5.125" hexagonal floral patterned insert tiles in the conservatory of the same home.

Similar iris tiles and tiles with other botanical motifs can be seen in the Grosse Pointe Memorial Church in Grosse Pointe Farms, Michigan, and many of the other installations covered elsewhere is this A-Z of Flint Faience.

Botanicals – leaves and flowers and such – were popular as individual tiles, as parts of larger tile panels or murals, as border tiles, and as inserts. They were just as popular in Arts & Crafts style tiles or Art Deco, stock designs, or custom work. The July 13, 1930 edition of the *Flint Journal* newspaper illustrated a wonderfully imaginative bathroom in the home of Eugene Zukor, located on Park Avenue in New York City. The tiles in the tub recesses were all unusual cat-tail designs in green and brown. These tiles have occasionally come up for sale on Internet auction sites.

Unusual rounded and carved floral tile in an "Indian flower" motif. Diameter 7.25". $350-400.

Raised line hexagon floral tile, measuring 2". $40-60.

A silhouette of white flowers on a blue background. Diameter 4.25". $100-125.

Unusual 3.5" hexagon shaped insert tile in raised line design installed in a bathroom in the former E.T. Strong home. *Courtesy of the Hamady Estate.*

Wonderful 3.5" hexagonal tile installed in a bathroom in the former E.T. Strong home, Flint, Michigan. *Courtesy of the Hamady Estate.*

Another large hexagonal tile in raised line design installed in the conservatory at the former E.T. Strong home in Flint, Michigan. 5.125" x 5.125". *Courtesy of the Hamady Estate.*

Large hexagonal tile in raised line design installed in the conservatory at the former E.T. Strong home, Flint, Michigan. 5.125" x 5.125". *Courtesy of the Hamady Estate.*

Buildings, Representations of

Buildings of a variety of types were represented as subject matter on Flint Faience tiles. Some were of an Arts & Crafts or Art Deco style (see Arts & Crafts and Art Deco entries for images and descriptions), others depicted Dutch windmills, and still another genre of buildings were almost cartoonish in their representation of what can only be described as "fat houses." The 6" square tile depicting a windmill in blue outline format on a white glazed background is quite different than the 4.25" insert tile of a windmill in the Ken Galvas collection that matches those on the sandbox in the kindergarten room at the Washington School in Wyandotte, Michigan. The matching windmill at the Washington School was inserted near to tiles depicting a little Dutch boy and a little Dutch girl. The 6" x 6" tile with the "fat house" motif in the Dale and Doris Barrett collection is nearly identical to one in the Roger Ellingsworth collection except for the white cloud in the former.

Blue and white outlined windmill. 6" x 6". *Courtesy of Dale and Doris Barrett.* $250-300.

"Fat house" tile in raised line design. 6" x 6". *Courtesy of Dale and Doris Barrett.* $650-700.

Molded windmill tile. 4.25" x 4.25" $100-125.

"Fat house" tile in raised line design. 6" x 6". *Courtesy of Roger Ellingsworth.* $650-700.

Burton, Howard B.

see also Architectural Faience: An Introduction, Zodiac, Wheatsworth Factory, Dryden Hotel, Flight Into Egypt, and Agriculture – Egypt

Howard Burton, c. 1929. *Courtesy of Kristine Burton.*

Howard Blaine Burton was born February 9, 1881 in Brocton, New York. He graduated from Cornell University, Ithaca, New York, on June 20, 1905 with a Bachelor of Architecture degree. On June 12, 1906, he married Cora Mae Allen in Brocton, New York, with their only child, Howard B. Burton, Jr. born on September 1, 1909.

Before joining Flint Faience & Tile Company, Burton was associated with several prominent architectural firms, including Carrere and Hastings (1905-1907), Henry Rutgers Marshall (1907-1909), McKim, Mead & White (1909-1910), Charles Platt (1911-1912), and John Russel Pope (1912-1915). Between 1915-1925, he worked with specialty contractors on design projects, including Rising & Nelson Slate Co., Vermont (1915-1918), Lunken Windor Co., Cincinnati (1919-1920), and Vendor Slate Co., Easton, Pennsylvania (1923-1925). He also worked as one of the staff of the *American Architect*. As Art Director and Architect for the Flint Faience and Tile Company between January 1926 and 1930, he was manager of Eastern sales, with duties specific to building materials products, design, installation, sales, travel and organization. Taine McDougal served as his boss. Burton is largely responsible for the Flint Faience & Tile Company literature that has survived to today, including the booklet *Architectural Faience: An Introduction* and issues of *AC Sparks* as well as *Catalog "G."* Additionally he can be credited with designing many of the most memorable Flint Faience tile installations, including the futuristic lobby walls, ceiling, wainscoting, floors, and loggia of the Dryden Hotel in New York City and the series of allegorical panels featuring agriculture for the Wheatsworth Company in Hamburg, New Jersey. He also designed three award-winning tile pieces, *Flight Into Egypt*, *Twelve Zodiacs*, and *Capricorn*, which were exhibited at the Metropolitan Museum of Art in October 1928 and traveled with the American Federation of Arts exhibition to eight other venues; and designed a bathroom for the Presidential Palace in Peru, circa 1929. His zodiac figure tile creations are well known, but he additionally created beautiful organic form vases with crystalline glazes.

With brief periods of unemployment, Burton continued his private practice – with his partner Max Bohm for most of the time between 1918-1940 – despite employment with other architectural firms and Flint Faience Tile Co. From 1934 to 1940, he served as associate architect with a low cost housing project in New York City. In 1942, he moved from the New York City area to Oklahoma City, where he worked as an architect with a government agency. He suffered a stroke in 1945 and could not continue working after that date. He died July 13, 1950 in Oklahoma City, Oklahoma. He is buried in St. Paul, Minnesota.

8.25" high glazed stoneware melon-form vase by Howard B. Burton. Diameter 6". *Courtesy of Kristine Burton. Photograph courtesy of Peter Lee.*

Champion, Albert

see chapter on History of Flint Faience Tiles: The Automotive Connection

• • • • • • • • • • • • • • • • • •

Children's Nursery Rhymes and Stories

see also Humpty Dumpty, Little Black Sambo

Probably no Flint Faience tile designs are more captivating to the viewer than those depicting nursery rhymes and stories from childhood. While occasionally found in private homes, these can most frequently be found in public school classrooms and libraries, adorning fireplaces, fountains, sandboxes, sinks and drinking fountains. Recognizable nursery rhymes and stories would include Mary Had a Little Lamb, Little Miss Muffet, Goldilocks and the Three Bears, Baa Baa Black Sheep, Jack and Jill, the Cow Jumped Over the Moon, This Little Piggy Had Roast Beef, Humpty Dumpty, and the Story of Little Black Sambo.

Large nursery rhyme panel, "Little Miss Muffet." 13.5" x 8.75". *Courtesy of Diane and Dan Veirs.* $3000+

Large nursery rhyme panel, "Mary had a Little Lamb." 13.5" x 8.75". *Courtesy of www.BungalowBill.com.*

Large nursery rhyme tile, "Goldilocks and the Three Bears." Personalized with "Nancy Joy Roy." 13.5" x 8.75". *Courtesy of www.BungalowBill.com.*

"Goldilocks and the Three Bears" tile with original hanger. 9" x 9". $2500+

'Jack and Jill" tile, measuring 9" x 9". $2500+

"Baa Baa Black Sheep" tile, measuring 6" x 6". $ 800-1000.

"Cow Jumped Over the Moon" tile, measuring 4.25" x 4.25". $350-400.

"This Little Piggy had Roast Beef" tile, measuring 6" x 6". *Courtesy of Dale and Doris Barrett.* $800-1000.

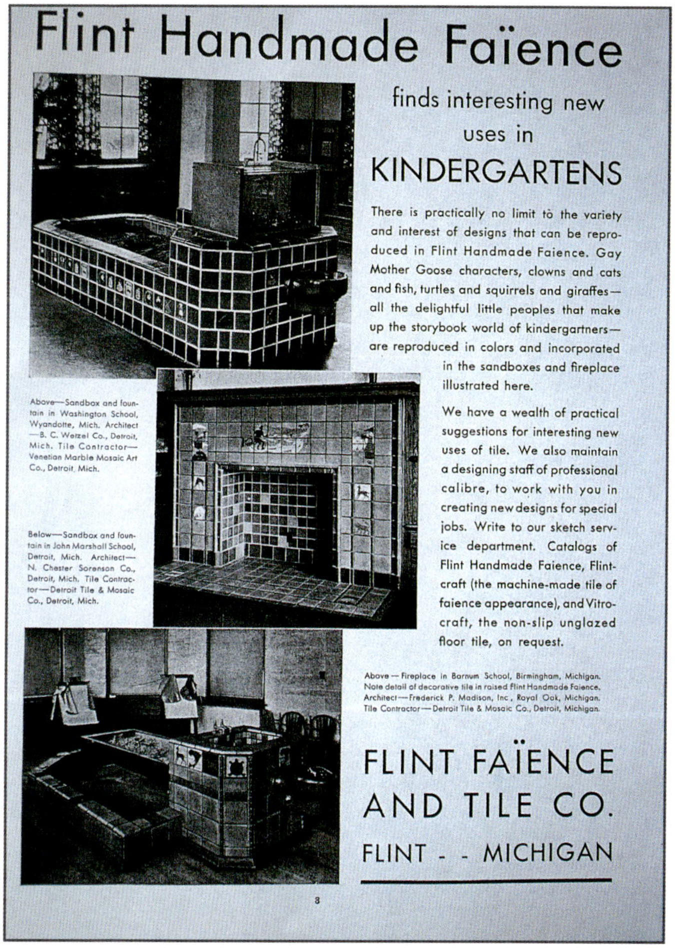

Flint Handmade Faïence

finds interesting new uses in

KINDERGARTENS

There is practically no limit to the variety and interest of designs that can be reproduced in Flint Handmade Faience. Gay Mother Goose characters, clowns and cats and fish, turtles and squirrels and giraffes— all the delightful little peoples that make up the storybook world of kindergartners— are reproduced in colors and incorporated in the sandboxes and fireplace illustrated here.

We have a wealth of practical suggestions for interesting new uses of tile. We also maintain a designing staff of professional calibre, to work with you in creating new designs for special jobs. Write to our sketch service department. Catalogs of Flint Handmade Faience, Flintcraft (the machine-made tile of faience appearance), and Vitrocraft, the non-slip unglazed floor tile, on request.

Above—Sandbox and fountain in Washington School, Wyandotte, Mich. Architect—B. C. Wetzel Co., Detroit, Mich. Tile Contractor—Venetian Marble Mosaic Art Co., Detroit, Mich.

Below—Sandbox and fountain in John Marshall School, Detroit, Mich. Architect—N. Chester Sorenson Co., Detroit, Mich. Tile Contractor—Detroit Tile & Mosaic Co., Detroit, Mich.

Above — Fireplace in Barnum School, Birmingham, Michigan. Note detail of decorative tile in raised Flint Handmade Faience. Architect—Frederick P. Madison, Inc., Royal Oak, Michigan. Tile Contractor—Detroit Tile & Mosaic Co., Detroit, Michigan.

FLINT FAÏENCE AND TILE CO.

FLINT - - MICHIGAN

3

Keramic Tile Journal, Volume 3, no. 6, 1931, Page 3, illustrating kindergarten rooms with children's nursery rhyme tile installations.

Flint Faience Tile Company created a selection of small 2.75" square decorative inserts for random placement among field tiles in nursery room walls and floors. These seven tiles with embossed process decorations of polar bears, ducks, squirrels, elephants, etc. were illustrated as nos. 6582, 6583, 6584, 6585, 6589, 6411 and 6412 on page 24 of *Catalog "G."* Flint Faience noted in one advertisement in the trade journal *Keramic Tile Journal* (*Keramic Tile Journal*, June 1931, 3) that "There is practically no limit to the variety and interest of designs that can be reproduced in Flint Handmade Faience. Gay Mother Goose characters, clowns and cats and fish, turtles and squirrels and giraffes – all the delightful little peoples that make up the storybook world of kindergartens – are reproduced in colors and incorporated in the sandboxes and fireplace illustrated here."

Illustrations of stock design nursery room inserts from page 24 of *Catalog "G."*

Churches

see also Religious Themes

Some of the churches that contain Flint Faience tile installations have direct connections to the employees and leadership of Flint Faience & Tile Co. and AC Spark Plug. For example, Flint Faience designer, Julio Haro, was a parishioner in St. Matthew Catholic Church in Flint, Michigan. Visible today in this church are beautiful tiles of lambs and other religious symbols along with colorful insert tiles among earthy toned field tiles. Although St. Matthew dates to 1911, the present site located on the southwest corner of Beach and Third streets was constructed beginning in 1919. Their recorded history notes that beginning in 1926 pews and marble altars were added and the decorating of the church was begun. The 1986 publication, *St. Matthew Church History 1911-1986*, notes "The Sanctuary floor is of hand made unglazed Faience tile of random design with decorative color inserts...the design and laying of this floor was done by a former parishioner, Julio Haro, who was a professional ceramist at AC Spark Plug." (St. Matthew Church, 1986, 7)

Exterior view of St. Matthew Church, Flint, Michigan. *Courtesy of St. Matthew Church, Flint, Michigan.*

Overview of the altar of St. Matthew Church, showing Flint Faience tiles. *Courtesy of St. Matthew Church, Flint, Michigan.*

Insert tiles in St. Matthew Church. *Courtesy of St. Matthew Church, Flint, Michigan.*

Albert Champion's memorial service was held at St. Paul's Episcopal Church in Flint, Michigan. Located at 711 South Saginaw Street, this splendid church (which dates historically to 1840, with the present church building constructed in 1873) contains a few installations of decorative Flint Faience tile in the chancel, including muted mauve field tiles with larger panels featuring religious motifs.

Lamb panel on left side of the altar. 12" x 18". *Courtesy of St. Matthew Church, Flint, Michigan.*

Center Cross design in front of the altar. 12" x 37". *Courtesy of St. Matthew Church, Flint, Michigan.*

Postcard of St. Paul's Episcopal Church, Flint, Michigan. *Courtesy of Ken Galvas.*

"IHS" tile in the chancel of St. Paul's Episcopal Church. *Courtesy of St. Paul's Episcopal Church, Flint, Michigan.*

"IHS" tile inserts in the chancel of St. Paul's Episcopal Church. *Courtesy of St. Paul's Episcopal Church, Flint, Michigan.*

Border tile detail in St. Paul's Episcopal Church. *Courtesy of St. Paul's Episcopal Church, Flint, Michigan.*

Several stock designs from *Catalog "G"* were most likely intended for use within a church setting. These include nos. 6789 and 6790 on page 8, roundels, 16" in diameter with raised line designs of a cross and roses in one and a little church in a valley in the other. Page 9 illustrates more than one stock design that might be favored by a church, including no. 6704, featuring a cross motif. One particularly beautiful pattern that was included in at least one church is stock design no. 6446, illustrated on page 21 of *Catalog "G."* In blue and gold glazes, this example of the 6" x 6" inlay process decorated tile is in the collection of Ken Galvas. This same tile pattern is part of the tile and brick installation on the exterior of the Sacred Heart Church in Flint, Michigan.

Typical inlay accent tile installed on the exterior of Sacred Heart Church in Flint, Michigan. 6" x 6". Stock design no. 6446. $100-125.

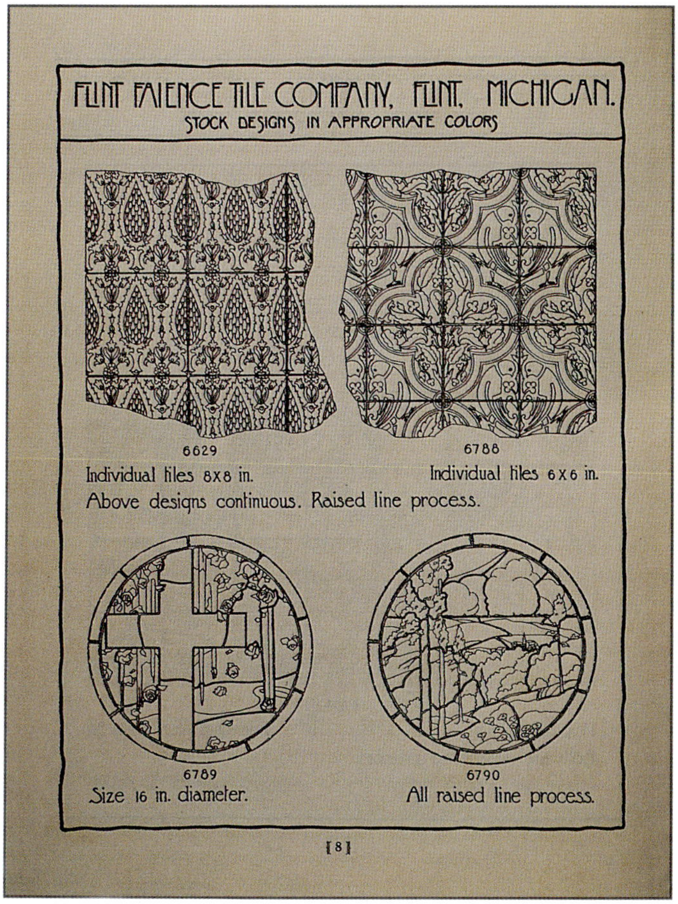

FLINT FAIENCE TILE COMPANY, FLINT, MICHIGAN.
STOCK DESIGNS IN APPROPRIATE COLORS

6629 6788

Individual tiles 8x8 in. Individual tiles 6x6 in.
Above designs continuous. Raised line process.

6789 6790

Size 16 in. diameter. All raised line process.

[8]

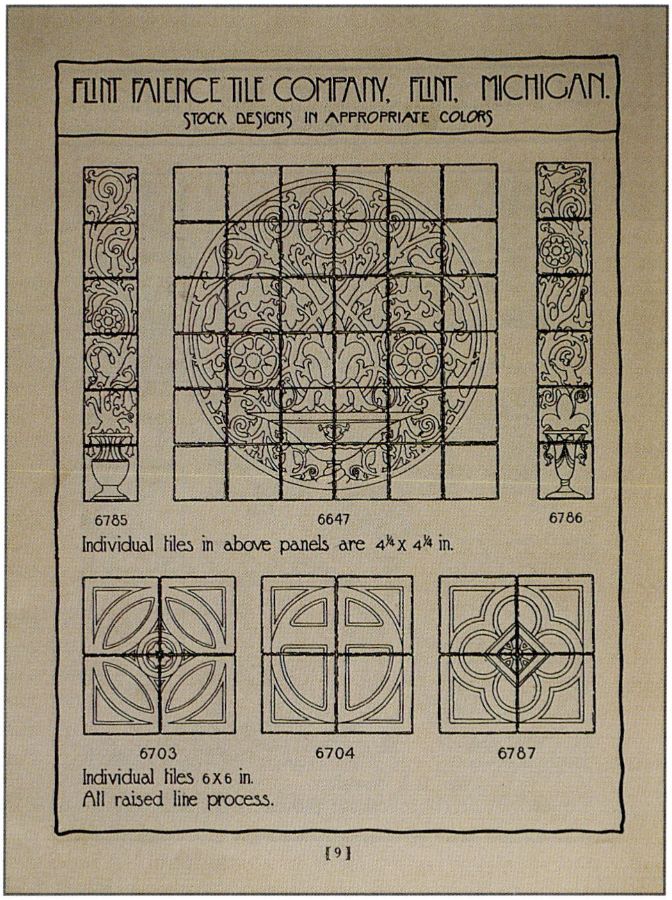

FLINT FAIENCE TILE COMPANY, FLINT, MICHIGAN.
STOCK DESIGNS IN APPROPRIATE COLORS

6785 6647 6786

Individual tiles in above panels are 4¼ x 4¼ in.

6703 6704 6787

Individual tiles 6x6 in.
All raised line process.

[9]

Stock designs, some with religious motifs, from pages 8 and 9 of *Catalog "G."*

Presentation drawings were prepared for a proposed Flint Faience tile floor in the First Baptist Church, Shaker Heights, Ohio. The watercolor over graphite on buff-white illustration board drawings were prepared by the company for The Smitley-Hamilton Company of Cleveland. The drawing measuring 19.875" x 24.125" depicts three proposed schemes for pavement, with decorative panels and inserts in three color schemes. The sketch was numbered X0937.

Other churches with significant Flint Faience tile installations include the Grosse Pointe Memorial Church in Grosse Pointe Farms, Michigan. The floors in the church feature beautiful insert tiles depicting lions, lizards, fish, iris, ducks, rabbits, turtles, polar bears, squirrels, a butterfly, and many geometric patterns.

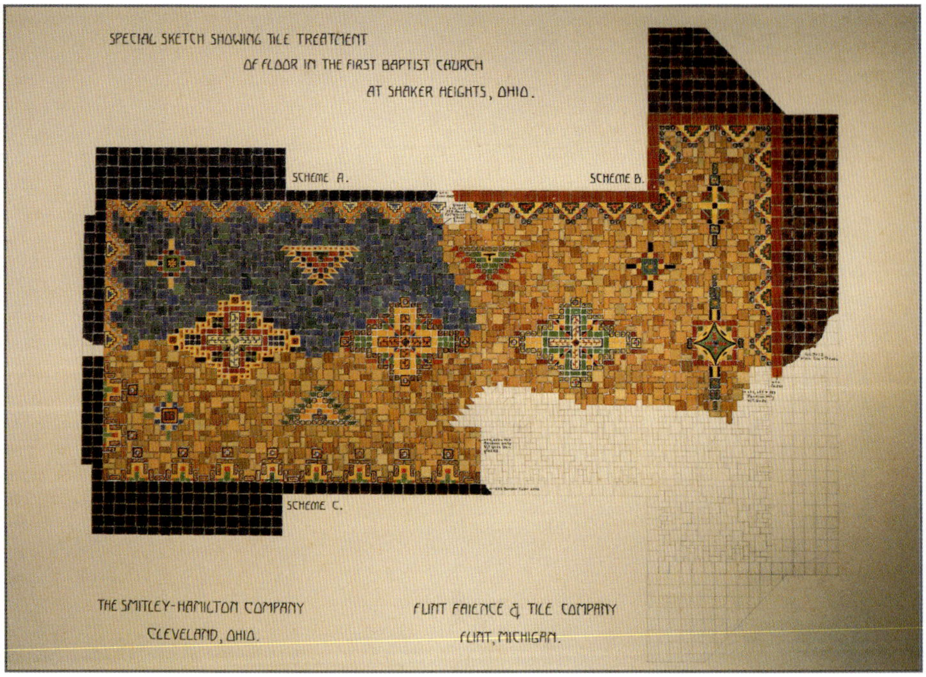

Original watercolor presentation drawing for the Shaker Heights First Baptist Church, Shaker Heights, Ohio. *Courtesy of Vance Koehler.*

Clowns

Clowns are not the most common Flint Faience tile subject matter, but they are not exactly rare. Usually clowns appear as part of a larger installation of interesting characters, such as witches, masks, Dutch boys and girls, and similar motifs. On the exterior of the sandbox in room 103 on the first floor of the Garfield School in Wyandotte, Michigan, constructed circa 1932, is a wonderful 6" square tile depiction of a smiling clown with the stereotypical red nose. The clown, installed on point, is near other interesting, brilliantly decorated tiles of fish, parrots, ships, and a rather evil looking bird. A less happy looking 4.25" square clown tile was installed next to a frightening masked face and court jester on the exterior of a sandbox at the Washington School kindergarten room in Wyandotte, Michigan.

Clown tile installed in the sandbox at Garfield Elementary School, Wyandotte, Michigan. 6" on point in raised line design. *Courtesy of Mary Wharton Thorson.*

Halloween mask tile installed in the sandbox, Washington Elementary School, Wyandotte, Michigan. 4.25" x 4.25". *Courtesy of Washington Elementary School.*

Occasionally clown tiles are found in private collections, such as the exquisitely drawn 4.25" square tile of a clown with a large polka dot hat and ruffled collar, all executed in raised line process, in the collection of Ken Galvas. One wonders what would have been installed next to it. The same question could be raised about a clown in another private collection, shown on a larger 8.25" square tile, who could be the twin or at least cousin of the previous one, with the pointed white hat with large black polka dots and the same ruffled collar. This larger tile, however, modeled in relief, is positioned on point, and is slightly more maniacal in facial expression than the other.

Clown tile in raised line design. 4.25" x 4.25". $300-400.

Large carved clown tile. 8.25" x 8.25". *Courtesy of Dale and Doris Barrett.* $800-900.

Colors or Colorants

see Glazes

Compass

see also Zodiac

The compass was not a common Flint Faience motif, but it is one of the most handsome of the innovative designs. The compass often accompanies a set of twelve zodiac tiles, as was the case with the compass installed in the small foyer at the former Taine McDougal home in Flint, Michigan. The home was built in 1928. The compass itself is composed of nine separate pieces and is 18" in diameter. It is interesting to note that this compass is accurate in its reading. The compass was the central motif, surrounded by four groupings of three zodiac tiles. Other images can be seen under the entry for the zodiac.

Large compass panel installed in the former Taine McDougal home in Flint, Michigan. Comprised of nine pieces with a diameter of 18". *Courtesy of Linda and Joseph Katrinic, Jr.*

This same compass can be seen as pattern no. 7148-2, 17.75" diameter, an original watercolor on a 4" x 6" index card now in the permanent collection of the Sloan Museum in Flint, Michigan. The watercolor indicates each of the glaze colors to be used in the tile production of the compass. The collection at the Sloan Museum also includes original watercolors on index cards of each of the twelve zodiac tiles, with glaze color numbers recorded.

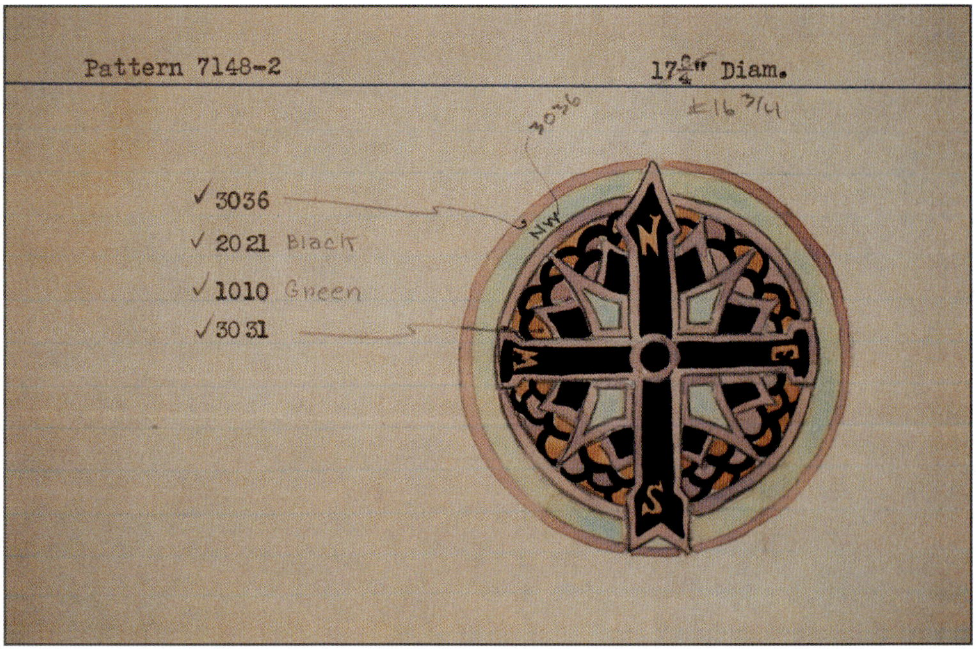

Watercolor sketch of a compass on an index card, showing glaze color selections. *Courtesy of the Alfred P. Sloan Museum.*

The Sloan Museum also has in its permanent collection an original pencil sketch for the compass, drawn on brown butcher paper. Some glaze color choices were indicated on this large 17" diameter sketch. This same compass can be seen being modeled in clay on the cover of the April 1929 issue of *AC Sparks*.

Detail of an original compass sketch. *Courtesy of the Alfred P. Sloan Museum.*

"Modeling a Special Design in Clay" from the cover of the April 1929 issue of *AC Sparks*. Flint Faience employee Karla Lind is shown modeling the compass motif. *Photo courtesy of the Archives, New York State College of Ceramics at Alfred University.*

Another large compass was designed for the residence of Colonel E.H.R. Green, in South Dartmouth, Massachusetts. An early advertisement in *Keramic Tile Journal* illustrated the entire complex project. For more information see the entry under Green.

Crystalline Glazes

Crystalline glazes were evidently very popular in Flint Faience tile installations. The *Architectural Faience* booklet issued by Flint Faience & Tile Company in 1929 lists and illustrates four available crystalline glazes – two green, one blue, and one amber. These glazes appear prominently on the foldout on page 2. The "W" or crystalline series (nos. W-8701, W-8704, W-8709, and W-8702) were described as "unique but extremely critical to produce. Not usable on decorated tile. Subject to widest variation. Price, three times 'standard'."

Keramic Tile Journal advertisement on page 5 of Volume 3, no. 10, 1931, illustrating a compass motif in the former Col. E.H.R. Green residence.

Page 2 foldout from *Architectural Faience: An Introduction*, illustrating four crystalline glazed tiles. *Courtesy of Jim Graham.*

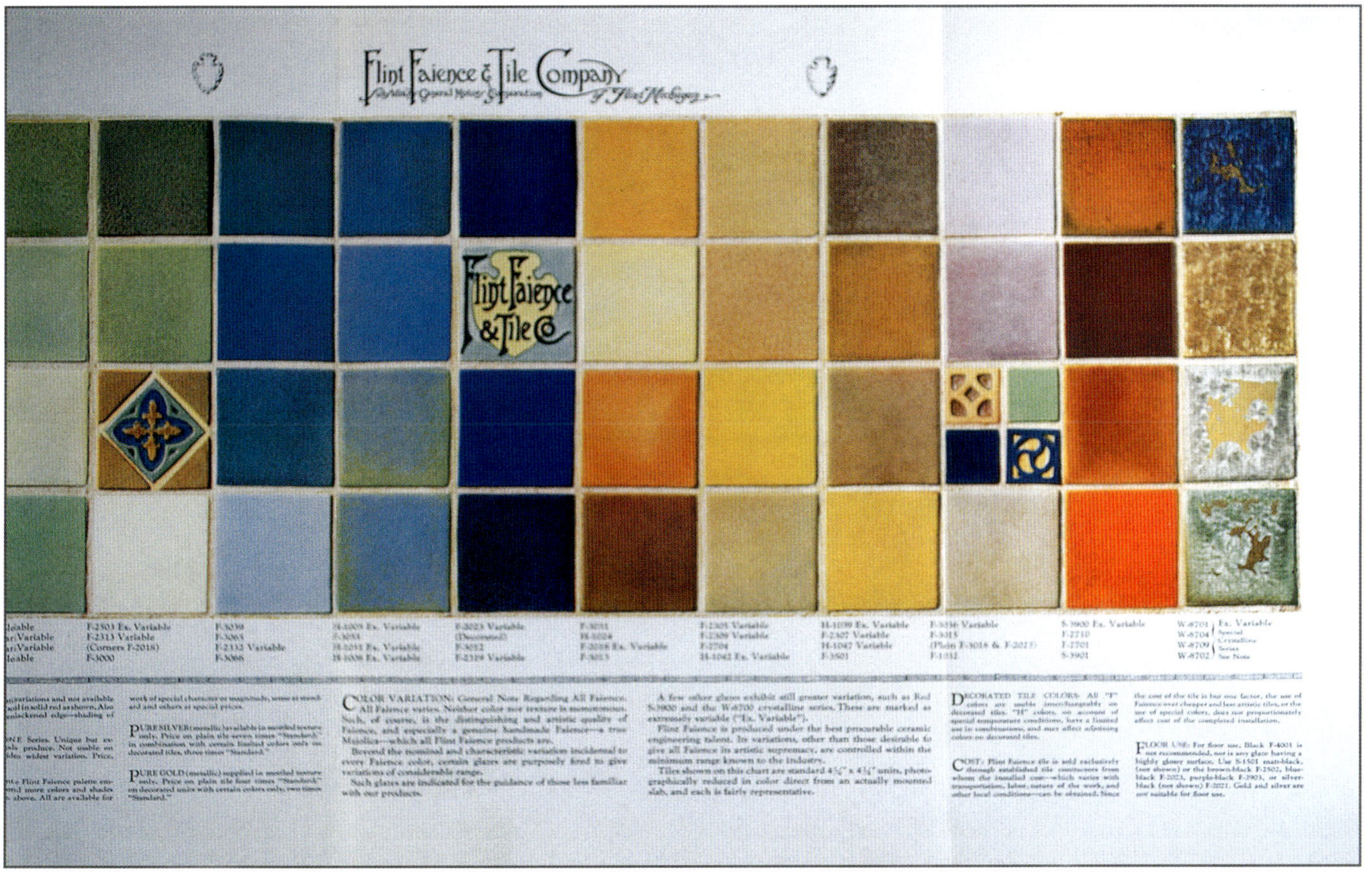

Crystalline glazed tiles and trivets can be seen in a number of installations and additionally as individual tiles in private collections. The Steve and Rosanne Heddy home, built between 1929-32 and located in Flint, Michigan, has many special Flint Faience features including a tiled butler's pantry and a fabulous tiled sunroom. The sunroom, which overall measures 128" x 162", is comprised of field tile and beautiful green crystalline insert tiles measuring either 3" x 2.75" or 6" x 6". A similar 2.75" square green crystalline insert tile is in the collection of Ken Galvas.

Crystalline insert tile, measuring 2.75" x 2.75" installed in the sunroom floor at the former Samuel Stewart home. *Courtesy of Stephen and Rosanne Heddy.*

Sunroom in the former Samuel Stewart home in Flint, Michigan. *Courtesy of Stephen and Rosanne Heddy.*

Crystalline glazed tile. 2.75". Note that a greater concentration of crystals generally translates to a higher retail price. $10-15.

There are five crystalline glazed tiles in the permanent collection of the Ross C. Purdy Museum of Ceramics at the American Ceramics Society headquarters in Westerville, Ohio. The Ken Galvas collection contains an assortment of tiles and trivets, some with quite stunning big green crystals. Several vases and a vase converted to a lamp with magnificent crystalline glazes also can be seen in the collection of Ken Galvas. The color palettes for these pieces range from blues to ambers.

Crystalline glazed trivet. Diameter 6". $75-100.

Crystalline glazed trivet. Diameter 6". $75-100.

Crystalline glazed trivet. Diameter 6". $75-100.

Crystalline glazed trivet. Diameter 6". $75-100.

Pair of crystalline glazed trivets, each with a diameter of 6". $75-100 each.

Two 4.75" x 4.75" crystalline tiles. *Courtesy of the Ross C. Purdy Museum of Ceramics at American Ceramic Society.*

Two crystalline glazed vases. Left 8.5". Right 8". $500-700 each.

Crystalline glazed vase with an elongated neck. Height 8.5". $300-400.

Crystalline glazed vase with a long wide neck. Height 7". $250-300.

Crystalline glazed lamp base. Vase height 11", overall height 21". $300-400.

Custom Designs

see also Binns, Dryden Hotel, the Wheatsworth Factory, Compasses, and Churches

Flint Faience Tile Company advertised on page 37 of their 1926 publication *Catalog "G"* that they will "gladly submit special water-colored sketches executed to conform to architect's, dealer's, or owner's suggestions." Their promotional material was specific in mentioning that the style of the custom design did not matter – classic, personal, or futuristic – all were possible at just a bit of an increase in time and cost. This was the case when Alfred University had sketches prepared of the proposed Flint Faience tiles to be designed and installed in the new Ceramics Building in Alfred, New York. The Archives of the New York State College of Ceramics contain the original watercolor sketches, with the glaze colors noted on each tile sketch. The tiles were very classical in design, showing potters at work forming, decorating, glazing, and loading a kiln. See illustrations and detailed descriptions under Binns entry.

Another of the amazing custom designed installations was that of the Dryden Hotel in New York City. Although created at nearly the same time as the very classical Alfred tiles, these futuristic tiles designed by Flint Faience Art Director Howard B. Burton are without equal in their stunning Art Deco motifs of exotic and magical cats, birds, plants, and flame motifs. See illustrations and descriptions under Dryden Hotel entry.

The same strong statements can be made about the stunning series of allegorical murals that were created for the Wheatsworth Factory in Hamburg, New Jersey, also by Howard B. Burton. All twenty tiled panels featured agricultural themes and most have an Arts & Crafts flavor. They have no equal. For more illustrations and details, see the Wheatsworth Factory entry.

Perhaps the most intriguing part of the custom design process is the presentation drawings that Flint Faience & Tile Company created for its special customers. Some of these proposals were approved, the tiles made, and the installation completed. Other projects never made it past the presentation stage. The First Baptist Church in Shaker Heights, Ohio had presentation drawings prepared by Flint Faience & Tile Company for The Smitley-Hamilton Company in Cleveland, circa 1928. Although the Church construction occurred, there is no evidence today that Flint Faience tile was used in the Church. Wonderful watercolor over graphite drawings of the Flint Faience proposal provide a glorious glimpse into what could have been. The complete presentation drawings can be seen under the entry for Churches.

Detail of watercolor presentation drawing "A" for the Shaker Heights First Baptist Church. *Courtesy of Vance Koehler.*

Detail of watercolor presentation drawing "B" for the Shaker Heights First Baptist Church. *Courtesy of Vance Koehler.*

Detail of watercolor presentation drawing "C" for the Shaker Heights First Baptist Church. *Courtesy of Vance Koehler.*

Decorations and Decorators

see also Raised Line

Flint Faience tiles were decorated by three processes. Each hand-decorated piece featured either inlaid or embossed processing (both molded) or raised line processing where the plain surfaces of tiles are decorated in a process closely related to that of cloisonné work. For more illustrations and detailed description of the raised line decorating process see separate Raised Line entry.

Relief tile of a maiden. 4.25" x 4.25". $125-150.

Pastoral scene in raised line design. 6" x 6". *Courtesy of Dale and Doris Barrett*. $800-1000.

Between 1921-33, there were less than twenty decorators and designers whose names have been recorded in their association with Flint Faience Tile Company. These include James McCabe, Eula Parks Irish, Jane Whitehead, Marjorie Milloy, Kathleen Wixson, Josephine Ellis, Karla Lind, Andrew Pereny, Margaret Scott, Helyn Thomas, Rhea Knisley, and Bessie Evans. Some historic photographs of Flint Faience employees have been published in the April 1929 issue of *AC Sparks*, in the *Flint Journal*, and in the 1929 promotional booklet, *Architectural Faience: An Introduction*.

Specific decorators have been associated with several important tile projects. These are largely known, not because they signed their decorations, but because mint sets of tiles and a few signed pieces became available at estate sales, or because relatives of the decorator have inherited these tiles and archival materials. For example, a mint set of sixteen tiles from the Dryden Hotel in New York City were acquired by a collector at the estate sale of Flint Faience & Tile Co. decorator Marjorie Milloy, who died in her nineties without any heirs in Flint, Michigan. While Ms. Milloy decorated the tiles, they were designed by Flint Faience Art Director Howard B. Burton.

Flint Faience decorator Andrew Pereny was born in New York in 1908, attended the Ohio State University, and was a member of the American Ceramic Society, being awarded a prize in an exhibition in 1933. He was employed by Rookwood Pottery in Cincinnati prior to his time as a decorator at Flint Faience. Additionally he was president of Pereny Pottery in Columbus, Ohio.

Flint Faience & Tile Company designers and decorators. c. 1929. Standing, left to right: James McCabe, Eula Parks (Irish), Jane Whitehead, Marjorie Milloy, Kathleen Wixson, Joesphine Ellis, Karla Lind, and Andrew Pereny. Seated: Margaret Scott, Helyn Thomas, Rhea Knisley, and Bessie Evans. *Courtesy of the Flint Journal*.

Page 8 AC Sparks April, 1929

Some of the designing and decorating staff of Flint Faience Tile Company.

Standing, left to right—James McCabe, Eula Parks, Jane Whitehead, Marjorie Milloy, Kathleen Wixson, Josephine Ellis, Karla Lind and Andrew Pereny.

Seated—Margaret Scott, Helyn Thomas, Rhea Knisley and Bessie Evans.

A corner in the decorating room. Here skilled decorators execute in many colors and by different processes the unlimited number of color schemes and designs available.

A few of the boys pose for their photograph as a car of Faience tile comes through the tunnel kiln.

A section of the new factory. Here a car of Faience tile may be seen emerging from one of the tunnel kilns.

Page 8 of the April 1929 issue of *AC Sparks* showing views of the designing, decorating and kiln areas with appropriate personnel. *Courtesy of the Archives, New York State College of Ceramics at Alfred University.*

An illustration from page 4 of *Architectural Faience: An Introduction,* showing "a corner of the decorating department." *Courtesy of Jim Graham.*

Detail from page 24 of *Catalog "G,"* illustrating seven special inserts for drug store walls and floors.

Drug Stores

Flint Faience Tile Company designed a selection of special 2.75" square tiles with inlay process decorations to be used as random decorative inserts in drug store walls and floors. Seven varieties are featured on page 24 of *Catalog "G"* with corresponding nos. 6576-6581 and no. 6413. E&B Brewery in Detroit has an exterior insert tile installation of this type. Both the caduceus stock design no. 6576 and stock design no. 6581 can be seen. None have appeared in any private collections to date.

Exterior of E&B Brewery in Detroit with caduceus tile drug store insert.

Exterior of E&B Brewery in Detroit with drug store motif tile inserts.

Dryden Hotel

The Dryden Hotel is certainly one of the most published and most magnificent of all the Flint Faience installations, unfortunately with few vintage tiles visible today. The Dryden Hotel, now the Dryden East, is located at 150 E. 39th Street in New York City. It was built in 1927-28 and designed by architect Henry Ives Cobb, with the Flint Faience tile installation designed by Howard B. Burton, Art Director and Architect with Flint Faience Tile Company. The tile contractor for the project was Wm. J. Adelson, Co., New York.

Dryden Hotel, c. 1928. *Photo courtesy of Kristine Burton.*

The entire loggia, walls and arched ceiling, wainscoting, and floors were completely designed in a fabulous futuristic application of Flint Faience tiles. One can tell from the historic photographs that this was a breathtaking installation just crazy with rich, warm colors. The wainscoting was Flint handmade Faience in "Berlin Blue (over-fired)" and the floors were unglazed Vitrocraft in the full color range. The futuristic loggia tiles include Art Deco-style geometric black cats with large golden eyes, exotic birds, flames, and foliage all in riotous hues of red, blue, green and gold.

Views of the Flint Faience tile installation in the Dryden Hotel, as published in *American Architect* in 1929.

The Dryden was such a magnificent accomplishment that photographs were published in the 1929 Flint Faience & Tile Company booklet *Architectural Faience: An Introduction*; the January 5, 1929 issue of the journal *American Architect*; and Volume III, No. 1, 1931 issue of *Keramic Tile Journal*.

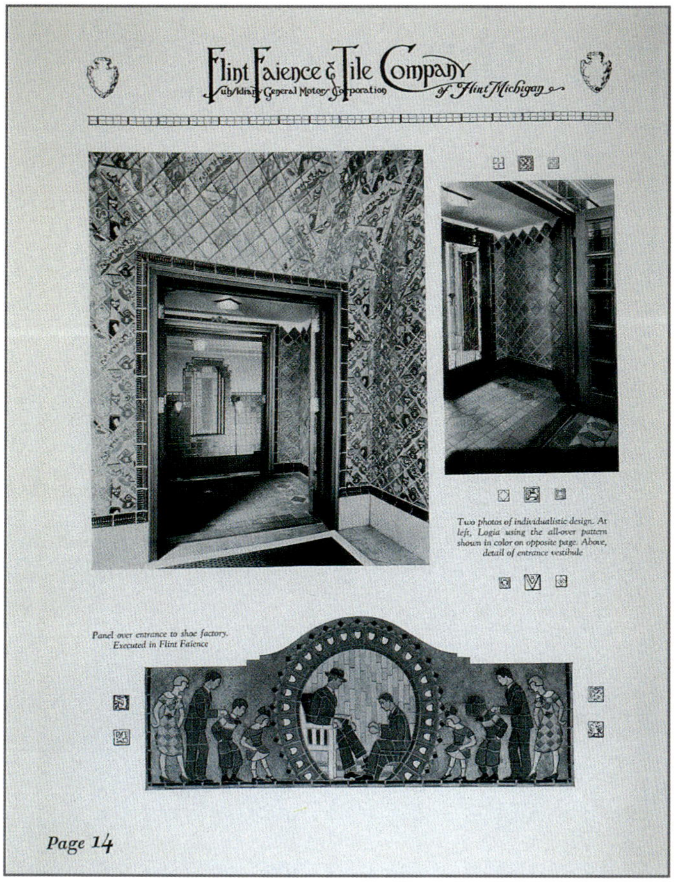

Flint Faience & Tile Company
Subsidiary General Motors Corporation
of Flint Michigan

Two photos of individualistic design. At left, Logia using the all-over pattern shown in color on opposite page. Above, detail of entrance vestibule

Panel over entrance to shoe factory. Executed in Flint Faience

Page 14

Two interior views of the Dryden Hotel, as published in 1929 on page 14 of *Architectural Faience: An Introduction. Courtesy of Jim Graham.*

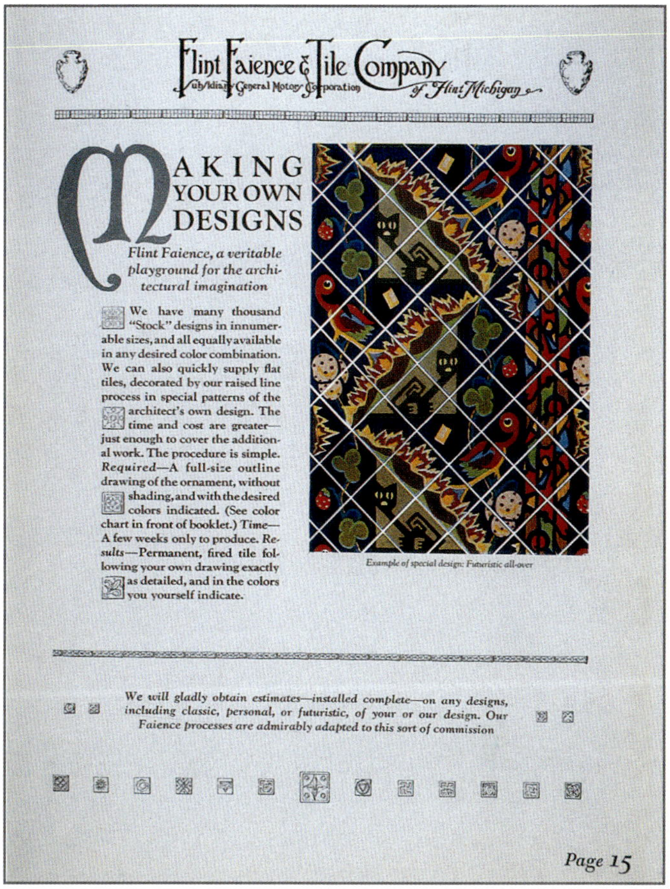

Flint Faience & Tile Company
Subsidiary General Motors Corporation
of Flint Michigan

MAKING YOUR OWN DESIGNS

Flint Faience, a veritable playground for the architectural imagination

We have many thousand "Stock" designs in innumerable sizes, and all equally available in any desired color combination. We can also quickly supply flat tiles, decorated by our raised line process in special patterns of the architect's own design. The time and cost are greater—just enough to cover the additional work. The procedure is simple. *Required*—A full-size outline drawing of the ornament, without shading, and with the desired colors indicated. (See color chart in front of booklet.) *Time*—A few weeks only to produce. *Results*—Permanent, fired tile following your own drawing exactly as detailed, and in the colors you yourself indicate.

Example of special design: Futuristic all-over

We will gladly obtain estimates—installed complete—on any designs, including classic, personal, or futuristic, of your or our design. Our Faience processes are admirably adapted to this sort of commission

Page 15

Color image of the Dryden futuristic tile, as published on page 15 of *Architectural Faience: An Introduction. Courtesy of Jim Graham.*

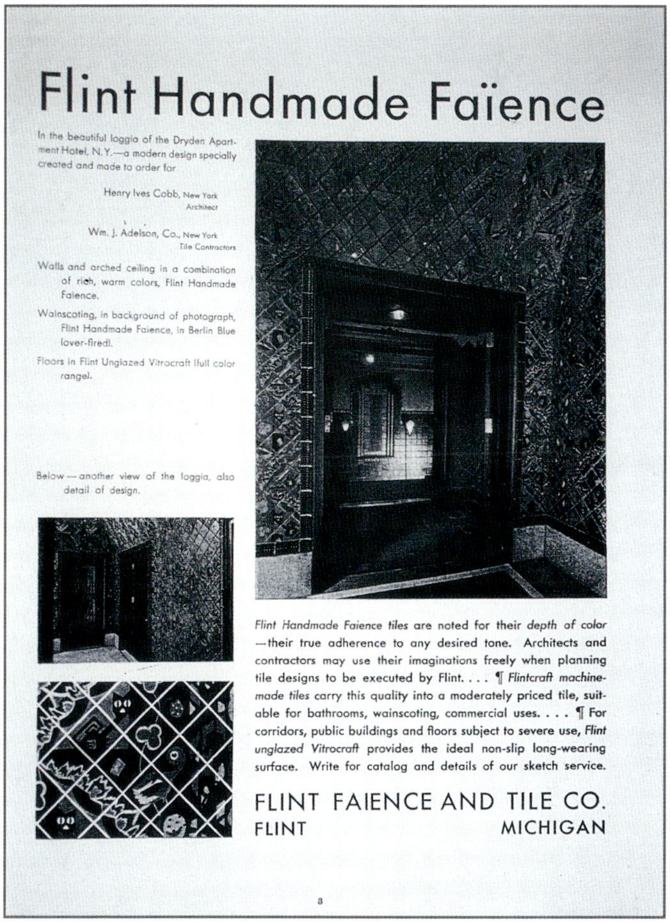

Flint Handmade Faïence

In the beautiful loggia of the Dryden Apartment Hotel, N.Y.—a modern design specially created and made to order for

Henry Ives Cobb, New York
Architect

Wm. J. Adelson, Co., New York
Tile Contractors

Walls and arched ceiling in a combination of rich, warm colors, Flint Handmade Faience.

Wainscoting, in background of photograph, Flint Handmade Faience, in Berlin Blue (over-fired).

Floors in Flint Unglazed Vitrocraft (full color range).

Below—another view of the loggia, also detail of design.

Flint Handmade Faience tiles are noted for their depth of color—their true adherence to any desired tone. Architects and contractors may use their imaginations freely when planning tile designs to be executed by Flint. . . . ¶ *Flintcraft machine-made tiles* carry this quality into a moderately priced tile, suitable for bathrooms, wainscoting, commercial uses. . . . ¶ For corridors, public buildings and floors subject to severe use, *Flint unglazed Vitrocraft* provides the ideal non-slip long-wearing surface. Write for catalog and details of our sketch service.

FLINT FAIENCE AND TILE CO.
FLINT MICHIGAN

3

The Dryden Hotel tile installation fully illustrated on page 3 of *Keramic Tile Journal*, Volume 3, no. 1, 1931.

A visit to the Dryden today reveals none of the futuristic Flint Faience tiles seen in early photographs and advertisements. Apparently, the tiles were either removed or more likely covered up by other two-dimensional wall coverings during various renovations over the years. A few tiles remain hidden from the public, to be seen in what is now a basement area of the building. There are field tiles in front of the elevator on the lower basement level and almost unrecognizable floor tiles in the basement, fragments of stair risers in the same area as well as tiles which have been painted over and more stair risers in the area which used to lead to the upstairs entranceway. Some of the remaining riser tiles match stock no. 6766 from *Catalog "G."* An identical 5" square tile is in the collection of Ken Galvas.

Tiled elevator foyer in the basement of the Dryden.

The Dryden East as it is known today. *Photo by Margaret Carney.*

Remnants of Flint Faience stair riser tiles in the Dryden, New York City.

Riser details from the Dryden.

Stairwell in the basement of the Dryden, showing original tile installation of Flint Faience tiles.

Raised line tile, stock design no. 6766 similar to those installed in the Dryden. 5" x 5". $100-125.

Because most of the Dryden tiles seem to have been covered, removed, or painted, most remarkable is the set of sixteen pristine, mint condition tiles from the collection of Ken Galvas. These tiles were obtained from the estate of Flint Faience tile decorator Marjorie Milloy, who died in the 1990s at age ninety-two with no heirs. They are simply stunning. Flint Faience & Tile Company proudly used illustrations of these futuristic tiles to illustrate advertising for "making your own designs."

Mint panel section of "futuristic all over" created for the Dryden Hotel, to have been installed on point. 18" x 18". *Photo by Dave Hodgkin*. $5000+.

Earhart, Amelia

An historic 1928 photograph of four women standing beside an enormous AC spark plug replica inside the ornately tiled salesroom at the Flint Faience & Tile Co. has an interesting story that accompanies it. A letter kept by one of those four women, written to noted aviatrix Amelia Earhart (b. July 24, 1897 Atchison, Kansas – died, July 2, 1937 en route from Lae, New Guinea to Howland Island), praises the contributions of Earhart while acknowledging the she used AC Spark Plugs on her historic non-stop flight across the Atlantic. The photo was taken to commemorate this event; a copy of the photograph was to accompany the letter sent to Amelia Earhart in 1928.

The letter to Miss Earhart was sent by four female employees of AC Spark Plug: Olive Cleveland, Alice White, Leone Chase, and Fleeta Richardson. It reads:

> On behalf of the thousands of women workers engaged in the spark plug industry here, and representative of those who have actually participated in constructing a unit used in your plane, we tender our sincere congratulations to you who have made history through your courageous flight across the Atlantic, the first woman to have accomplished such a daring feat.

An article which released the contents of the letter in the August 1928 issue of *AC Sparks* (AC Spark Plug Company, August 1928, 3) noted that Amelia Earhart's plane made the sixth consecutive Atlantic flight from West to East in which AC Spark Plugs were used, the first of which, of course, was that of Colonel Charles Lindbergh.

Employees of AC Spark Plug, c. 1928 in the Flint Faience display room. Left to right: Olive Cleveland, Alice White, Leone Chase, and Fleeta Richardson. *Photo courtesy of the* Flint Journal.

Employees

see also Bergmans, Burton, Champion, Decorations and Decorators, Haro, and Zodiac (McDougal)

When American tile production was at its peak in 1929, it is estimated that there were around 9,500 employees at the various U.S. tile companies. (Sims, 1998, 9) There are no reliable statistics on the peak number of tile workers at the Flint Faience & Tile Company plant, but certain names recur more often than others in the literature. In addition to the decorators, designers, architects, and administrators already described, there are other employees of note.

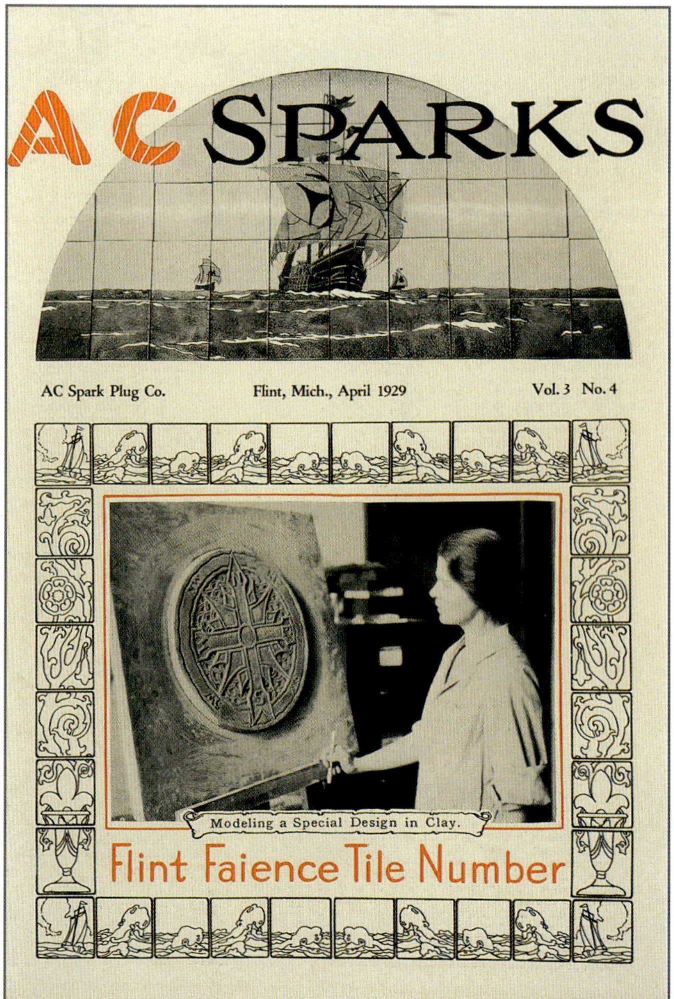

Karla Lind shown modeling at Flint Faience & Tile Company. Illustration from April 1929 issue of *AC Sparks. Courtesy of the Archives, New York State College of Ceramics at Alfred University.*

Karla Lind was born in Denmark on the Island of Bornholm. Before she became chief modeler at Flint Faience & Tile Company in April 1928, she worked as a decorator at a Danish pottery, Michael Anderson & Sons Ceramic Factories, and took night courses at the Ronne Technical School. From 1925-28 she worked as a modeler in St. Petersburg, Florida. While in her position as chief modeler at Flint Faience, she additionally taught modeling in the evening at the Flint Institute of Arts in 1928. Another modeler was J. Emmett Schultz, who also taught at the Flint Institute of Arts.

J.D. Whitmer graduated from the Ohio State University in 1908, and worked at American Encaustic Tiling Company from 1910-1928, before becoming plant superintendent and chief engineer at Flint Faience & Tiling Company in February 1928.

Edward L. Morrissey began his work in Flint as office manager in September 1924. He was later made sales manager, working with W.S. Isherwood, AC general sales manager. He worked for AC for thirty-two years, 1924-56. In 1949, he began working in the personnel department and in 1954 he was placed in charge of insurance and pension programs. He died on February 4, 1965.

Ralph E. Stoneburner was general foreman of Flint Faience & Tile Co. beginning in 1921. He had previously worked for Weller Pottery, Roseville Pottery, and American Encaustic Tiling Company. He was hired at AC in 1918 to be in charge of the kiln and sagger departments.

John L. Hale was assistant sales chief at Flint Faience & Tile Company beginning in 1928, working as assistant to E.L. Morrissey, sales manager. Previously he had worked in sales for AC.

Other related AC and Flint Faience & Tile Company employees include: Louis Berg, manager of manufacturing for all AC products; Charles Carroll, production manager; Charles E. Edwards, representative, Flint Faience & Tile Company district office, Birmingham, Alabama; Emile Francoise, representative, Flint Faience & Tile Company district office, Detroit, Michigan; W.S. Isherwood, AC general sales manager; F. Girard Lambert, representative, Flint Faience & Tile Company district office, Cleveland, Ohio; F.W. Matson, representative, Flint Faience & Tile Company district office, Chicago, Illinois; and P.W. Rhame, chief inspector; Helen Saigon was the first woman draftsman at Flint Faience, hired in 1924.

J.D. Whitmer as illustrated in April 1929 issue of *AC Sparks. Courtesy of the Archives, New York State College of Ceramics at Alfred University.*

Edward L. Morrissey as illustrated in April 1929 issue of *AC Sparks. Courtesy of the Archives, New York State College of Ceramics at Alfred University.*

John L. Hale as illustrated in April 1929 issue of *AC Sparks. Courtesy of the Archives, New York State College of Ceramics at Alfred University*

Ralph E. Stoneburner as illustrated in April, 1929 issue of *AC Sparks. Courtesy of the Archives, New York State College of Ceramics at Alfred University.*

Exotics

see also Furniture and Julio Haro

Although it is unclear whether the subject matter of some tiles should be regarded as exotic or simply tiles with an international flavor, there are a number of Flint Faience tiles that seem to fall into this captivating category. This would include the turbaned portrait paperweights illustrated under the entry for Bookends, Paperweights, etc. Other tiles with depictions of international personages, sometimes a bit stereotypical in design, include tiles in both private collections and within several installations. One tile, with a design of a Japanese woman wearing a kimono and holding an umbrella with a bamboo-type raised line border, hanging paper lanterns, and peaked mountains in the background, is in the private collection of Dale and Doris Barrett who inherited it from the estate of Josephine Ellis, one of the decorators at Flint Faience Tile Company. The Orient is once again the theme of an almost Art Deco rendition of an Asian person, a 6" x 6" tile, oriented on point, and installed on the sandbox in the Humpty Dumpty fireplace room at the Garfield School in Wyandotte, Michigan. Other images on the sandbox include a ship, a clown, a fish, and a parrot.

Asian figure tile in raised line design installed on the sandbox at the Garfield School, Wyandotte, Michigan. 6" x 6". *Courtesy of Mary Wharton Thorson.*

Raised line tile with a Japanese theme. 6" x 6". *Courtesy of Dale and Doris Barrett.* $600-800.

While little Dutch boys and girls have been featured on tiles installed in elementary schools, two individual tiles in private collections have as their theme a Dutch girl holding a rabbit. They are near a large red tulip and her dress has a plaid design. Perhaps it is another children's nursery rhyme or just a charming subject decorated with the raised line process. Both the tile in the Galvas collection and one in the Barrett collection are 6" square. While both girls wear wooden shoes, the plaid colors on the dress have been varied from tile to tile.

Tile depicting a Dutch girl holding a rabbit. 6" x 6". $700-900.

Variations on glaze palette shown in 6" x 6" tile motif of Dutch girl holding a rabbit. *Courtesy of Dale and Doris Barrett.* $700-900.

There are several tile designs that collectors refer to as Egyptian motifs, but probably they are depicting other peoples. There are two nearly identical 4.25" tiles in the Ken Galvas collection that feature a smiling face with a headband over long hair or a headdress. The tiles definitely have an exotic or international flavor and are beautifully decorated utilizing the raised line process. Another genre of decorations with an international flavor is the stock design no. 4726 featuring what appears to not be an Egyptian person, but rather a Pre-Columbian figure, perhaps a Remojadas smiling figure. Two tiles in the Ken Galvas collection are of this group; one 3.5" square is bisque and the other measuring 3.375" has a glossy black glaze overall. A similar tile in the Ruth Hylen collection has the incised signature of Julio Haro on the back. Illustrations of the Hylen tile and backstamp can be seen in the chapter on Identification and Marks.

Smiling faces tiles . 4.25" x 4.25". $275-325 each.

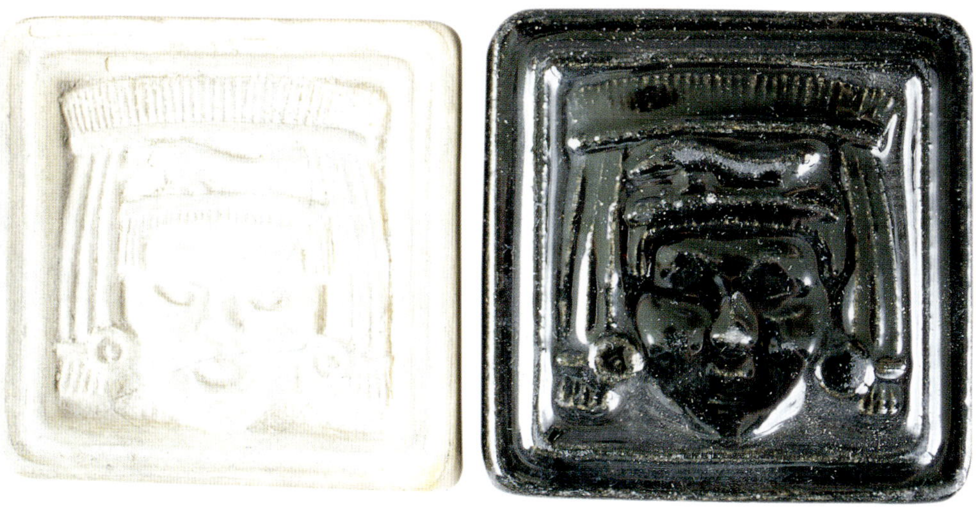

Molded tiles with faces. 3.5" x 3.5". $75-100 bisque. $100-125 monochrome glaze.

Still another tile with an international or exotic flavor is the 6" x 6" tile featuring two Spanish, Mexican, or Latin dancers in the Dale and Doris Barrett collection. Both dancers wear traditional costumes and are posed ready to dance across the tile. It reminds one of the large tile panel, created by Julio Haro and depicting a Mexican theme, that was published in several key journals yet whose whereabouts are currently unknown. The illustrations of this panel, consisting of fifteen central tiles and border tiles, reveal a Mexican woman holding a parrot and standing in a garden, while a man in a traditional Mexican poncho strums the guitar. It was published numerous times, including as the color inset in the 1926 Flint Faience Tile Company *Catalog "G."* A similar watercolor sketch is in the collection of the Sloan Museum in Flint, Michigan. The central figure is that of a "Tehuana," a woman from the Isthmus of Tehuantepec in Southern Mexico. These women are depicted in colorful costumes comprised of bright hued skirts with rich embroidered embellishments. The Tehuana conduct the business and marketing in their society and the family funds are usually the spectacular jewelry which adorns them. Julio Haro isn't the only artist who proudly depicted the Tehuana – the artist Frida Kahlo painted her self-portrait as a Tehuana in 1943.

Tehuana tile panel by Julio Haro. Inset in *Catalog "G."*

Spanish dancer tile, executed in raised line design. 6" x 6". *Courtesy of Dale and Doris Barrett.* $500-600.

Watercolor painting of a Mexican scene attributed to Julio Haro, now in the collection of the Sloan Museum. *Courtesy of the Alfred P. Sloan Museum.*

Postcard of a Tehuana. *Courtesy of Andrew Lopez.*

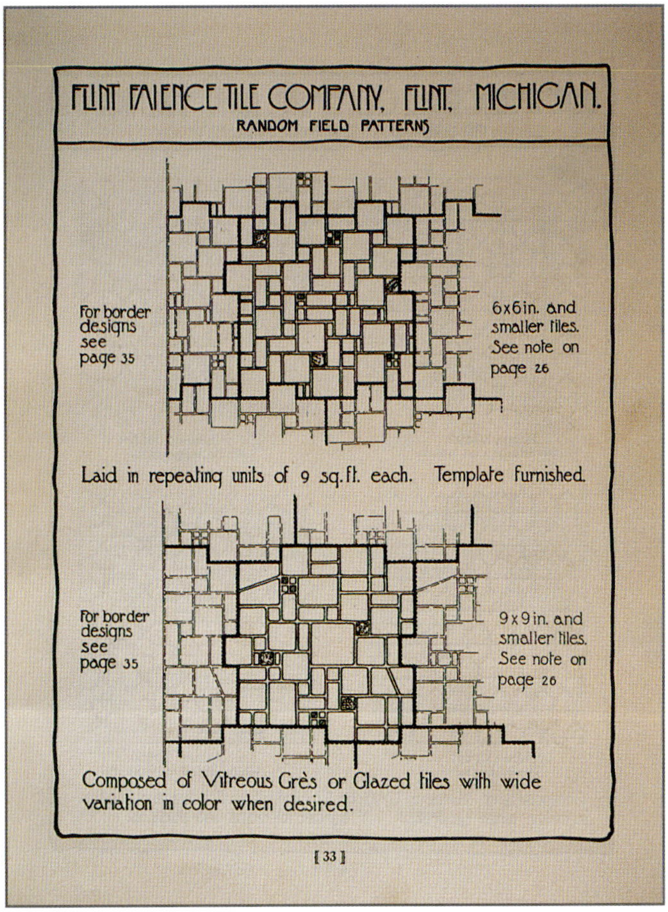

Illustrations of stock design field tile patterns from page 31 of *Catalog "G."*

Field Tiles

Random field tile patterns and borders are illustrated on pages 33 through 35 of the 1926 Flint Faience Tile Company *Catalog "G."* The field tiles were composed of vitreous grès or glazed tiles with a wide variation in color if desired. Recommended patterns were given stock design numbers and many of those illustrated utilized elongated hexagonal tiles for dramatic effects. Field tiles without inserts can be seen in the floor in front of the elevator at the Dryden Hotel in New York City. Another dramatic field tile pattern can be seen in the tiled area around the swimming pool at the Park Gables in Chicago.

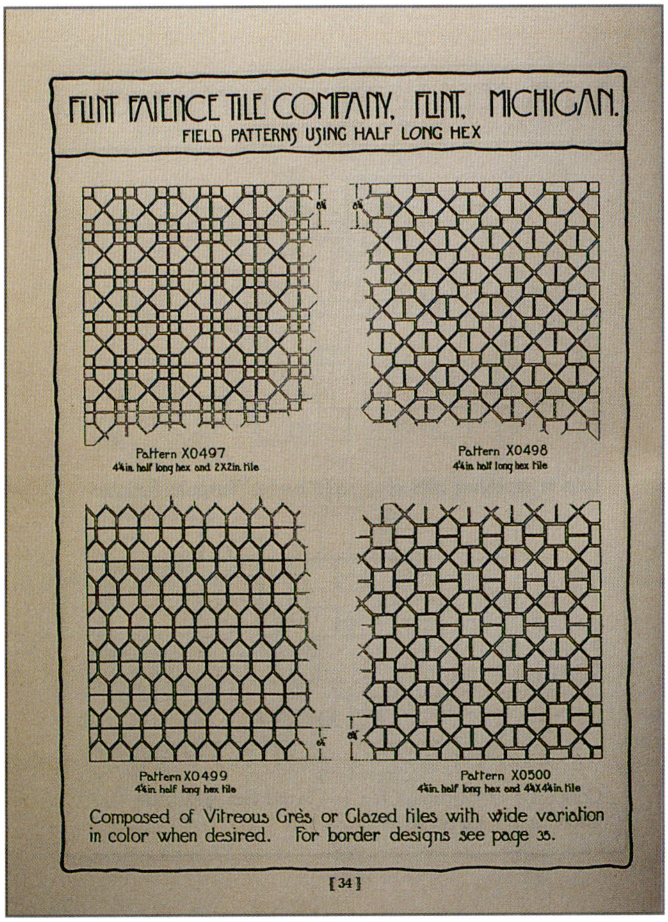

Illustrations of stock design field tile patterns from page 34 of *Catalog "G."*

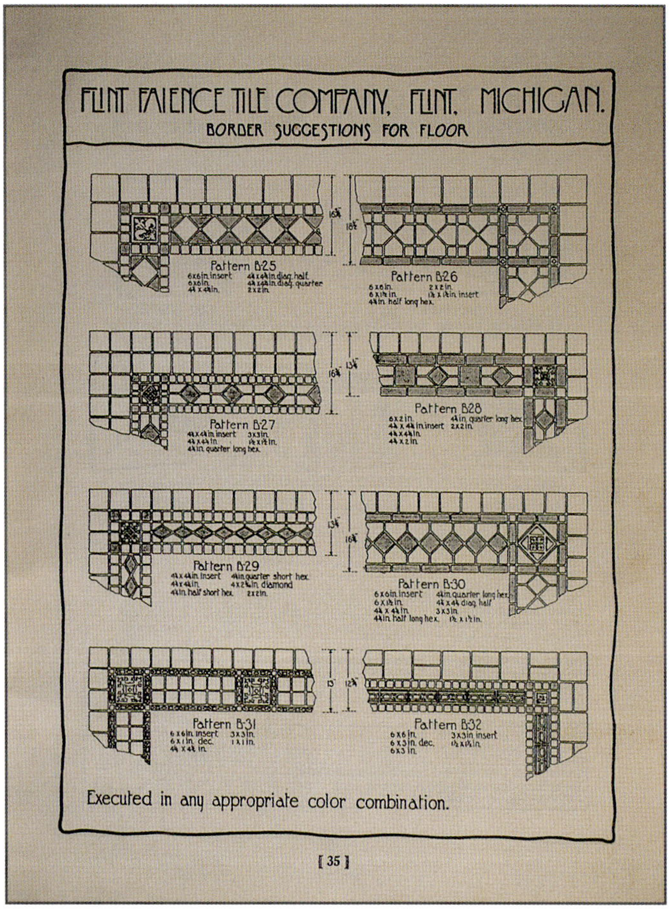

Illustrations of stock design field tile patterns from page 35 of *Catalog "G."*

Dryden Hotel elevator floor field tiles.

Flint Faience field tiles as seen in the Park Gables swimming pool periphery.

Fireplaces

see also Religious Themes, Humpty Dumpty, Little Black Sambo, Ships, Animals, Fish and Sea Life, and Schools

What architectural feature adds more drama (and warmth) to a home or school than a fireplace? The architects designing the kindergarten rooms and libraries in elementary schools of the late 1920s and early 1930s frequently chose to include a charming tiled fireplace. It was a rarity if homes of this era chose to not have a fireplace and often Flint Faience tiles were selected. While the school and library fireplaces were tiled with ships and storybook characters and animals, the home fireplaces were generally comprised of beautiful field tiles in earthy tones of brown, amber, and gold.

Catalog "G," issued by Flint Faience Tile Company in 1926, illustrates several stock design fireplace mantels and arches on pages 3 through 6. Sites with Flint Faience tiled fireplaces include St. Paul's Catholic School (1927) in Grosse Pointe Farms, Michigan with religious themes dominating the tile decorations in Room 100. Washington School, Wyandotte, Michigan, contains a reinstalled fireplace in the school library (moved from the second floor to the first) featuring a scene of three sailing ships and related subjects. In the kindergarten room of the same school there is an 85" wide fireplace with animals and birds in large panels ranging from ten 6" tiles to two 8" tiles and 6" individual tiles (a polar bear, giraffe, elephant, lion, owl and moon, crowing rooster, and a duck and chicken in an Arts & Crafts idyllic setting). An Art Deco style fireplace with sailing ships is in the second floor library of the Garfield School in Wyandotte, Michigan (1932), a school where there are also two other stunning fireplaces. In room 103 in the Garfield School there is an exquisite 83" wide fireplace depicting the children's nursery rhyme Humpty Dumpty, and in room 109 the imaginative story of Little Black Sambo is depicted in 6" and 9" tile panels. Henry Ford Elementary School, located in Dearborn, Michigan has a charming 78" wide fireplace in Room 103, the kindergarten room. It contains thirty-two insert tiles, each 2.75" of wolverines, myna birds, snails, camels, rams, kangaroos, pumas, tigers, porcupines, tigers, donkey, goats, fox, vultures, woodpeckers, parrots, penguins, kingfishers, pigeons, llamas, elephants, hippopotamus, and coyotes.

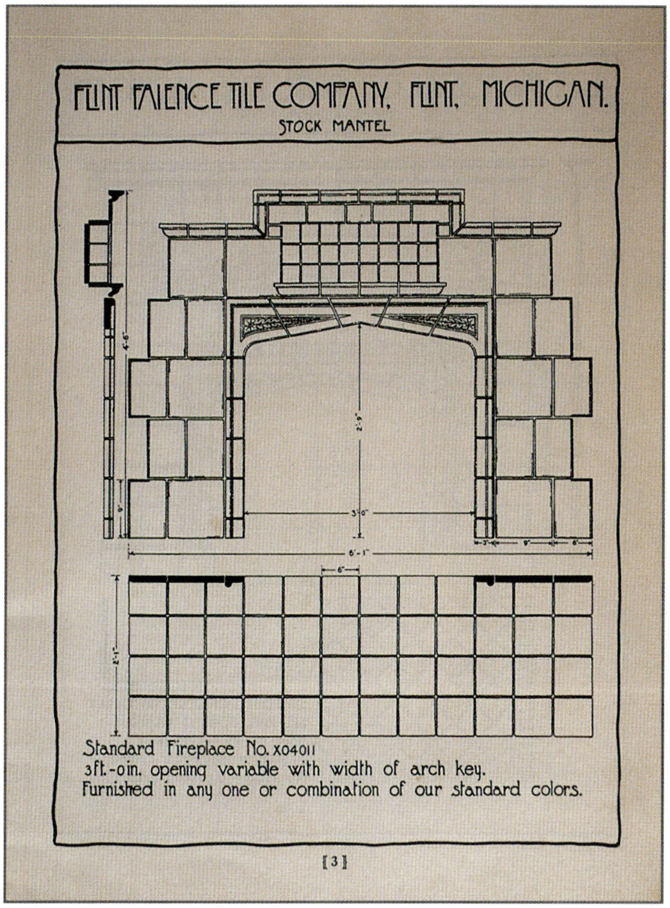

Standard fireplace stock design no. XO4011 as illustrated on page 3 of *Catalog "G."*

Kindergarten fireplace in the Henry Ford Elementary School, Dearborn, Michigan.

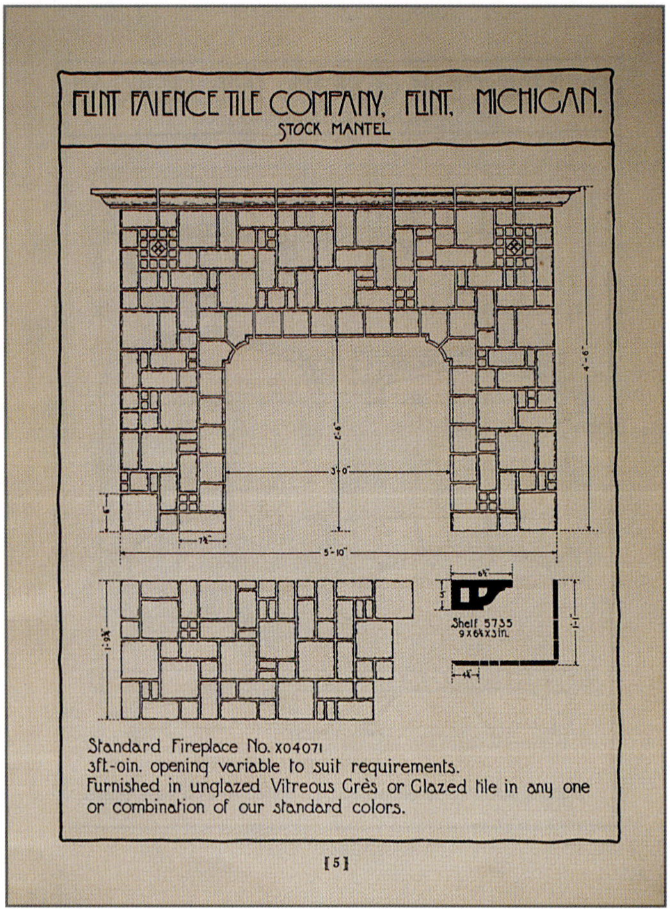

Standard fireplace stock design no. XO4071 from page 5 of *Catalog "G."*

A fireplace with a slightly more dramatic variation on the stock design fireplace arches illustrated in *Catalog "G"* can be seen in the former Prosper Champion home in Flint, Michigan. Note the colorful inserts among the field tiles on the floor facing the fireplace located in the living room. Most of the inserts are those categorized as "Gothic" in *Catalog "G"* page 24, nos. 6513, 6543, and 6514. The fireplace is 83" across and 22" deep, with a height of 40". Built in 1928, this home also contained a tiled sunroom (with tiled radiator grills), bathrooms, an entrance foyer, and heraldic tiles on the home's exterior.

Fireplace in the former Prosper Champion home, Flint, Michigan. *Courtesy of Jim Fitzell and Jessica Higgins.*

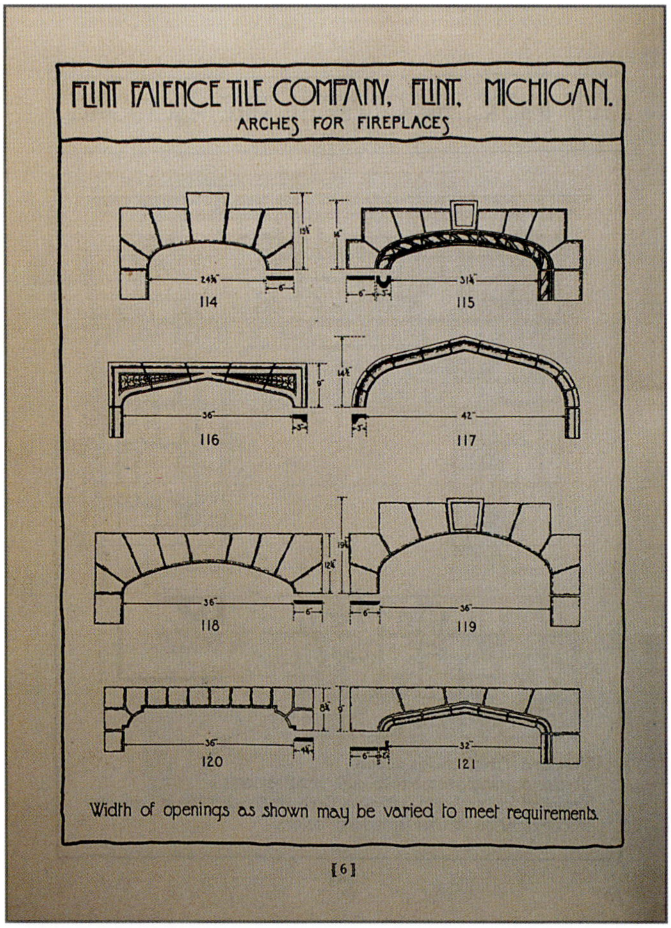

Arches for fireplaces as illustrated on page 6 of *Catalog "G."*

Unique among Flint Faience fireplace tile installations is the crystalline glazed fireplace facing in the F. A. Bower House in Flint, Michigan. The tiles are of lavender and grey hues, and the fireplace uses the heat source known as Magic Coal Electric Fire. No doubt this made the upstairs sitting room quite comfortable on a cold winter night in Michigan. It is not unusual for these types of fireplace facings to have electrical outlets as part of the central installation as they heated via electricity rather than wood, coal, or gas.

Several fireplace facings with colorful Flint Faience tiles were included in the restroom areas of the Warner Theatre in Erie, Pennsylvania. See the entry under Theatres for illustrations and detailed descriptions.

Crystalline tiles and Magic Coal Electric Fire in the F.A. Bower residence in Flint, Michigan. *Courtesy of Ken Kayser.*

Firing

see Kilns

Fish and Sea Life

see also Ships

Fish and other sea life are another popular tile motif for Flint Faience. In fact, the fish tiles often show a sense of artistic license, unseen in many other more realistic portrayals. For instance, the four individual 6" square fish on the fireplace at the Washington Elementary School Library in Wyandotte, Michigan are shown in all types, poses, and postures, and with odd "facial" expressions. Another fish with character is located in the Roger Ellingsworth collection. The tile is 4.25" square and matches the one on the Washington School fireplace facing. A similar tile, but with the fish less tilted, is illustrated on page 2 of the 1929 Flint Faience & Tile Company promotional booklet, *Architectural Faience: An Introduction*.

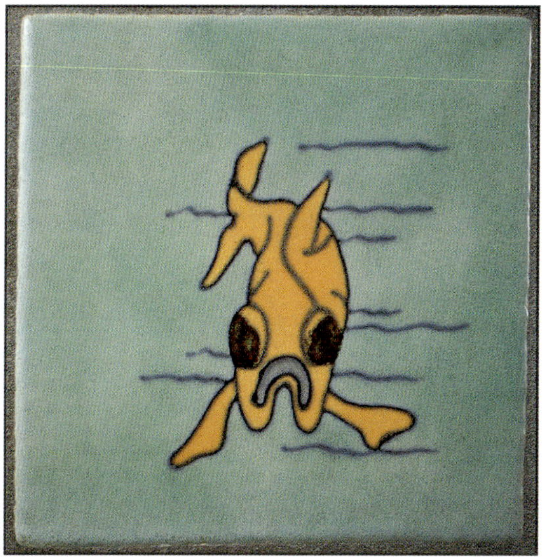

6" fish tile as seen in the fireplace in the library at Washington Elementary School, Wyandotte, Michigan. *Courtesy of Washington Elementary School, Wyandotte, Michigan.*

Fish tile. 4.25" x 4.25". *Courtesy of Roger Ellingsworth.* $200-250.

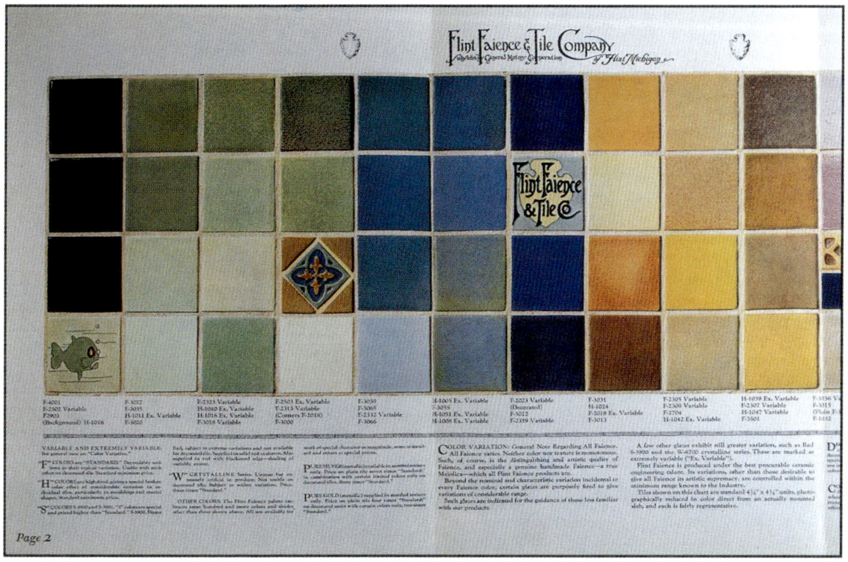

Illustration of a fish tile from page 2 foldout in *Architectural Faience: An Introduction. Courtesy of Jim Graham.*

Fireplace in the library of the Washington Elementary School. Tiles in this fireplace were removed from an original second floor fireplace and reinstalled in their current location on the first floor. *Courtesy of Washington Elementary School, Wyandotte, Michigan.*

The same school fireplace shows other sea life among the ships on the main tile panel, which is comprised of twelve 6" tiles mounted in two horizontal rows. Writhing serpents frolic along with the wind and sun.

Whimsical seascape panel in the reinstalled fireplace in the Washington Elementary School. *Courtesy of Washington Elementary School. Wyandotte, Michigan.*

Other more realistic portrayals of fish can be seen on the drinking fountain and sink in the John Marshall Elementary School kindergarten room, in Detroit. These fish motifs of blue fish and green fish were shown among other water motifs, such as a lobster and a duck. Each tile measures 6" square. A similar, but slightly larger 8.25" x 8.25" fish tile is in the private collection of Roger Ellingsworth.

Two fish tiles installed in the combination sink, fountain, and sandbox of the John Marshall School in Detroit, Michigan. 6" x 6" each. *Courtesy of the John Marshall Elementary School.*

Large fish tile executed in raised line design. 8.25" x 8.25". *Courtesy of Roger Ellingsworth*. $1200-1500.

Fleur-de-lis insert tile in the sunroom of the Samuel Stewart home, measuring 6" x 6". *Courtesy of Stephen and Rosanne Heddy*.

Fisher Building, Detroit

see Art Deco

Fleur-de-lis

The term fleur-de-lis has been defined as a heraldic device comprised of a stylized three-petalled iris. Fleur-de-lis were popular designs for insert tiles commonly seen in Flint Faience floor installations of field tiles. One example of use in an installation would be the sunroom of the Samuel Simon Stewart home, built between 1929-1932 in Flint, Michigan. A 6" square tile decorated with a fleur-de-lis in warm amber and black hues is installed among field tiles for a stunning effect. A modified fleur-de-lis design on a 6" square tile, installed on point, can also be seen as an insert tile in the Stewart sunroom floor. It has added embellishments of a blue diamond and dots as part of the decorative scheme. A similar tile, stock design no. 6450, is located in the Ken Galvas collection. Individual tiles with a simple fleur-de-lis pattern are in various glazes and in private collections, too. Some are 3" square, others are 2" or 6" square. This was a stock design featured in *Catalog "G"* on page 23.

Fleur-de-lis insert tile in the sunroom floor of the Samuel Stewart home, measuring 6" x 6". *Courtesy of Stephen and Rosanne Heddy*.

Fleur-de-lis insert tile, stock design no. 6450. 6" x 6". $100-150.

Fleur-de-lis insert tile, stock design no. 6544. $30-50.

Black and gold glazed fleur-de-lis insert tile, stock design no. 6522. 3" x 3". $30-50.

A variety of 2" insert tiles in the fleur-de-lis pattern, stock design no. 6539. $30-40 each.

Stock design no. 6518 featured a more embellished version of the standard Flint Faience fleur-de-lis pattern. A 2.875" example is in the Ken Galvas collection along with a 6" square tile in the stock design no. 6454 pattern, a geometric which utilizes four fleur-de-lis within the overall design.

Fleur-de-lis pattern insert tile, stock design no. 6518. 2.875" x 2.875". $30-50.

Geometric insert tile incorporating some fleur-de-lis patterns, stock design no. 6454. 6" x 6". $100-150.

Flight Into Egypt

Flight Into Egypt is the title given to one of the premiere tile panels designed by noted architect and designer Howard B. Burton during his five year association with the Flint Faience & Tile Company. It was comprised of one central tile with twenty-four smaller border tiles, the central tile depicting Joseph walking alongside Mary and Jesus seated on a donkey on a starry night. Not only was *Flight Into Egypt* illustrated in several publications, it was additionally exhibited in the traveling 1928-29 International Exhibition of Ceramic Art organized by the American Federation of Arts which opened at the Metropolitan Museum of Art in New York City and was on view there October 1-28, 1928. The exhibition traveled to eight major cities in the United States. In addition to this Flint Faience masterpiece by Howard B. Burton, the exhibition also featured ceramics created by Charles Fergus Binns, Mary Chase Perry Stratton, and Eric Saarinen (Pewabic Pottery), Henry Varnum Poor, Adelaide Alsop Robineau, Frank Holmes (Lenox China), Leon Victor Solon (tile designs executed by American Encaustic Tiling Company), and Carl Walters, to name just a few.

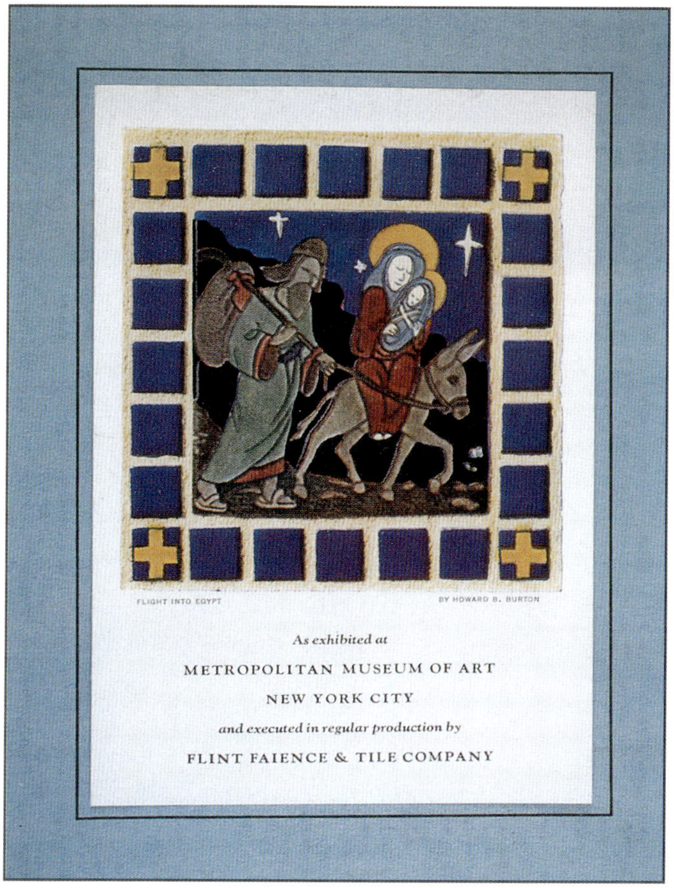

"Flight into Egypt" as published in 1929 as the frontispiece for *Architectural Faience: An Introduction. Courtesy of Jim Graham.*

While the *Flight Into Egypt* tile panel that was exhibited at the Metropolitan Museum of Art remains in a private collection, another version without the tile border can be seen in the private collection of Dale and Doris Barrett, who obtained it from the estate of Josephine Ellis, a decorator at Flint Faience Tile Company. A third version, also without the border tiles, is in the collection of Rick Reigle, obtained from the estate of Eula Irish.

"Flight into Egypt," measuring 6" x 6". *Courtesy of Dale and Doris Barrett.* $1000-1500.

Flight Into Egypt wasn't the only tile work by Howard Burton juried into the exhibition organized by the American Federation of Arts. Another tile, measuring 7.25" x 8", a nativity scene titled *Capricorn* (for December 25th), was also exhibited. An example of this tile is now in a private collection. Kristine Burton, granddaughter of Howard B. Burton, can be credited with surmising that *Capricorn* was the title of this nativity scene tile, based on December 25th being under the sign of Capricorn. A third selection by Burton, twelve tiles labeled in the A.F.A. catalog as "zodiacs," was included in this special international exhibition. There are several zodiac tile sets in circulation, all designed by Howard Burton. It is not known which of these was the third selection for inclusion in this Metropolitan Museum of Art exhibition and traveling A.F.A. show.

"Capricorn" nativity tile, measuring 7.25" x 8". *Courtesy of Dale and Doris Barrett.* $1500+

Flintcraft

Flintcraft was a new glazed tile product available from the Flint Faience & Tile Company and advertised in 1930-31 in *Keramic Tile Journal*, an important trade journal

FLINTCRAFT . . . a Machine-Made Tile of Faïence Appearance

200 colors make possible the creation of an UNLIMITED VARIETY of INTERESTING DESIGNS—at moderate cost

When the cost of a tile installation is limited, resourceful designers turn to Flintcraft. Flintcraft offers a richer effect than ordinary commercial colored tiles, and yet is only slightly higher in cost. A palette of over 200 colors stimulates the creation of interesting patterns. Flintcraft colors are rich, deep and uniform. The glaze is exactly the same as on our handmade faïence.

Three panels reproduced here give only a faint idea of the design possibilities of Flintcraft. Our sketch service department is prepared to suggest an unlimited number of designs and color combinations.

Below is a massive design in orange, yellow and black. 3" squares, 3" diagonal halves and 6" x 1" strips are used. Here again only three colors combine to produce an effective pattern. Can you imagine the great variety of combinations possible with 200 colors?

Using only three (blue-grey, maroon and black) of the 200 colors and only four simple shapes (4¼" squares, 3" squares, 3" diagonal halves, and 6" x 1" strips)—our sketch service department produced the design above. This design, of course, may be carried out in many other color combinations.

Here is a modern design in pastels—a combination of two shades of blue and cream. 4¼" x 4¼" squares, 3" diagonal halves, and 6" x 1" strips are used.

FLINT FAÏENCE AND TILE CO.
FLINT - - - - MICHIGAN
Flint Handmade Faïence—Flintcraft—Vitrocraft, the Non-Slip Floor Tile. Catalogs—Estimates—Color Sketches for Installations cf Any Size on Request

5

Advertisement for Flintcraft from *Keramic Tile Journal* Volume 3, no.7, 1931, page 5.

of the time. It was a machine made, economical tile which was originally available in ten special colors (and later in two hundred) and in any Flint Faience color on special order. It was deemed appropriate for use where "uniform joints" were preferred. These tiles were dry pressed and bear the symbol of a Flint arrowhead as the backstamp. The chapter on Identification and Marks also illustrates the impressed arrowhead alongside a "Flintcraft" impressed backstamp.

Flint Faience arrowhead backstamp on Flintcraft tile.

Probably the most amazing tile installation utilizing Flintcraft was the creation of "a famous Italian decorator's version of Apelles' 'Anadyomene'… reproduced in this inexpensive, enduring, colorful material, for a decorative panel in a modern residence." (*Keramic Tile Journal,* November 1931, 5) The modern residence was the home of Herbert K. Dalton in Rumson, New Jersey. The Flint Faience version was designed by Julio Haro. The architect involved was Alfred Brusselle of New York City and the tiling contractor was Robert L. Duche, Red Bank, New Jersey.

Anadyomene, an epithet of the goddess Aphrodite/Venus, means "rising from the sea." A painting with the title *Aphrodite Anadyomene* was created by the Greek painter Apelles (c. 352-308 B.C.), court artist to the kings of Macedonia including Philip II of Madeon. In his peak years, 332-329 B.C., Apelles worked at the court of Alexander the Great. Not a single trace of his work survives to this day, though descriptions of his paintings can be found in ancient literature. He has been credited with having painted the first self portrait in the world. His *Aphrodite Anadyomene* depicted Venus rising from sea foam and wringing her wet tresses, and was painted for the sanctuary of Aesculaplus on the island of Cos. The Flint Faience tile version was appropriately designed to rise out of the soapsuds of a bathtub in New Jersey. Other well-known artists who have created paintings or sculpture depicting the Venus Anadyomene include Titian, ca. 1520; Ingres, 1808-48; and Cy Twombly, 1981.

Flintcraft advertisement from *Keramic Tile Journal,* Volume 3, no. 11, 1931, page 5, featuring "Anadyomene."

Installed Flintcraft tiled panel "Anadyomene." *Photograph by Adam Goldberg with assistance from Dr. Dan Goldberg. Courtesy of Mindy and Nate Kestenman.*

Floors

see also Field Tiles, Flintcraft, and Vitrocraft

Flint Faience tiles were available for floor and wall installations during their entire history (1921-33). Flint Faience hand-made tiles were available in some 150 colors, in plain, decorated and special designs. Vitrocraft, formerly known as "Vitreous Grés [sic]", an unglazed tile for residential or public floors, was also hand-made and available in four color ranges. Flint Faience lastly introduced Flintcraft, an economical machine-made glazed tile which was available circa 1930 in ten special colors (and later in two hundred), and in any Flint Faience color on special order.

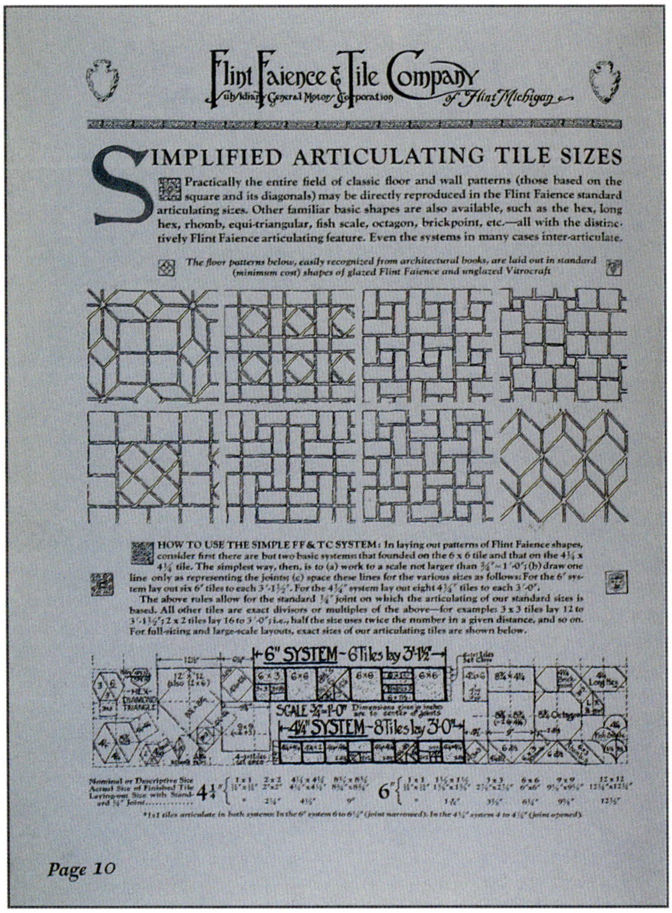

Flint Faience & Tile Company
Subsidiary General Motors Corporation of Flint Michigan

SIMPLIFIED ARTICULATING TILE SIZES

Practically the entire field of classic floor and wall patterns (those based on the square and its diagonals) may be directly reproduced in the Flint Faience standard articulating sizes. Other familiar basic shapes are also available, such as the hex, long hex, rhomb, equi-triangular, fish scale, octagon, brickpoint, etc.—all with the distinctively Flint Faience articulating feature. Even the systems in many cases inter-articulate.

The floor patterns below, easily recognized from architectural books, are laid out in standard (minimum cost) shapes of glazed Flint Faience and unglazed Vitrocraft

HOW TO USE THE SIMPLE FF & TC SYSTEM: In laying out patterns of Flint Faience shapes, consider first there are but two basic systems: that founded on the 6 x 6 tile and that on the 4¼ x 4¼ tile. The simplest way, then, is to (a) work to a scale not larger than ¾" = 1'-0"; (b) draw one line only as representing the joints; (c) space these lines for the various sizes as follows: For the 6" system lay out six 6" tiles to each 3'-1½". For the 4¼" system lay out eight 4¼" tiles to each 3'-0".

The above rules allow for the standard ¼" joint on which the articulating of our standard sizes is based. All other tiles are exact divisors or multiples of the above—for example: 3 x 3 tiles lay 12 to 3'-1½"; 2 x 2 tiles lay 16 to 3'-0"; i.e., half the size uses twice the number in a given distance, and so on. For full-sizing and large-scale layouts, exact sizes of our articulating tiles are shown below.

6" SYSTEM - 6 Tiles lay 3'-1½"

SCALE ¾"=1'-0"

4¼" SYSTEM - 8 Tiles lay 3'-0"

Page 10

Illustrations of floor patterns from page 10, *Architectural Faience: An Introduction. Courtesy of Jim Graham.*

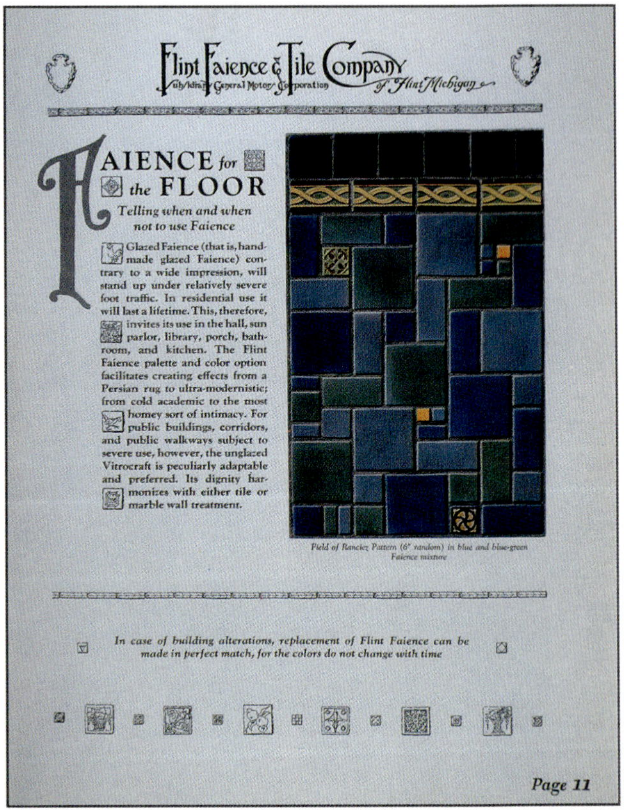

Flint Faience & Tile Company
Subsidiary General Motors Corporation of Flint Michigan

FAIENCE for the FLOOR

Telling when and when not to use Faience

Glazed Faience (that is, hand-made glazed Faience) contrary to a wide impression, will stand up under relatively severe foot traffic. In residential use it will last a lifetime. This, therefore, invites its use in the hall, sun parlor, library, porch, bathroom, and kitchen. The Flint Faience palette and color option facilitates creating effects from a Persian rug to ultra-modernistic; from cold academic to the most homey sort of intimacy. For public buildings, corridors, and public walkways subject to severe use, however, the unglazed Vitrocraft is peculiarly adaptable and preferred. Its dignity harmonizes with either tile or marble wall treatment.

Field of Ranciez Pattern (6" random) in blue and blue-green Faience mixture

In case of building alterations, replacement of Flint Faience can be made in perfect match, for the colors do not change with time

Page 11

Flint Faience floor tiles as illustrated on page 11, *Architectural Faience: An Introduction. Courtesy of Jim Graham.*

These floor tiles were often utilized in automobile showrooms, swimming pool environments, cafeterias, churches, elevator lobbies and school hallways. Flint Faience & Tile Company Floor Flyer A-304 included color and design suggestions.

The Enduring Distinction of Flint Faience Tile Floors

FLINT Faience and unglazed Vitrocraft, in addition to their beauty, provide an enduring surface, easy to clean and have an upkeep cost of practically nothing. Both have a strong hand-made body; are impervious to stains, hot liquids, oils and dirt. Faience with its glass-like surface, in any of its innumerable colors, cleans with merely a damp cloth. Its heavy glaze will, in any residential use, outlast the building.

Unglazed Vitrocraft is vitrified all the way through—hence impervious. Its non-slip surface is also easy to clean—far easier than most materials in its price class. Vitrocraft is among the hardest floor materials in existence, is one-third the cost of many, and will withstand the heaviest of public traffic.

Cover of Flint Faience & Tile Company Floor Flyer A-304. *Courtesy of the Archives, New York State College of Ceramics at Alfred University.*

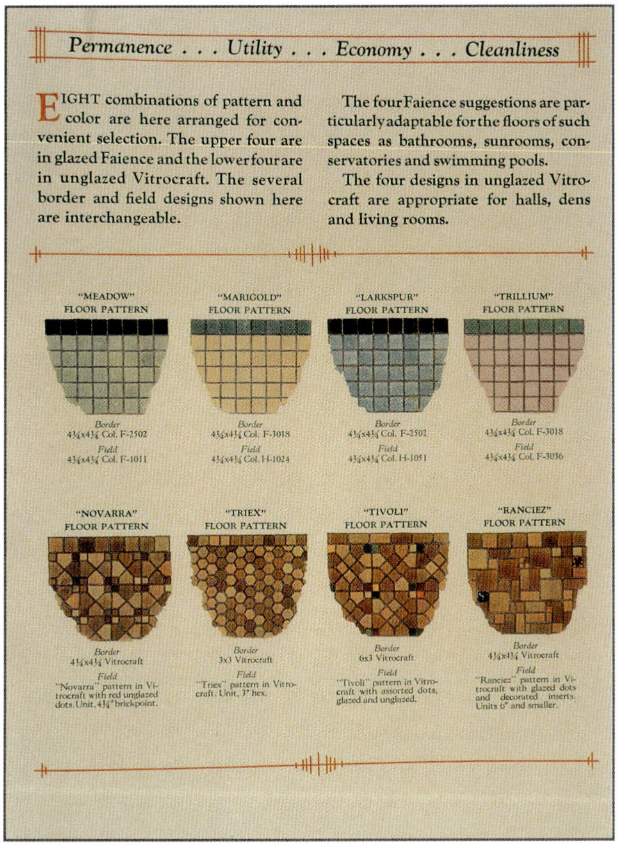

Detail from Floor Flyer A-304. *Courtesy of the Archives, New York State College of Ceramics at Alfred University.*

Detail from Floor Flyer A-304 showing various uses for tiled flooring. *Courtesy of the Archives, New York State College of Ceramics at Alfred University.*

Flowers

see Botanicals

Ford, Edsel and Eleanor

see also Kitchens and Bathrooms

The Eleanor (1896-1976) and Edsel (1893-1943) Ford home built 1926-29 is located on an 87 acre estate on the shores of Lake St. Clair in Grosse Pointe Shores, Michigan. It was designed in the Cotswold style by noted architect Albert Kahn. While the exterior and much of the interior is in the Cotswold style, some rooms are decorated in the sharply contrasting modern style. The Fords moved into their new 30,000 square foot, 60-room home at the end of the year in 1929. Flint Faience tiles were chosen for the kitchen and bathroom areas of the home, with the most remarkable thing about the bathrooms being that there were twelve of them in the home (see illustrations and descriptions under Bathrooms and Kitchens). The home also contains fine furnishings, including original paintings by Paul Cezanne, Henri Mattise, and Diego Rivera. Edsel Ford became President of the Ford Motor Company in 1919 at the age of twenty-five. The home has been preserved and is open to the public on a regular schedule.

Fort Shelby Hotel, Restaurant

The April, 1929 issue of *AC Sparks* (AC Spark Plug Company, 1929, 7) noted that the Fort Shelby Hotel in Detroit had a major installation of Flint Faience tiles in its hotel restaurant. Also known as The Shelby, the hotel was named after Fort Shelby because it was built on the site where the British ceded the Straits of Detroit to the Americans during the War of 1812. It was built in two phases, by two notable architects. The original building, located at 525 West Lafayette Street, was completed in 1917 and designed by Schmidt, Garden and Martin of Chicago. The 1927 addition was the creation of Albert Kahn of Detroit.

The 20-story addition included at least one prominent restaurant that utilized Flint Faience tiles in a significant installation. Within a basement restaurant called the Terrace Room was a fountain and tiled walls and columns around the room. This once-prestigious hotel, later known as the Pick-Fort Shelby, closed in 1973 due to declining patronage, the tiled walls long before covered with other flat wall surfaces. In the 1970s, the Terrace Room had become the Subway Disco. Apartments, restaurants, and bars remained a bit active, but each of these components declined until only the lobby bar named Shelby's remained. It closed in 1998. In more recent years the basement area where the Terrace Room was located was partially inundated by water. Nonetheless, it was listed on the National Register of Historic Places on November 25, 1983. There are urban legends surrounding this site and the possible presence of ghosts of notorious inhabitants.

Postcard of the Fort Shelby Hotel, Detroit, Michigan, which contained a major installation of Flint Faience tiles in its restaurant. Note that more was paid for the postcard today than it cost to stay here when the postcard was printed. "The Fort Shelby, with 900 rooms, is one of Detroit's largest hotels. Towering 22 stories above the city, it commands a remarkable view of the Detroit River and Canada beyond. Rates are from $2.50. All rooms have bath, circulating ice water, and Servidor."

Fountains and Drinking Fountains

Flint Faience tiled fountains and drinking fountains took several forms depending on whether they were part of a school, home, or other public building. Some schools of the late 1920s and early 1930s contained elaborately tiled fountains in their libraries, simple monochrome-tiled drinking fountains in the school hallways, or drinking fountains that were part of sandbox, sink, and drinking fountain installations in kindergarten rooms with wonderful nursery rhyme motifs and wild animals. Wonderful, understated drinking fountains can be seen in the hallways of the Henry Ford Elementary School in Dearborn, Michigan. The 4.25" tiles are monochrome, with Art Deco hues in pink and black matte glazes.

Hallway drinking fountain, Henry Ford Elementary School, Dearborn, Michigan.

Detail of hallway drinking fountain, Henry Ford Elementary School, Dearborn, Michigan.

Fountain cap detail in raised line design and border tile details 4.5" x 6" from the fountain in the conservatory in the former E.T. Strong home, Flint, Michigan. *Courtesy of the Hamady Estate.*

However, Flint Faience tile fountains that were inside private homes were never subdued. For example the conservatory/solarium in the former E.T. Strong home in Flint, Michigan, built in 1929, has a brilliant polychrome tiled fountain with a pronounced Italian flavor. The center figure is white marble. This centrally located fountain is surrounded by richly colored hexagonal floor tiles, stunning stair risers, alcoves, and wonderful natural lighting all illustrated under other entries.

Side panel of the fountain in the conservatory in the former home of E. T. Strong. Tiles measure 8" x 8". *Courtesy of the Hamady Estate.*

Fountain in the conservatory in the former E. T. Strong home, Flint, Michigan. *Courtesy of the Hamady Estate.*

Another amazing Flint Faience tiled fountain is located at the Brookside School Library at Cranbrook in Bloomfield Hills, Michigan. It measures 95" x 36.25" overall and contains the sculpture of three frogs. Ceramic tile fountains were common enough that they adorned pages 1 and 2 of the 1926 trade journal published by Flint Faience Tile Company, now referred to simply as *Catalog "G."*

Fountain in the library at Brookside School, Birmingham, Michigan. *Courtesy of Cranbrook.*

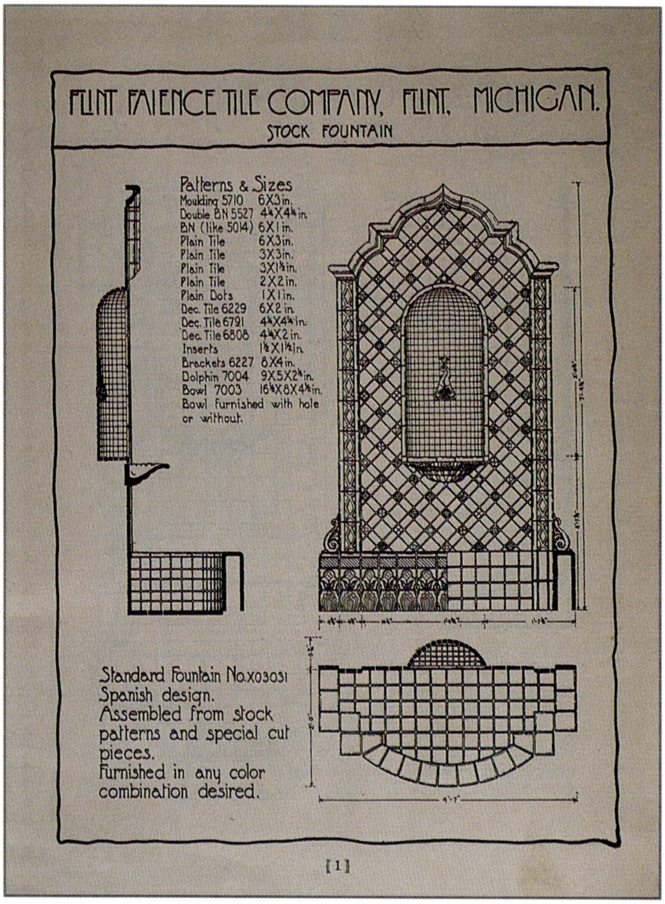

Stock fountain designs from page 1 of *Catalog "G."*

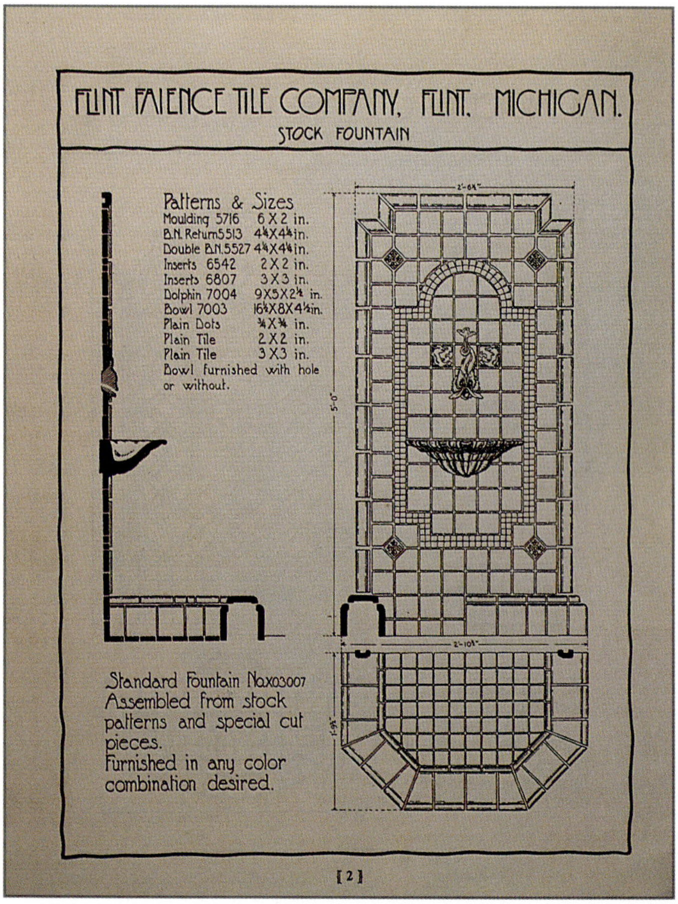

Stock fountain designs from page 2 of *Catalog "G."*

Not all school drinking fountains were the same, as illustrated by the colorful random patterned drinking fountains in the hallways at the Garfield School in Wyandotte, Michigan that date circa 1932. There are four similar drinking fountains in the school, each with a pair of entwined celadon-glazed carp in the central tile panel above the fountain. The drinking fountain tile installation is 64" tall and 53" wide with the carp tile measuring 9.125" x 15.25". The nearby Washington School kindergarten room, also in Wyandotte, Michigan, has a traditional drinking fountain built into a Flint Faience tile combination drinking fountain, sandbox, and terrarium. Although the actual drinking fountain is new, it retains the spirit of the original. All tiles are 4.25" square.

Combination drinking fountain, sandbox, and terrarium in the Washington Elementary School, Wyandotte, Michigan. *Courtesy of Washington Elementary.*

Drinking fountain in the Garfield Elementary School in Wyandotte, Michigan. The fountain is 64" tall and 53" wide. The center panel of intertwined carp is 9.125" x 15.25". *Courtesy of Mary Wharton Thorson.*

Foyers

see also Zodiac, and Art Deco

In their own promotional literature, A-303, the Flint Faience & Tile Company illustrated an exquisite entrance hallway or foyer and noted that this is "where the visitor gains his first impression of the home." No one created more dramatic tiled foyers than Flint Faience Tile Company. The small but exquisite entrance foyer of the former Taine McDougal home, located in Flint, Michigan and now owned by Linda and Joe Katrinic, Jr., contains a tile compass surrounded by the twelve zodiac tiles set as inserts among a dark charcoal tiled background. Each zodiac tile is 4.25" square while the centered compass is comprised of nine tile pieces with an overall diameter of 18". This zodiac set is identical to the set illustrated on the 4" x 6" index cards with watercolor sketches and glaze color numbers located in the Sloan Museum in Flint. See illustrations and detailed descriptions under Zodiac and Compass entries.

Illustration of hall entranceway foyer featured in Flint Faience & Tile Company Flyer A-303. *Courtesy of the Archives, New York State College of Ceramics at Alfred University.*

In sharp contrast to the Taine McDougal compass and zodiac foyer, is the Art Deco style stairwell foyer in the 1929 Bower home, located in Flint, Michigan and now owned by Ken and Susan Kayser. Radiating out from the 12" diameter carved center tile depicting the winged Mercury and his shield are vibrantly colored tiles in oranges, blues, and gold hues, varying from 2" to 3" to 4" to 6" square.

Foyer in the former Bower house in Flint, Michigan, featuring "Mercury." *Courtesy of Ken Kayser.*

Detail of the tiled foyer in the former Bower house, Flint, Michigan. *Courtesy of Ken Kayser.*

If having a Flint Faience tiled foyer could ever be considered "standard," then the 50" x 61" entrance foyer of the former Prosper Champion home could be considered the norm. Colorful 2" x 2" tiles are inserted among 4" x 4" pentagon shaped earth-toned field tiles. Constructed in 1928, the Prosper Champion home is located in Flint, Michigan. Prosper Champion was the brother of Albert Champion, and apparently also owned his own spark plug company at one time.

Foyer in the former Prosper Champion home, Flint, Michigan, built c. 1928. *Courtesy of Jim Fitzell and Jessica Higgins.*

Fruit

The subject of fruit is a remarkably popular Flint Faience design, despite the fact that other food groups are seldom, if ever, represented. The only other reference to food in the Flint Faience repertoire would be the special custom designs for the Wheatsworth Factory in Hamburg, New Jersey. That site featured twenty allegorical tiled panels, all of which involved the subject of agriculture and specifically wheat products, including breakfast cereal and stacks of steaming pancakes. See entry for the Wheatsworth Factory for illustrations and detailed descriptions.

If fruit is shown, then grapes are usually among the chosen fruit. Two 8.5" x 10" tiled panels with grapes and vines in the Galvas collection are presented with an Art Deco flavor when judged both stylistically and by glaze palette. These two tiles can be compared to a relatively simple, straightforward treatment of the subject, with the grapes and vines almost glowing against a glossy black background glaze on a 6" square tile in the same collection. Another 6" tile adds a basket and other fruit to the composition, providing stock design no. 6660 from *Catalog "G."*

Large carved Art Deco tile with grapes, illustrating different glaze palette, also measuring 8.5" x 10". $1400-1600.

Large carved Art Deco tile with grapes, measuring 8.5" x 10". $1400-1600.

Tile with grape motif in raised line design. 6" x 6". $450-550.

Carved tile depicting a basket of fruit, stock design no. 6660. 6" x 6". $ 400-500.

Fruit compote tile executed in a wax resist. Wax resist tiles seem to be less plentiful than raised line tiles. Stock design no. 6641. 6" x 6". $350-400.

While not plentiful, tiles with designs of fruit compotes exist in a variety of glazes and hues. Some appear to have been produced by wax resist methods and others are raised line decoration. These are plentiful in *Catalog "G"* as stock designs, such as no. 6661 (6") or nos. 6692 and 6693, featuring two tiles measuring a total of 18" x 9". Still another variation on stock design no. 6641 is the 6" x 6" fruit in compote motif, oriented on point, which can be seen with three small glaze palette changes on three separate tiles in the Galvas collection.

FLINT FAIENCE TILE COMPANY, FLINT, MICHIGAN.
STOCK DESIGNS—EXECUTED IN ANY COLOR COMBINATION

6709 6736 6641 6733 6602
6820 6819 6851 6849 6850
6660 6661 6715 6711 6665
6800 6805 6799 6804 6801
6718 6719 6720 6721 6760

Raised line process inserts. Size 6x6 in.

[20]

A series of stock designs, some with fruit motifs, from page 20 of *Catalog "G."*

Fruit compote tile executed in a wax resist, showing glaze variations. Stock design no. 6641. 6" x 6" . $ 350-400.

Fruit compote tile executed in a wax resist, showing glaze variations. Stock design no. 6641. 6" x 6". $ 350-400.

Even border tiles sometimes had fruit decorations (with grapes, of course). A beautiful set of two 6" x 6" border tiles with designs of grapes, cherries, pears, and pomegranates can be seen in the Dale and Doris Barrett collection.

Other Flint Faience tile installations included grape decorations, including the University of Detroit Mercy Faculty Building Chapel Sacristy 7" square grapes tile within a 22" x 22" diamond shaped setting. Other fruit symbols can be seen in the drinking fountain installation at St. Paul's Catholic School in Grosse Pointe Farms, Michigan.

Border tiles with fruit motifs, shown together. *Courtesy of Dale and Doris Barrett*. $600-800.

Two border tiles in a raised line design with fruit motif. 6" x 6". *Courtesy of Dale and Doris Barrett*. $300-400 each.

Furniture

see also Identification chapter

Aside from architectural furniture most frequently seen in school rooms and solariums, such as fireplaces, fountains, sandboxes, sinks, and drinking fountains, the only other furniture which utilized Flint Faience tiles are fireplace screens and small tables with tiled tops and wrought iron bases. These have not been documented in the literature.

Flower basket tile top table. 13.75" x 13.75" x 18.5". $750-850.

As noted in the chapter on Identification, sometimes vintage Flint Faience tiles have been inset into newer bases that are not original with the tiled table top. An authenticated wrought iron tile top table contains a central panel with daisies in a blue vase, surrounded by stylized flower motif tiles. The table measures 13.75" x 13.75" x 18.5" high. A look at details of the wrought iron work lets one know whether or not this is an original factory table frame or a later concoction. See the chapter on Identification for more details.

"Magical Oak" tile top table. 19.25" x 13" x 18.5". $1800-2000.

Spanish design tiles are showcased on this tile top table. 27" x 18" x 23" high. *Courtesy of Robert Rozycki*. $1200-1500.

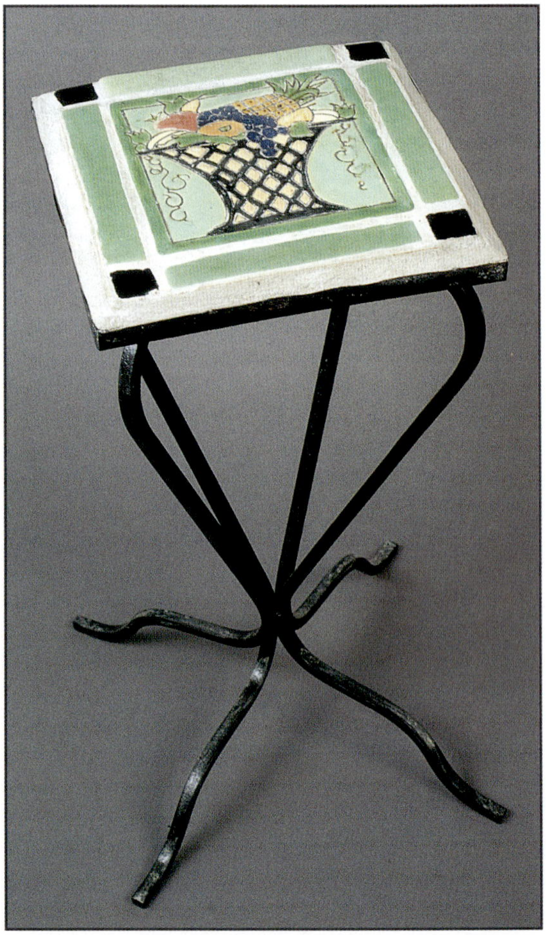

Flower basket tile top table. Not the original base. 9.5" x 9.5" x 20.5". $300-400.

Jolly Roger tile top table. 12" x 12" x 24.5" $400-500. *Courtesy of Rick and Linda Fusco.*

Sometimes just the unmounted table top tiles have found their way into private collections; such is the case with a four-piece round table top with a diameter of 12", in the Ken Galvas collection.

Four piece tile top executed in raised line design. No base. 12". $750-850.

Honeycomb tile top table. Not an original base. 18.5" x 13" x 20". $400-500.

A stunning fireplace screen was created by Julio Haro and is now in a private collection. It depicts a Mexican Tehuana in her brightly colored costume, a popular subject matter for designer Julio Haro, artist Frida Kahlo, and others (see also Exotics entry).

Fireplace screen with Tehuana motif by Julio Haro. *Courtesy of Private Collection.*

General Motors Building

see Tree of Life

Geometric

Geometric isn't a term used by Flint Faience Tile Company but it is probably the most convenient term for describing the many tiles produced by the company that were decorated by the inlay or raised line process, mostly for use as inserts in floor and wall installations. These tiles have symmetrical design patterns that are not formalized as animals or other easily labeled or recognized designs. Most of these geometrics are referred to by collectors by their stock design number, such as no. 6501, which was used to illustrate the wide variety of colorations available for each tile design available in the 1929 Flint Faience & Tile Company booklet *Architectural Faience: An Introduction.* An example of tile no. 6501 measuring 4.125" square, pale blue with gold, blue, and red glazes can be seen in the collection of Ken Galvas. This same tile can be seen as an insert among field tiles in many installations.

Detail of page 22 of *Catalog "G,"* illustrating geometric patterns including stock design no. 6501.

Example of geometric insert tile no. 6501. 4.125" x 4.125". $75-100.

Geometric can also be used to describe some of the floor tile design patterns executed in Flint Faience tiles. *Architectural Faience* illustrated many elaborate floors, among them a stunning box design in Flint Faience. Other more traditional geometric floor patterns can be seen in the historic black and white photograph published in November 1932, which shows Emile Francois, the tile expert, sitting amid a permanent Flint Faience tile display in the Builders Exchange Building in Cleveland.

4¼ Decorated tile No. 6501 in the following colorations:

-8	-10	-19	*(also 1 x 1 tile*
-7	-1	-13	*No. 6773 in 10*
-20	-31	-34	*colorations)*
-23	-9	-11	

Detail of illustrations of geometric stock design no. 6501 from page 7, *Architectural Faience: An Introduction. Courtesy of Jim Graham.*

Emile "Edgar" Francois shown among geometric floor patterns in the permanent display of Flint Faience tiles in the Builders Exchange Building in Cleveland. *Keramic Tile Journal*, November, 1932.

Insert tile with geometric stock design no. 6451. 6" x 6". $100-150.

Insert tile in geometric stock design no. 6531, measuring 6.125" x 6.125". $100-150.

Insert tile with geometric stock design no. 6436. 4.25" x 4.25". $100-125.

Geometric insert tile, stock design no. 6556. 4.25" x 4.25". $100-125.

A different glaze palette shown on geometric insert tile stock design no. 6556. *Courtesy of Baggs Memorial Library, the Ohio State University.*

Geometric insert tile, stock design no. 6434. 4.25" x 4.25". $100-125.

Geometric insert tile, stock design no. 6514. 4.25" x 4.25". $100-125.

Two geometric patterned insert tiles, stock design no. 6555. 4.25" x 4.25". $100-125 each.

Black and gold glazed insert tile, stock design no. 6553. 4.25" x 4.25". $100-125.

Pair of insert tiles in geometric stock design no. 6519. 3" x 3". $40-60 each.

Blue and gold glazed geometric insert tile in stock design no. 6523. 2.75" x 2.75". $30-40.

Insert tile in raised line design, geometric stock design no. 6624. 3" x 3". $50-75.

Glaze variation seen on geometric insert tile, stock design no. 6523. 2.85" x 2.85". $30-40.

Colorful geometric insert tile, stock design no. 6426. 3" x 3". $40-60.

Geometric insert tile, stock design no. 6418. 2.75" x 2.75". $30-40.

Blue and gold glazed geometric insert tile, stock design no. 6521. 2.75" x 2.75". $30-40.

Geometric swastika insert tile, stock design no. 6524. 2.75" x 2.75". $30-40.

Grouping of three geometric insert tiles, stock design no. 6524. 2.75" x 2.75". $30-40 each.

Geometric insert tile with wheel pattern, stock design no. 6416. 2.75" x 2.75". $30-40.

Geometric insert tile with stock design and "O" pattern no. 6616. 2.85" x 2.85". $50-60.

Geometric insert tile with endless knot pattern, stock design no. 6588. 2.75" x 2.75". $30-40.

Geometric insert tile in stock design no. 6541. 2" x 2". $25-30.

Two geometric insert tiles, stock design no. 6520. 2.75" x 2.75" $30-40 each.

Two related geometric insert tiles in stock design no. 6537. 2" x 2". $25-30 each.

Grouping of "spinning" geometric insert tiles, stock design no. 6537. 2" x 2". $25-30 each.

Grouping of seven geometric patterned insert tiles, stock design no. 6536. 2" x 2". $25-30 each.

Grouping of "reverse spinning" geometric insert tiles, stock design no. 6537. 2" x 2". $25-30 each.

Blue and black glazed geometric insert tile, stock design no. 6664, with raised line design. 2" x 2". $35- 40.

Grouping of eight geometric insert tiles, stock design no. 6542. 2" x 2". $25-30 each.

Checkerboard patterned insert tiles, stock design no. 6540. 2" x 2". $25-30 each.

2" x 2" geometric insert tile, stock design no. 6507. $25-30.

1.5" x 1.5" geometric border tile in raised line design. $10-15.

Grouping of seven 2" x 2" geometric insert tiles, stock design no. 6534. $25-30.

1" x 1" geometric insert tile in raised line decoration, stock design no. 6773. $10-15.

Blue "X" insert tile, stock design no. 6775, measuring 0.875" x 0.875". $10-15.

Glazes

see also Crystalline Glazes

Flint Faience tiles were available in a wide selection of colors that featured matte, enamel, crystalline or glossy glazes. The 1929 Flint Faience & Tile Company publication titled *Architectural Faience: An Introduction* described and illustrated dozens of available glaze colors and types and noted that they have "available some 150 plain colors." (Flint Faience & Tile Company, *Architectural Faience: An Introduction*, 1929, 5) They continued, "Flint Faience colors are fired, not for ceramic expediency, but for their decorative utility." Portions of the color variations have been reproduced in the entries for Crystalline Glazes, Fish and Sea Life, and others. Undoubtedly new glazes were developed throughout the twelve years that the company produced tiles. Different promotional literature cited differing numbers of available glazes; sometimes 200, and sometimes infinite numbers of available glazes were mentioned. A later 1920s *Sweet's Catalogue* notes 150 colors and "some 50 shades of blue." (B1870, 1928-29)

When describing the use of Flint Faience tiles for the floor, the author of the *Architectural Faience* promotional booklet noted that the durability of the tiles in residential settings such as hallways, sun rooms, libraries, porches, bathrooms, and kitchens gave the tile great appeal, but the Flint Faience color palette and color options could create effects varying from "a Persian rug to ultra-modernistic; from cold academic to the most homey sort of intimacy." (Flint Faience & Tile Company, *Architectural Faience: An Introduction*, 1929, 11)

Flint Faience & Tile

COLOR Printing

Ink pigment on special paper has done its best to suggest the depth of quality—the beauty and richness of the Flint Faience glazes.

Fired at 1900 to 2400 degrees, and with hand-dipped glaze of appreciable thickness, Flint Faience has a distinctive quality.

Other glazes than shown *although equally striking*, but whose individuality of texture, sheen, gloss or elusive crystallization, could not be caught by the color camera, had to be omitted—with regret.

Samples of our entire color palette in the actual tile themselves are on display at our branches and in the showrooms of representative tiling contractors.

All glaze colors come from the fire with variation from tile to tile, it being impossible, of course, to show by a single tile the beauty characteristic of an assembled installation

H-1005 Ex. Variable
F-3055
H-1051 Ex. Variable
H-1008 Ex. Variable

F-2023 Variab
(Decorated)
F-3012
F-2319 Variab

COLOR VARIATION: General Not
All Faience varies. Neither color n
Such, of course, is the distinguishin
Faience, and especially a genuine ha
Majolica—which all Flint Faience prod
Beyond the nominal and characterist
every Faience color, certain glazes are
variations of considerable range.
Such glazes are indicated for the guid
with our products.

Page 3

Examples of available Flint Faience glazes and pertinent information from page 3 of *Architectural Faience: An Introduction*. *Courtesy of Jim Graham.*

Examples of available Flint Faience glazes illustrated on page 2 of *Architectural Faience: An introduction. Courtesy of Jim Graham.*

Flint Faience & Tile Company acknowledged that because all their tiles were "genuine handmade Faience – a true Majolica – which all Flint Faience products are...," there would be nominal and characteristic variation incidental to every Faience color. Additionally they cautioned that some types of glazes such as Red S-3900 and the W-8700 crystalline series could have extreme variations in the color results. The subdued and brilliant colors of Flint Faience glazed tiles are illustrated here in mostly monochrome glazes on tiles in both private collections and vintage installations.

The standard glazed tiles were fired at 1900 to 2400 degrees after hand-dipping each tile to apply the glaze. The promotional brochures intended for use primarily by architects were not meant as a substitute for seeing actual samples of the entire color palette on tiles that were displayed in the company's branch offices and the showrooms of representative tile contractors. At one time branch offices were located in New York, Chicago, Detroit, Birmingham, and, of course, Flint, Michigan.

Monochrome glazed tiles of various sizes: 6", 4.25", 2", and 1.5". $5-10 each.

Parlor floor in the University of Detroit Mercy's Faculty Building, with colorful inserts. *Courtesy of the Jesuit Community at the University of Detroit Mercy.*

Monochrome tile with muted matte glaze, measuring 4.25". *Courtesy of Baggs Memorial Library, the Ohio State University.*

Glaze tests sometimes utilized the vase format. Such was the case in three test glaze vases, each measuring 5" tall that are labeled 1, 2, 3. These iridescent type glazes are occasionally found on Flint Faience tiles. The set now in the Ken Galvas collection was purchased from the estate of Ralph Stoneburner, who was a general foreman of the Flint Faience & Tile Company.

Three glaze test vases with trial glazes numbered 1, 2, 3, each 5" tall. $150-175 each.

Drinking fountain with brightly glazed tilework and carp motif, c. 1932, Garfield Elementary School, Wyandotte, Michigan. *Courtesy of Mary Wharton Thorson.*

Gothic

Flint Faience Tile Company designed a selection of 2.75" decorative inserts for random placement in wall and floor installations which they labeled as "Gothic." These included such motifs as a crown, an heraldic lion, a winged creature (or two), and a lantern – a total of fourteen different designs, all illustrated on page 24 of *Catalog "G."* These random pattern designs were decorated in either inlay or embossed processes.

There are examples of some of these Gothic insert tile designs in private collections. Four stock designs, nos. 6546 (lanterns), 6513 (crowns), 6543 (a heraldic bird), and 6517 (a dragon form), are all included in the Ken Galvas collection. Each is 2.75" square.

Gothic style tile inserts as illustrated on page 24 of *Catalog "G."*

Lantern design insert tiles of the Gothic type, stock design no. 6546, measuring 2.65" x 2.65". $40-50 each.

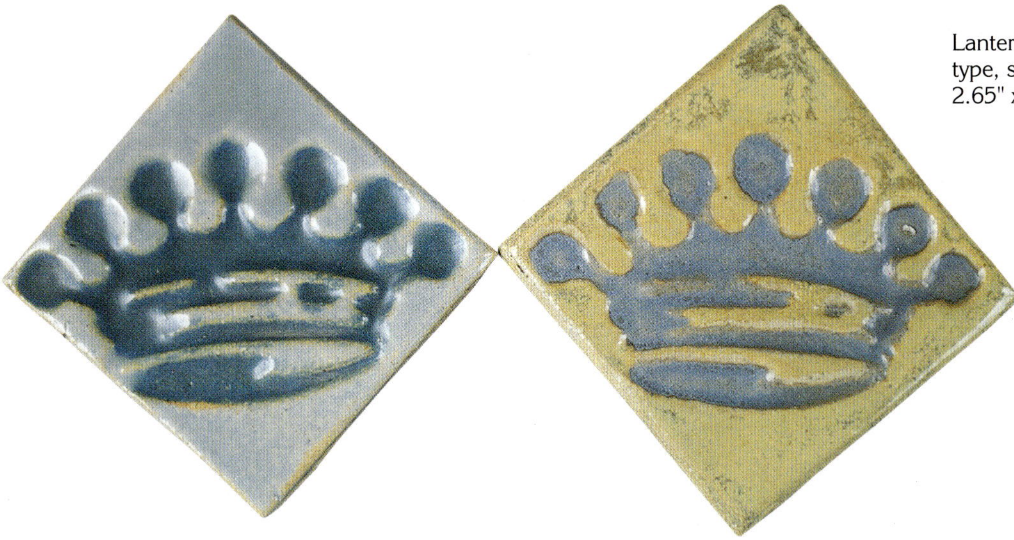

Crown insert tiles, from the Gothic category, stock design no. 6513, measuring 2.75" x 2.75". $40-50 each.

Framed black bird insert tile from the Gothic category, stock design no. 6543, measuring 2.75" x 2.75". $50-60.

Dragon insert tile from the Gothic category, stock design no. 6517, measuring 2.75" x 2.75". $50-75.

Advertisement in *Keramic Tile Journal*, Volume 4, no. 6, June 1932, page 4, illustrating Col. E.H.R. Green's home exterior, compass and tiled terrace.

Green, Col. E. H. R., Residence

Many splendid private residences contained beautiful Flint Faience tiles, including that belonging to the late Col. E.H.R. Green of South Dartmouth, Massachusetts. A tile compass, complete with nautical motifs, was chosen "to fit the fancy of a man whose hobbies run to charts and ships and out-of-the-way ports." (*Keramic Tile Journal*, October 1931, 5) Set in the center of a tile-paved terrace, the design was created by Alfred A. Williams of Boston, a representative of Flint Faience and Tile Company. Tarello Tile Co., New Bedford, Massachusetts, served as the tile contractor.

Colonel Edward Green was not just the son of Hetty Green, who was known to be the richest woman in the world at the time of her death in 1916. Legend has it that he was active in Texas politics and maintained his voting residence in Texas by leaving a suit of clothes and one of his wooden legs in a rented room in one of the fine residences of Terrell, Texas. (4/5/01 www.terrellheritagesociety.org/texas%20 midland%20railway%car.htm) There is a museum dedicated to the legendary frugal Hetty Green located in New Bedford, Massachusetts. There you can learn about Hetty and her son Edward, among other miserly millionaires. One story told about Hetty's eccentric frugality notes that her excessive penny-watching sometimes had a disastrous result. Is it possible that her "unwillingness to pay for a doctor to treat an injury to Ned's [Edward's] leg resulted in amputation"? (5/10/03 www.virtualvermont.com/history/hgreen.html)

Postcard illustrating the residence of Col. E.H.R. Green. *Courtesy Ken Galvas.*

There are individual tiles in private collections that match some of those at the former E.H.R. Green residence. For example, stock design no. 6428, a 3" square insert tile decorated by the inlay process, is in the collection of Ken Galvas. A raised line rope design, part the nautical theme, can be seen in the collection of Roger Ellingsworth. The coil of rope pattern may seem like an odd design, but it was actually one of the tiny insert tiles chosen to adorn the title page of *Architectural Faience: An Introduction*.

Geometric tile, stock design no. 6428 similar to tiles at the former Col. E.H.R. Green residence. Tile measures 3" x 3". $40-50.

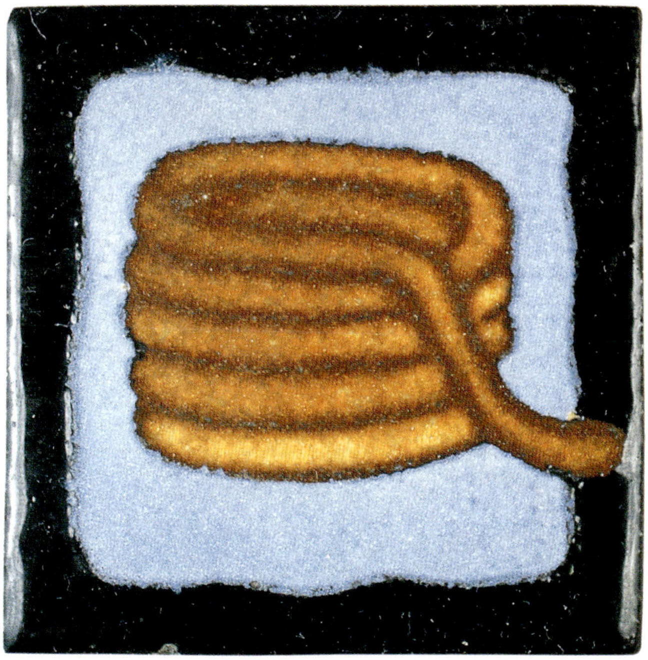

Raised line coil of rope nautical insert, measuring 3" x 3". *Courtesy of Roger Ellingsworth.* $100-125.

Handmade

see also Marketing

Handmade is the word used over and over to describe Flint Faience tiles. Their promotional literature, always aimed at the architect client or tiling contractor, stressed that "true Faience as made by us today is genuinely handmade at every process after the preliminary machine-milling of the plastic 'body.'" (Flint Faience & Tile Company, *Architectural Faience: An Introduction*, 1929, 13) This was truly a buzzword of the 1920s and assisted in marketing these unique artistic yet practical tiles.

The April 1929 issue of *AC Sparks* proudly noted "Flint Faience tiles are not machine-made tiles. They are moulded by hand, glazed and fired. This gives them their glowing beauty, irregularity of surface and design and great durability." (AC Spark Plug Company, 1929, 3) This theme runs throughout the company's promotional literature, with perhaps the highlight being in their 1929 brochure known as A-303, where they exclaim, "Like the old pieces which reach Museum importance, Flint Faience is similarly hand-made at every step." (Flint Faience & Tile Company, *Bathroom Flyer A-303*, 1929, cover)

Lest the reader be misled by this description, Josephine Ellis and her co-workers did not have to tediously sculpt every single embossed and inlaid tile. Plaster-of-Paris molds were cast from the original model and the clay was then pressed into these molds, hence the phrase "molded by hand." The hand-decorated process is described under the entry Raised Line.

Prototype star mold made by Josephine Ellis, measuring 4" x 4". *Courtesy Dale and Doris Barrett.*

Haro, Julio

Julio Haro was born October 28, 1898, in Mexico City. He attended the Art Division of the architectural school at the Academy of San Carlos in Mexico City. He came to the United States in 1921. Haro's first boss as he was hired at Flint Faience and Tile Company was Carl Bergmans. Haro was the Chief Designer at Flint Faience & Tile Company from 1921 to 1933. Historic documents tell us that some of his various titles included: in 1921, Tile Worker; June 1, 1923, Tile Decorator (the same year he created his first tile panel); March 28, 1925, Acting Foreman; July 16, 1925, Tile Supervisor. After the tile plant closed in 1933, Haro took on other design responsibilities as artist designer in the Engineering Department at AC Spark Plug. He designed beautiful instrument cluster panels for automobile dashboards, although his tile creations remained the highlight of his long career with AC Sparkplug. He retired in 1963 after forty-two years of service to AC and passed away in 1971 at the age of seventy-two. Haro was included in three editions of *Who's Who in American Art*. He was a founding member of the Flint Institute of Arts and the International Institute of Flint, Michigan, both of which still play a vital role in the community today.

Carl Bergmans (left) and Julio Haro at work at the Flint Faience Tile Company. *Courtesy of the Alfred P. Sloan Museum, acc. no. 86.15.51.*

Many Flint Faience tile panels and installations can be credited to Julio Haro. Watercolor and oil paintings still surface in the marketplace that reveal the strong ties to Haro's Mexican roots. He designed the Flint Faience installations in Edward T. Strong's residence in Flint, Michigan; the Aphrodite panel for the Dalton residence in Rumson, New Jersey; several rooms at the University of Detroit; the Leland Hotel in Detroit; the IMA Auditorium; and the First National Bank in Flint. Julio Haro also designed the 4,400 individual tiles for the swimming pools of the S.S. *Manhattan* and S.S. *Washington*. The four lunettes featuring Spanish galleons with full sail for the United States Customs House in San Juan, Puerto Rico were also designed by Haro, as were the cafeteria and new car showrooms at the GM Building and more than one large stunning tiled panel including the wonderful one with a Mexican theme (whereabouts currently unknown) which was published many times. The Mexican theme panel was included as the cover of the July 1930 issue of *Keramic Tile Journal*, *Catalog "G,"* and recently as the cover of the book *Ceramic Tile in 20th Century America* by John J. Sekora. This panel demonstrates Haro's sensitivity to the customs and traditions of his southern Mexican homeland. The creation of the Spanish theme for the Faculty Building at the University of Detroit Mercy stands as a testament to his mastery of design. When viewing the building it is hard to comprehend how a material as hard and unyielding as tile can give such a deep feeling of warmth and welcome to the visitor. It becomes easy to understand what Haro's wife Maria meant when she said, "he never enjoyed the other jobs as much as the tile." (Crawford, 1982, n.p.)

Cover of the *Keramic Tile Journal*, July 1930, featuring a tile mural with a Mexican theme created by Julio Haro. *Courtesy Vance Koehler.*

Julio Haro's creative endeavors did not stop with the work he did for Flint Faience Tile Company and AC for forty-two years. Newspaper articles record that in his spare time he created at least one Cathedral-like backdrop for a concert performance in Flint at the I.M.A. auditorium. He painted the original watercolor and it was transferred by a Minneapolis studio, enlarged, onto a canvas backing.

Julio Haro, c. 1963, shortly before his retirement. *Courtesy of the Alfred P. Sloan Museum.*

Heraldic lion crest on the exterior of the former Prosper Champion home, in Flint, Michigan. *Courtesy of Jim Fitzell and Jessica Higgins.*

Heraldic

see also Fleur-de-lis

While heraldic shields weren't the most prolific of Flint Faience tile motifs, they did play a prominent role in the exterior of at least one significant residence. The front of the Prosper Champion (brother of AC founder, Albert Champion) home in Flint, Michigan has two heraldic shields inset into the brick façade, which lend a certain elevated status to the dwelling, despite their unknown derivation. One crest depicts a lion, while the other shield form contains fleur-de-lis, stripes, and ribbons. If one investigates private residences of this era, heraldic shields are a prevalent theme in stained glass windows as well.

The Prosper Champion home, built in 1928, additionally has a Flint Faience tile sunroom floor with a tiled radiator grill, a tiled fireplace in the living room, a colorfully tiled entrance foyer, and a wonderful pinkish-lavender, green and black tiled bathroom, among other ceramic features.

Fleur-de-lis shield on the exterior of the former Prosper Champion home in Flint, Michigan. *Courtesy of Jim Fitzell and Jessica Higgins.*

Individual tiles with heraldic themes can be seen in various private collections in the United States. These tiles were standard patterns available through their catalog sales, as seen in the Flint Faience Tile Company *"Catalog G"* from 1926, p. 20, no. 6820 and p. 21, no. 6445.

6" x 6" heraldic tile, stock design no. 6445. $150-200.

6" x 6" heraldic tile, stock design no. 6820. $150-200.

Detail of heraldic tile stock design no. 6820 from page 20 of *Catalog "G."*

FLINT FAIENCE TILE COMPANY, FLINT, MICHIGAN.
STOCK DESIGNS-EXECUTED IN ANY COLOR COMBINATION

6530 6533 6532 6401 6527
6528 6531 6559 6529 6558
6457 6455 6446 6443 6450
6454 6449 6444 6451 6447
6445 6456 6453 6448 6452

Inlay process inserts. Size 6 x 6 in.

[21]

Page 21 of *Catalog "G"* illustrating various heraldic tile stock designs.

Many consider the griffin, a winged mythical beast, as a heraldic emblem. These are quite commonly found on Flint Faience insert tiles, as can be seen in stock design no. 6538, a 2.75" square tile from the Ken Galvas collection. This griffin is almost iridescent in lavender and pink hues. The rectangular modeled tile of a rampant lion in the Ken Galvas collection could also be considered of this heraldic genre. Other heraldic insert tiles can be seen *in situ* in such installations as those at the Grosse Pointe Memorial Church, Grosse Pointe Farms, Michigan and other locations.

Griffin tile, stock design no. 6538, measuring 2.75" x 2.75". $40-50.

Carved rampant lion tile, measuring 10" x 5". $600-800.

History of Flint Faience

see chapter History of Flint Faience

Holiday Themes

Easily recognizable among holiday-type theme tiles are those that have a Halloween flavor, such as the black cat with the arched back shown against a yellow background, 4.25" square, from the Ken Galvas collection. It is identical in design to one installed in the Washington School kindergarten room sandbox in Wyandotte, Michigan, except that their black Halloween cat is shown against a green background to match all the undecorated tiles in the installation. The same sandbox has another 4.25" square Halloween theme tile in the form of a black glazed witch stirring a glowing red cauldron. A much less scary witch with a broom and a black and white cat can be found decorating a raised line process tile 6" square. The caped figure is leaning toward a small child in a curious manner. This charming Halloween tile is in the collection of Ken Galvas.

Other holiday themes include Christmas motifs such as the 4.25" tile depicting a Christmas tree with lighted candles in the collection on loan to the Western Reserve Historical Society in Cleveland.

Tile depicting black cat with arched back and yellow background glaze. 4.25" x 4.25". $125-150.

Black cat tile installed on the sandbox at the Washington Elementary School, Wyandotte, Michigan. 4.25" x 4.25". *Courtesy of Washington Elementary School.*

4.25" x 4.25" tile depicting a witch stirring a cauldron installed on the sandbox at Washington Elementary School, Wyandotte, Michigan. *Courtesy of Washington Elementary School.*

Rare 6" x 6" Halloween tile. $1000-1200.

Hospitals

While it is possible that for aesthetic, therapeutic and sanitation reasons many hospitals used Flint Faience ceramic tiles in interior hallways, floors, and dining areas, not many have been identified and documented. A 1931 issue of *Keramic Tile Journal* (*Keramic Tile Journal*, September 1931, 5) illustrates three different views of the hydrotherapy suite at the McLean Hospital in Belmont, Massachusetts.

The advertisement on page five in the leading trade journal of the day touted "Flint Handmade Faience colored tiles are a factor in mental treatment in this hydrotherapy suite." Flint Faience worked most directly with architects in placing their tile, and never advertised in the popular ladies magazines. The hospital architect was Eugene T. Nolte of Braintree, Massachusetts and the tiling contractor was Rinaldi Tile Company, Inc. of Cambridge, Massachusetts. "Soft green tile walls with a trim of yellow-red flecked with rose" were chosen since "Certain tones of green, psychiatrists agree, have a soothing effect on mental patients" while "Yellow-red suggests sunlight – enlivens the spirit and helps to overcome mental depression." Shades nos. 300 and 3501 were selected because "they most nearly satisfied the exacting requirements of the learned doctor" [Dr. Tillotson].

McLean Hospital is now part of a 44-building hospital complex that is part of Harvard University. The hydrotherapy suites were demolished during renovations in the past quarter century. McLean Hospital is located at 115 Mill Street.

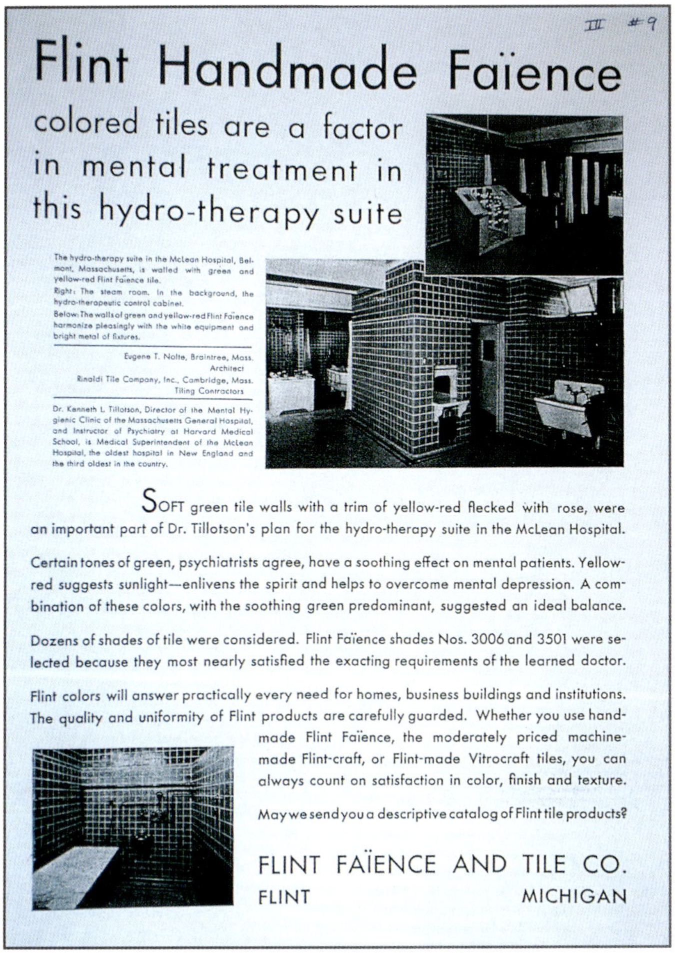

III #9

Flint Handmade Faïence

colored tiles are a factor in mental treatment in this hydro-therapy suite

The hydro-therapy suite in the McLean Hospital, Belmont, Massachusetts, is walled with green and yellow-red Flint Faïence tile.

Right: The steam room. In the background, the hydro-therapeutic control cabinet.

Below: The walls of green and yellow-red Flint Faïence harmonize pleasingly with the white equipment and bright metal of fixtures.

Eugene T. Nolte, Braintree, Mass.
Architect
Rinaldi Tile Company, Inc., Cambridge, Mass.
Tiling Contractors

Dr. Kenneth L. Tillotson, Director of the Mental Hygienic Clinic of the Massachusetts General Hospital, and Instructor of Psychiatry at Harvard Medical School, is Medical Superintendent of the McLean Hospital, the oldest hospital in New England and the third oldest in the country.

SOFT green tile walls with a trim of yellow-red flecked with rose, were an important part of Dr. Tillotson's plan for the hydro-therapy suite in the McLean Hospital.

Certain tones of green, psychiatrists agree, have a soothing effect on mental patients. Yellow-red suggests sunlight—enlivens the spirit and helps to overcome mental depression. A combination of these colors, with the soothing green predominant, suggested an ideal balance.

Dozens of shades of tile were considered. Flint Faïence shades Nos. 3006 and 3501 were selected because they most nearly satisfied the exacting requirements of the learned doctor.

Flint colors will answer practically every need for homes, business buildings and institutions. The quality and uniformity of Flint products are carefully guarded. Whether you use handmade Flint Faïence, the moderately priced machine-made Flint-craft, or Flint-made Vitrocraft tiles, you can always count on satisfaction in color, finish and texture.

May we send you a descriptive catalog of Flint tile products?

FLINT FAÏENCE AND TILE CO.
FLINT MICHIGAN

Advertisement illustrating the hydrotherapy suite at the McLean Hospital, published on page 5 in the *Keramic Tile Journal,* Volume 3, no. 9, 1931.

Salvaged relief tile from the Winchester Hospital, Flint, Michigan. *Courtesy of the Alfred P. Sloan Museum.*

Winchester Hospital, once located on Flushing Road in Flint, Michigan, and built circa 1923, also utilized Flint Faience tiles. In this case, the tiles were located on the building exterior rather than on the interior as was the case with McLean Hospital. One tile can be seen today in the Sloan Museum in Flint, while many are part of the private collection of Gerard Burnash who salvaged the tiles when the building was demolished in 1997. These Winchester Hospital tiles include large 9.25" squares with designs of iron crosses in brilliant reds, blue, and oranges, 4.25" x 8.5" modeled iris tiles, and stunning 9.75" square tiles that remind one of a stained glass window with and without diamond-shaped centers.

Salvaged tile from the Winchester Hospital, Flint, Michigan, executed by a wax resist method. 9" x 9". c. 1923. *Courtesy of Gerard Burnash.*

High relief iris tile, stock design no. 6204, measuring 8.75" x 4.25", salvaged from the Winchester Hospital, Flint, Michigan. Note that these tiles were mounted and grouted to a pre cast slab of concrete that was then installed into the exterior of the building. *Courtesy of Gerard Burnash.*

Salvaged tile from Winchester Hospital in Flint, Michigan, affixed to a pre cast slab of concrete. Center tile 10" x 10". *Courtesy of Gerard Burnash.*

10" x 10" salvage tile from Winchester Hospital, Flint Michigan, stock design no. 7007 in high relief. *Courtesy of Gerard Burnash.*

Hotels

see also Dryden Hotel and Fort Shelby Hotel, Restaurant

Hotels formed a major component of buildings that utilized Flint Faience tiles. The 1929 *AC Sparks* listing of recent Faience installations cited three hotels in New York City (the Dryden Hotel, Hotel Murray, and the San Carlos Hotel) as well as the Fort Shelby Hotel restaurant in Detroit. (The Fort Shelby Hotel restaurant is detailed under the entry for Fort Shelby Hotel.) The Hotel Murray and the San Carlos Hotel have both undergone massive renovations with no Flint Faience tile remaining or visible. A September 2002 visit to the San Carlos site showed the building completely gutted, and renovations underway. The Dryden Hotel, with its futuristic tiles and wonderful architectural features, is illustrated and detailed under the separate Dryden Hotel entry.

There were other hotels with Flint Faience tile installations but hotels changed owners and renovations occurred, so seldom were the tile installations left intact. It is known that Flint Faience Tile Company designer Julio Haro created at least one tile installation for the Leland Hotel in Detroit. No further information is available and there is no evidence of such an installation at the hotel today, which is now a Ramada Inn. A historic black and white postcard gives an idea of the Leland Hotel at its prime.

Postcard of the Leland Hotel, Detroit, Michigan. *Courtesy of Margaret Carney.*

Another magnificent hotel that was recorded to have a major Flint Faience tile installation is the Mayflower Hotel in Washington, D.C. No evidence of tile work is discernible today in this grand hotel now known as the Renaissance Mayflower Hotel and located at 1127 Connecticut Avenue, N.W.

Postcard of the Mayflower Hotel, Washington D.C. *Courtesy of Ken Galvas.*

With so many mysteries about hotel tile installations that have disappeared it is uplifting to learn of a flourishing hotel, over seventy-five years of age, with at least part of its original tile installations intact and even restored. The Vinoy Park Hotel, located at 501 Fifth Avenue N.E., in St. Petersburg, Florida, was built in 1925 and is now listed on the National Register of Historic Places. Designed by Henry L. Taylor of New York, who was also responsible for designing St. Mary's Church, the Jungle Hotel, and the Florida Theatre in St. Petersburg, the Vinoy's architectural style may be described as Mediterranean Revival. The contractor, from Tampa, was George A. Miller, and the $3.5 million 375-room hotel was completed in just under ten months. The lobby is designed of glazed quarry tile with hand-painted decorative inserts – in spectacular Flint Faience. The Vinoy Park Hotel is now the Renaissance Vinoy Resort and Golf Club. They are proud of their renovations and feature details of the Flint Faience insert tiles in their glossy promotional materials.

Postcard of the Vinoy Park Hotel, St. Petersburg, Florida. *Courtesy of Ken Galvas.*

Tiled lobby promenade in the present day Renaissance Vinoy Resort and Golf Club in St. Petersburg, Florida. *Courtesy of Renaissance Vinoy Resort and Golf Club.*

2.75" x 2.75" insert tile, stock design no. 6514 from the renovated Renaissance Vinoy Resort and Golf Club. *Courtesy of Renaissance Vinoy Resort and Golf Club.*

Geometric insert tile, stock design no. 6501, measuring 4.25" x 4.25" as seen today in the renovated Vinoy Resort and Golf Club. *Courtesy of Renaissance Vinoy Resort and Golf Club.*

Original Flint Faience griffin insert tile, stock design no. 6538, measuring 2.75" x 2.75" in the present day Renaissance Vinoy Resort and Golf Club. *Courtesy of Renaissance Vinoy Resort and Golf Club.*

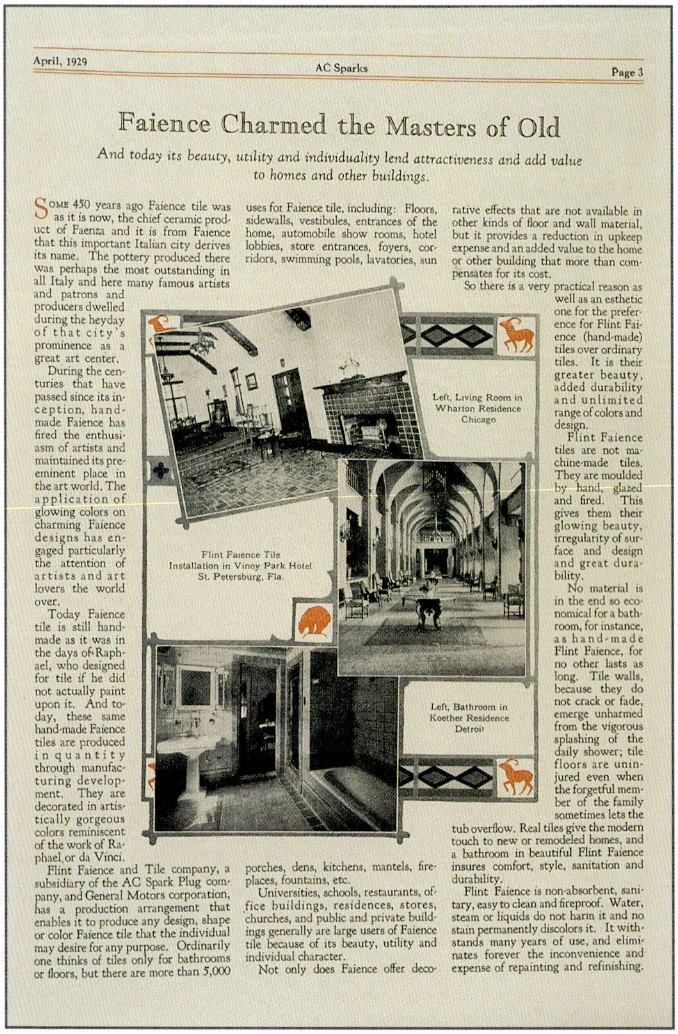

April, 1929 — AC Sparks — Page 3

Faience Charmed the Masters of Old

And today its beauty, utility and individuality lend attractiveness and add value to homes and other buildings.

SOME 450 years ago Faience tile was as it is now, the chief ceramic product of Faenza and it is from Faience that this important Italian city derives its name. The pottery produced there was perhaps the most outstanding in all Italy and here many famous artists and patrons and producers dwelled during the heyday of that city's prominence as a great art center.

During the centuries that have passed since its inception, hand-made Faience has fired the enthusiasm of artists and maintained its pre-eminent place in the art world. The application of glowing colors on charming Faience designs has engaged particularly the attention of artists and art lovers the world over.

Today Faience tile is still hand-made as it was in the days of Raphael, who designed for tile if he did not actually paint upon it. And today, these same hand-made Faience tiles are produced in quantity through manufacturing development. They are decorated in artistically gorgeous colors reminiscent of the work of Raphael, or da Vinci.

Flint Faience and Tile company, a subsidiary of the AC Spark Plug company, and General Motors corporation, has a production arrangement that enables it to produce any design, shape or color Faience tile that the individual may desire for any purpose. Ordinarily one thinks of tiles only for bathrooms or floors, but there are more than 5,000 uses for Faience tile, including: Floors, sidewalls, vestibules, entrances of the home, automobile show rooms, hotel lobbies, store entrances, foyers, corridors, swimming pools, lavatories, sun porches, dens, kitchens, mantels, fireplaces, fountains, etc.

Universities, schools, restaurants, office buildings, residences, stores, churches, and public and private buildings generally are large users of Faience tile because of its beauty, utility and individual character.

Not only does Faience offer decorative effects that are not available in other kinds of floor and wall material, but it provides a reduction in upkeep expense and an added value to the home or other building that more than compensates for its cost.

So there is a very practical reason as well as an esthetic one for the preference for Flint Faience (hand-made) tiles over ordinary tiles. It is their greater beauty, added durability and unlimited range of colors and design.

Flint Faience tiles are not machine-made tiles. They are moulded by hand, glazed and fired. This gives them their glowing beauty, irregularity of surface and design and great durability.

No material is in the end so economical for a bathroom, for instance, as hand-made Flint Faience, for no other lasts as long. Tile walls, because they do not crack or fade, emerge unharmed from the vigorous splashing of the daily shower; tile floors are uninjured even when the forgetful member of the family sometimes lets the tub overflow. Real tiles give the modern touch to new or remodeled homes, and a bathroom in beautiful Flint Faience insures comfort, style, sanitation and durability.

Flint Faience is non-absorbent, sanitary, easy to clean and fireproof. Water, steam or liquids do not harm it and no stain permanently discolors it. It withstands many years of use, and eliminates forever the inconvenience and expense of repainting and refinishing.

Left, Living Room in Wharton Residence Chicago

Flint Faence Tile Installation in Vinoy Park Hotel St. Petersburg, Fla.

Left, Bathroom in Koether Residence Detroit

Vinoy Park Hotel as illustrated in the publication *AC Sparks*, April, 1929. *Courtesy of the Archives, New York State College of Ceramics at Alfred University.*

The Mincks-Adams Hotel, known as the Adams Building, is located at 403 South Cheyenne Avenue in Tulsa, Oklahoma, and was constructed during 1927-28 for I.S. Mincks, who unfortunately lost the building during the Depression. The exterior glazed terra cotta veneering in elaborate Rococo style was created by Northwestern Terra Cotta Company and the building was placed on the National Register on November 7, 1978. Flint Faience tiles can be seen in the historic black and white image included in the trade publication *Keramic Tile Journal*, Volume III, No. 3, March 1931. In this image, a section of the lunch counter at the Mincks Hotel, complete with a floor in unglazed non-slip Vitrocraft is visible, as is the counter shown in blue Faience. The architect for the project was Alfred C. Fabry, and the tiling contractor was Consolvo Tile & Mantel Co., both of Tulsa.

The Adams Building has been renovated and the amazing Flint Faience tile installations have never looked better – in hallways, on columns, floors, and walls.

Lunch counter of the Mincks Hotel, as shown in the *Keramic Tile Journal,* Volume 3, no. 3, March 1931.

Wall panel detail from the Mincks Hotel, presently known as the Adams Building. *Courtesy of BoxerProperty.com.*

Column detail in the Mincks Hotel, presently known as the Adams Building. *Courtesy of BoxerProperty.com.*

Floor inserts in the Mincks Hotel, presently known as the Adams Building. *Courtesy of BoxerProperty.com.*

Column detail in the cafeteria area of the Mincks Hotel, presently known as the Adams Building. *Courtesy of BoxerProperty.com.*

Humpty Dumpty

see also Children's Rhymes and Stories

Humpty Dumpty is the featured theme on the tiled fireplace in room 103 at the Garfield School in Wyandotte, Michigan. This popular nursery rhyme is one of several "theme" fireplaces in the 1932 era school, which additionally includes a fireplace depicting the Story of Little Black Sambo in another classroom and a somewhat Deco designed tile mural with three ships, located in the school's library. The same school has four Flint Faience tiled drinking fountains with celadon-looking carp intertwined and a sandbox with wonderful 6" tiles of Teddy Bears with Flowers, Old King Cole, a Spotted Dog, etc. Humpty Dumpty's tiled fireplace is 83" wide and 60" high. There are five large 9" square tiles sequentially depicting the Humpty Dumpty nursery rhyme, beginning with Humpty Dumpty sitting on the wall, his great fall, all the king's horses, all the king's men, and "here fell Humpty Dumpty."

Fireplace with Humpty Dumpty theme in Garfield Elementary School, Wyandotte, Michigan, measuring 83" x 60". *Courtesy of Mary Wharton Thorson.*

"Humpty Dumpty Sitting on a Wall" tile from the fireplace at Garfield Elementary School, Wyandotte, Michigan. Tile 9" x 9". *Courtesy of Mary Wharton Thorson.*

"Humpty Dumpty Had a Great Fall" tile from the fireplace at Garfield Elementary School, Wyandotte, Michigan. Tile 9" x 9". *Courtesy of Mary Wharton Thorson.*

Top right:
"All The King's Horses" depicted on a 9" x 9" tile in the fireplace at Garfield Elementary School, Wyandotte, Michigan. *Courtesy of Mary Wharton Thorson.*

Center right:
"All the King's Men" depicted on a 9" x 9" tile in the fireplace at Garfield Elementary School, Wyandotte, Michigan. *Courtesy of Mary Wharton Thorson.*

Bottom right:
"Here Fell Humpty Dumpty" depicted on a 9" x 9" tile in the fireplace at Garfield Elementary School, Wyandotte, Michigan. *Courtesy of Mary Wharton Thorson.*

The Humpty Dumpty fireplace tiles are beautifully created by the raised line technique and are some of the most imaginative and detailed of any of the nursery rhyme installations. Other tiles in raised line depicting the Humpty Dumpty nursery rhyme, not from this series, can be found in private collections. One example would be the 6" x 6" tile in the collection of Ken Galvas which depicts a very smug Humpty Dumpty sitting on the wall (before the impending fall).

"Humpty Dumpty Sitting on a Wall" depicted on a 6" x 6" tile. $900-1200.

Identification

see chapter on Identification and Marks

Inserts

see also Geometrics, and Signage

Inserts were the usually brightly glazed and decorated tiles with inlay, raised line, or embossed decorations installed among various patterns of field tiles in floors and walls. Their sizes varied but stock design insert tiles commonly came in 6" x 6", 4.25" x 4.25", 3" x 3", 2.75" x 2.75", 2" x 2", 1.5" x 1.5", and 1" x 1", according to *Catalog "G,"* published in 1926 by Flint Faience Tile Company.

The beautiful large parlor in the Faculty Building at the University of Detroit Mercy has a woven pattern of field tiles and colorful 2.75" square inserts. The sunroom in the Samuel Simon Stewart home in Flint, Michigan also has dramatic 6" square inserts. Some insert tiles were not square or rectangular, but round or hexagonal. For example, the conservatory room with a stunning tiled fountain in the former E.T. Strong home in Flint has unusual 5.125" hexagonal insert tiles. One of the bathrooms in the same home has Flint Faience tiled walls and floors, some with almost an optical illusion effect. This bathroom utilized colorful 3.5" hexagonal tile inserts among the lavender floor tiles arranged in a honeycomb pattern. Apparently, colorful bathrooms were in vogue during the late 1920s, because another bathroom in the same home – this one with a salmon pink hue – had still another dramatic application for colorful insert tiles.

The use of inserts within the tiled floor basket weave design in the parlor of the Faculty Building at the University of Detroit Mercy. *Courtesy of the Jesuit Community at the University of Detroit Mercy.*

Example of an insert tile measuring 2.75" x 2.75", stock design no. 6514 installed in the parlor floor of the Faculty Building at the University of Detroit Mercy. *Courtesy of the Jesuit Community at the University of Detroit Mercy.*

Example of an insert tile, measuring 2.75" x 2.75", stock design no. 6535 installed in the parlor floor of the Faculty Building at the University of Detroit Mercy. *Courtesy of the Jesuit Community at the University of Detroit Mercy.*

Sunroom floor showing the use of insert tiles in the former Samuel Stewart home, Flint, Michigan. *Courtesy of Stephen and Rosanne Heddy.*

Example of an insert tile, measuring 2.75" x 2.75", stock design no. 6418 installed in the parlor floor of the Faculty Building at the University of Detroit Mercy. *Courtesy of the Jesuit Community at the University of Detroit Mercy.*

Insert tile measuring 6" x 6", stock design no. 6533 installed in the sunroom floor of the former Samuel Stewart home, Flint, Michigan. *Courtesy of Stephen and Rosanne Heddy.*

Conservatory in the former home of E. T. Strong, Flint, Michigan, illustrating the use of colorful insert tiles. *Courtesy of the Hamady Estate.*

Hexagonal raised line insert tiles, each measuring 5.125", installed in the conservatory in the former home of E.T. Strong, Flint, Michigan. *Courtesy of the Hamady Estate.*

Hexagonal raised line insert tiles, each measuring 3.25", installed in one of the bathrooms in the former E.T. Strong home, Flint, Michigan. *Courtesy of the Hamady Estate.*

Bathroom wall with insert tiles in the former E.T. Strong home, Flint, Michigan. *Courtesy of the Hamady Estate.*

Bathroom in the former E.T. Strong home. *Courtesy of the Hamady Estate.*

Insert tiles, glazed or bisqued, were sometimes used to decorate the exteriors of buildings such as the E&B Brewery in Detroit. Even the glazed insert tiles have faded from more than seventy years in the sun and daily weather. Insert tiles in private collections are numerous and are illustrated and described in many entries here including geometrics, botanicals, and animals. Stock design no. 6505, a 1.5" square insert tile decorated by the inlay process, is located in the Ken Galvas collection.

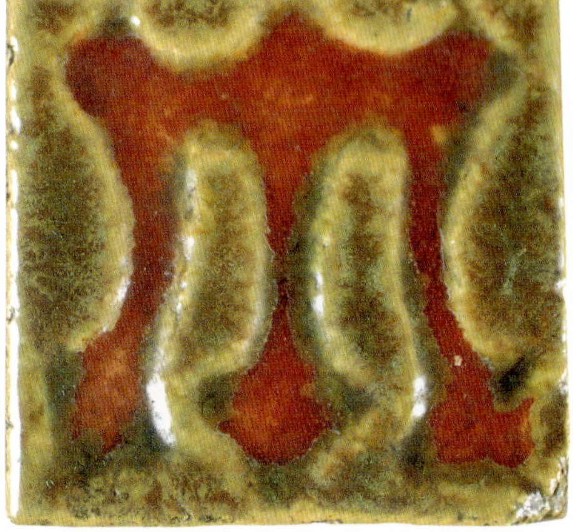

Small 1.5" insert tile, stock design no. 6505. $10-15.

As mentioned before, insert tiles do not have to be tiny. Some floors used insert tiles of varying sizes within the same installation. A more unusual example of a 6" x 6" insert tile is stock design no. 6559, a trident, a type of weapon, from the Ken Galvas collection. A tile matching this pattern is one of many decorative tiles installed in the fireplace facing of a Syracuse, New York residence in the mid-1920s by the architect Howard Yates. The stair risers in the same Syracuse home utilized this trident pattern, among others.

Trident insert tile, stock design no. 6559, measuring 6" x 6". $150-200.

Installations

see also chapter on Installations or Public Collections

Flint Faience tile installations are numerous, including floors in sun rooms, hallways, foyers, kitchens and bathrooms; walls, furniture, fountains, stair risers, fireplaces, murals, sandboxes, drinking fountains, bathrooms, swimming pools, and signage, in schools, universities, churches, auditoriums, banks, automobile showrooms, apartment houses, hospitals, theatres, hotels, restaurants, presidential palaces, factories, Y.M.C.A.'s, a U.S. customs house, private residences, Masonic temples, steamships, and more.

A listing of all known Flint Faience tile installations (including some proposed and others extant) plus museum collections, listed alphabetically by location, can be found in the chapter titled Installations or Public Collections. A brief chronology of significant installations would include the swimming pool at the Rockefeller Playhouse at Kykuit in Poncantico Hills, New York, constructed between 1925-27; the swimming pool at the Park Gables Apartments in Chicago, 1927; the Dryden Hotel in New York City, 1927-28; the series of allegorical panels created in 1928 for the Wheatsworth Factory in Hamburg, New Jersey; the Warner Theatre in Erie, Pennsylvania, 1929-31; and the tiles for the new ceramics building at the New York State School of Clay-Working and Ceramics, 1931-32. While many of the installations that have been documented are within the greater metropolitan Detroit and Flint, Michigan regions, Flint Faience installations can be found across much of the United States, with installations also in Puerto Rico and Peru.

Keramic Tile Journal

see also Julio Haro

Keramic Tile Journal was one of the leading tile trade journals of the day, and responsible for supplying much of the information known today about Flint Faience tile installations. Flint Faience advertised in almost every issue and there were a number of articles in the journal featuring Flint Faience tiles between 1929 and 1933, including photographs of special installations. The journal was an official publication of the Tile & Mantel Contractors' Association of America. The audience was focused on tile contractors and architects.

First published in 1929, Vol. I, the journal ceased publication in 1953 with Volume XXV. The issues that are relevant to Flint Faience tile collectors include 1929-1933, Vol. I through V. The covers of the journal occasionally included Flint Faience tile installations, such as the large panel with a Mexican flavor designed by Flint Faience Tile Company chief designer Julio Haro. See entry for Julio Haro for the cover illustration and detailed description. Other *Keramic Tile Journal* covers reflect the stylistic designs that were popular at the time.

Cover of *Keramic Tile Journal,* January 1932 issue.

Cover of *Keramic Tile Journal,* June 1932, issue.

Kilns

If it weren't for the management of AC Spark Plug Company wanting to more fully utilize their spark plug tunnel kilns which sat idle during part of the manufacturing process, there would not likely have been Flint Faience Tile Company.

Much is known about the tunnel kilns at AC Spark Plug, in which both the Flint Faience tiles and spark plugs were fired. This is largely due to articles that were published in the 1920s, including "Data on the Operation of a Continuous Tunnel Kiln at the Plant of the A.C. Spark Plug Company," from the June 1922 issue of the *Journal of the American Ceramic Society*. This article details the preheating zone, hot zone, cooling zone, pusher, burner equipment, fuel, pyrometer equipment, cars, and standard conditions of operation for the tunnel kilns and the firing of spark plugs. A later article in the July 1929 issue of *Ceramic Industry*, called "Water Cooled Tunnel Kiln Burning Tile," examined the impact of additions to the number of tunnel kilns at the Flint Faience & Tile Company as well as other expansion plans recently completed due to increased demand for their product. Detailed descriptions of firing practices and equipment are presented in this long article.

It is also known that prior to firing, most Flint Faience tiles were formed in plaster molds and allowed to carefully dry after being removed from the molds. They were fired at 2200 degrees Fahrenheit in the tunnel kilns at the AC Plant. If necessary, the tiles were glazed after this bisque or first firing. Each tile was dipped by hand into the raw glaze, which in the glost firing developed into a beautiful color, dependent on the color oxides utilized. The glost or glaze firing also occurred in the tunnel kiln. The cars moved slowly through the 75-foot kiln just a few feet an hour. The journey through the kiln took anywhere from seven to nine hours. The cooling process which began past the center of the long tunnel kiln was an even more delicate process. Cooling too rapidly would cause cracks or checks in the faience tile.

Vitrocraft tile, Flint Faience's unglazed floor tile, was fired for nine days in a periodic kiln, where two days were required to bring the temperature to the maximum, two days with this temperature sustained, three more days to cool the tiles, and one day to unload the kiln. Oil was the fuel used for both the standard glazed tiles and unglazed Vitrocraft. In an unpublished transcript on AC Spark Plug Company stationery (with a handwritten notation in the upper right hand corner reading "Received by McD in Paris Aug 27-1928") titled *Report on Survey of Tile Plant* and now in the permanent collection of the Sloan Museum, Flint, Michigan, there is mention of improving the efficiency of use of both the periodic and tunnel kilns. It was noted that "When loading and unloading periodic kiln from now on a crew will be maintained continuously from start to finish, thereby reducing the cycle probably two days. In the past the cycle has been twelve days. We expect to cut this to ten or less." Comments about the tunnel kilns were as follows, "The tunnel kiln until the last few days was operated on a twelve hour shift and 25 minute schedule. An eight hour shift was instituted last week and schedule changed to twenty minutes. When the change was made to eight hour shift each kiln operator was specifically charged with the responsibility of producing first class tile by proper firing and unloading. Since this procedure has been in effect, grog and dirt have been entirely absent, and nothing to my knowledge has been broken by improper handling, loading or unloading." Other firing practice changes noted in this document included changing the kiln schedule to accommodate the firing of crystalline glazes, etc.

This 1928 tile plant survey, clearly an internal document for AC Plant eyes only, notes the productivity of the kilns, great variance in glaze color results, and the problem of too many tiles having to be refired. The periodic kiln capacity was 6000 feet every ten days or 600 feet per day. The tunnel kiln produced an average of

400 square feet of vitreous, but the capacity of the periodic kiln did not allow a build up of a surplus of bisque (and the tunnel kiln was intended just for producing glazed tile). The author of the survey concluded that another periodic kiln and another tunnel kiln were needed immediately, with the periodic kiln being used to fire surplus bisque and shapes and the tunnel kiln "for all ware requiring variation in temperature from regular tile." (AC Spark Plug Company, August 27, 1928, 3) The report implied that if a choice were to be made, the author would recommend another tunnel kiln.

One interesting observation is that the Flint Faience & Tile Company letterhead in 1929 included a logo with three old-fashioned bottle kilns, although the tile business was started in order to utilize the existing sparkplug tunnel kilns to a greater extent. Bottle kilns were also illustrated on the cover of *Catalog "G,"* as well as in the logo on the title page, although these types of kilns were not utilized in the Flint Faience manufacturing process. Flint Faience did utilize periodic kilns in their manufacturing process, but no evidence has been shown that these periodic kilns were bottle kiln style.

Car of tile emerging from the tunnel kiln at the Flint Faience & Tile Company plant in Flint, Michigan, c. 1929. *Photo courtesy of the* Flint Journal.

Postcard showing an aerial view of the AC Sparkplug Plant on Dort Highway, with an inset of the tunnel kilns used to fire spark plugs and Flint Faience tile in the upper left corner. *Courtesy of Margaret Carney.*

Flint Faience & Tile Company letterhead featuring a logo with three bottle kilns. *Courtesy of Ken Kayser.*

Bottle kiln logo from title page of Flint Faience Tile Company *Catalog "G."*

Cover of Flint Faience Tile Company *Catalog "G,"* illustrating bottle kilns.

Kindergartens

see Schools

Kitchens and Pantries

In their own promotional brochure, Flint Faience & Tile Company claimed that kitchens were "the laboratory of the home." (Flint Faience & Tile Company, *Bathroom Flyer A-303*, 1929, n.p.) Big kitchens, little kitchens, it didn't matter – just as long as they were tiled kitchens. Almost always quietly conservative, Flint Faience tiled kitchens were beautiful and functional, and looked clean and sanitary from floor to walls. Modern appliances of the day – refrigerators, freezers, gas stoves and sinks – were built-in among these monochrome tiles. The large kitchen in the Edsel and Eleanor Ford home located in Grosse Pointe Shores, Michigan, is comprised entirely of 6" x 3" tiles, glazed a monochrome yellow-eggshell-taupe hue.

Kitchen illustrated in Flint Faience promotional brochure A-303. *Courtesy of the Archives, New York State College of Ceramics at Alfred University.*

Tiled kitchen in the main house of Edsel and Eleanor Ford. *Courtesy of Edsel and Eleanor Ford House.*

"Butler's Pantries" almost deserve their own alphabetical entry, but the obvious close proximity to kitchens and the functional link makes this a logical "kitchens" connection. At the top of the list of notable pantries would be the one in the Samuel Stewart home in Flint, Michigan. Construction of this beautiful home was begun in 1929 and completed in 1932. While the sunroom in this home is stunning, so is the impact of the 4.25" square pristine eggshell hue tiled walls with green tiled trim in the butler's pantry.

Kitchen in the main house of Edsel and Eleanor Ford. *Courtesy of Edsel and Eleanor Ford House.*

Exterior of the former home of Samuel Stewart, Flint, Michigan. *Courtesy of Stephen and Rosanne Heddy.*

Tiled butler's pantry in the former home of Samuel Stewart. *Courtesy of Stephen and Rosanne Heddy.*

Tiled pantry walls and trim in the former home of Samuel Stewart, built c. 1929. *Courtesy of Stephen and Rosanne Heddy.*

The kitchen of the former E.T. Strong residence in Flint, Michigan has been altered over the years. It no longer reflects its past glory when it was noted that "the kitchen walls are smartly tiled in pearl grey and dull black Flintcraft." (*Keramic Tile Journal*, December 1931, 5). The journal illustration, though black and white, is revealing.

III #12

FLINT FAIENCE TILES . .

in the residence of
E.T. Strong, President,
Buick Motor Co.,
Flint, Michigan

Joseph M. Savage, Flint - - Architect
Ernest Phelps, Flint - Tiling Contractor

The hallway is paved with handmade Flint Faience tile in contrasting black and white.

In the conservatory, the paving is hexagonal Flint handmade Faience tiles of variegated greens and blues.

Simplicity and warmth are preserved in the breakfast room with a floor of reddish-yellow Flint handmade Faience, with insets in contrasting colors.

The kitchen walls are smartly tiled in pearl gray and dull black Flintcraft.

Flint service provides a grade of tile to meet every architectural requirement, a shape for every purpose, a color to suit each taste. Consider what this means: You can get all the tiles required for a job of any size, through the same dealer, from the same manufacturer. You can count on complete delivery at one time. You can be sure that colors will always match, even when you use different grades of tile. May we send you a descriptive catalog of Flint handmade Faience, Flintcraft (the machine-made tile of faience appearance), and Vitrocraft (the non-slip, unglazed floor tile).

FLINT FAÏENCE AND TILE CO.
FLINT - - - MICHIGAN

5

Keramic Tile Journal, Volume 3, no.12, 1931, page 5, illustrating the tiled kitchen in the former home of E.T. Strong, Flint, Michigan.

Kykuit

see Rockefeller Playhouse

Lamps

see Vases and Flowerpots

Little Black Sambo

see also Children's Rhymes and Stories

More than one hundred years ago, *The Story of Little Black Sambo* was written and illustrated by Helen Bannerman. While the story and its illustrations have sparked controversy in recent decades, in the 1920s and 1930s there was no such discussion. In fact, this popular children's story was the subject of tiles manufactured by at least two tile companies, Pewabic Pottery of Detroit, Michigan, and the Flint Faience Tile Co. of Flint, Michigan. The Flint Faience tiles illustrating *The Story of Little Black Sambo* can be seen today in the fireplace in Room 109 of the Garfield Elementary School in Wyandotte, Michigan, which dates circa 1932. One Pewabic tile of the same theme is in a private collection.

Besides the story's popularity and the number of prominent illustrators who published their own versions of it, another indication that *The Story of Little Black Sambo* was not viewed as politically incorrect in the early 1930s is that these tiles traveled to New Orleans in 1930 and can be seen with the Flint Faience & Tile Company's exhibition at the international tile conference in a photograph from the *Flint Saturday Night* newspaper, published May 3, 1930.

Fireplace with tiled narrative of *The Story of Little Black Sambo* in the Garfield Elementary School, Wyandotte, Michigan. Overall fireplace measures 60" x 81". *Courtesy of Mary Wharton Thorson.*

Tile made by Pewabic Pottery with a theme of *The Story of Little Black Sambo*, measuring 9" x 6.375". *Courtesy of Norman Karlson.*

The charming fireplace (5' tall and 81" wide) is comprised of field tiles in earthtones and raised line tiles illustrating the complete story in seven separate panels. Four of the panels are 9" x 9" tiles, two are comprised of two 9" tiles on top of one another, and the large central panel includes ten 6" tiles in two rows. The 9" tiles illustrate the various tigers wearing Little Black Sambo's new red shirt, blue trousers, shoes, and umbrella. The double tiles depict Little Black Sambo in his fine new clothes and his father carrying the jar of *ghi*, or melted butter. The large multi-tiled central panel shows the happy family cooking pancakes with the tiger butter.

The Garfield school is full of Flint Faience tiles; these include another room's fireplace illustrating the nursery rhyme Humpty Dumpty; four drinking fountains; a sandbox with more nursery rhyme tiles; and a fireplace in the school library with three sailing ships in a somewhat Art Deco fashion. All are illustrated elsewhere in this book.

Fireplace detail from the Garfield Elementary School, Wyandotte, Michigan, featuring *The Story of Little Black Sambo*. Tile panel 9" x 18". *Courtesy of Mary Wharton Thorson.*

Fireplace detail from the Garfield Elementary School, featuring *The Story of Little Black Sambo*. Tile 9" x 9". *Courtesy of Mary Wharton Thorson.*

Fireplace detail from the Garfield Elementary School, featuring *The Story of Little Black Sambo*. Tile 9" x 9". *Courtesy of Mary Wharton Thorson.*

Fireplace detail from the Garfield Elementary School, featuring *The Story of Little Black Sambo*. Tile 9" x 9". *Courtesy of Mary Wharton Thorson.*

Fireplace detail from the Garfield Elementary School, featuring *The Story of Little Black Sambo*. Tile 9" x 9". *Courtesy of Mary Wharton Thorson.*

Fireplace detail from the Garfield Elementary School, featuring *The Story of Little Black Sambo*. Tiles 9" x 18". *Courtesy of Mary Wharton Thorson.*

Central tiled panel of the Little Black Sambo fireplace at Garfield Elementary School, Wyandotte, Michigan. Panel comprised of ten 6" tiles. *Courtesy of Mary Wharton Thorson.*

Lorch Hall

see Signage

Manufacturing Techniques

see Kilns, Glazes, Raised Line, and Hand-made

Marks

see chapter on Identification and Marks

Marketing

At first it seems somewhat surprising that Flint Faience and Tile Company did not market their fine tile to the homeowner or customer directly, and did not advertise in the popular home journals of the day. But after a little thought and reading the philosophy behind their marketing strategy – as well as reading a speech given by Flint Faience art director and architect, Howard B. Burton to the Tile Manufacturers' Representatives Club in New York City called "History of Faience Tile" – the logic is irrefutable. Flint Faience Tile Company marketed their tile to architects and tile contractors because, as Howard Burton noted, "'selling the architect' has its hardly-to-be-over-estimated importance." (Burton, 1930, 29) In this published article, basically a recounting of his address, he raised the questions "What order was not placed because an architect or several architects were known to have approved that material on other work? Who ever landed his initial order from a new factory without having spoken of what architects had already used their material?" (Burton, 1930, 29) He believed, as his company leaders did, that the "Architectural Influence" was profound. He emphatically stated that selling the architect on tile was modern merchandising and the number of new orders were the measure of the success of this merchandising strategy.

Sweet's Architectural Catalogue 1927-28 Section B (copyright 1927) listed on page B1435 prominent architects who had utilized Flint Faience Tile, including Dwight James Baum, Carrere & Hastings, Howard Greenley, Raleigh Jas. Hughes, W.S. Ferguson, Albert Kahn, Malcomson & Higgenbotham, McKim, Mead &

White, Parker, Thomas & Rice, Geo. B. Post & Sons, Schmidt, Garden & Erkison, Smith, Hinchman & Grylls, Starrett & Van Vleck, Philip S.Tyre, R. Clipston Sturgis, and York & Sawyer.

The bottom line of Howard Burton's speech was the same message found in similar articles of the day, where ceramic tile was battling substitution materials such as glass, oil-cloth, paint, cork, marble, gypsum, cement, linoleum, stone, wall paper, aluminum, painted sheet iron, asbestos, etc. In the end, and literally at the end of his speech, Burton concluded, "...it is those who sell, who know the public pulse, who should have greater voice and part in bringing tile up out of the basement toilets and establish it on the high plane enjoyed by other fine materials some possessing but a fraction of Tile's venerable and artistic ancestry." (Burton, 1930, 29)

In marketing, the hand-made nature of Flint Faience tiles was stressed over and over again. Only their glazed floor tile called Flintcraft was acknowledged as being machine-made. It was always glossed over that the term "faience" historically referred to tin-glazed earthenware. When promoting faience tiles, drama was not underutilized. One article that described the history of faience (not just Flint Faience) concluded, "Faience tile, the same faience that charmed da Vinci and Raphael; that adorned the palaces of kings and emperors centuries ago, today is used in the dwelling places of royalty the world over and in the homes and buildings of Americans in many walks of life." (McGinnis, 1930, 27)

Tile trade journals had more than one article relating to marketing and tile sales. Another article on the subject, titled "Salesmanship – Tiling Contractor Definitely Proves That Selling Principles Apply to the Tile Industry the Same as They Do in Any Other Business," noted that a new sales arena was the recessed tile work for Frigidaires and that this "new place for tile...offers a splendid opportunity for creative selling." (Morrissey, 1931, 27) Once again in this article the story was tile vs. the substitute material and that selling is the theme song of every product, not just tile. Flint Faience was also careful to only sell their product through recognized tile contractors, to insure proper installation.

There exists one interesting document regarding Flint Faience & Tile Company sales policies, plans, and merchandising which is now in the collection of the Sloan Museum (acc. no. 72.25.9). The report, titled "Suggested Sales Plan & Policy for the Flint Faience & Tile Company," was issued sometime in 1928, under a cover letter by W.S. Isherwood, who was General Sales Manager. Page 1 lists the "channels through which business should flow," as (in order of importance): Architects, General Contractors, Contractors, Special Dealer Accounts, Dealers, Decorating Companies, Consumers, Special Selling Organizations, and Factory Selling Organizations. The report then elaborates on each "general procedure for soliciting business from the various channels," e.g. "Architects should be contacted with to sell them on our product so that they, in turn, will talk and specify our tile." (Flint Faience & Tile Company, 1928, 2) The report even specifies a price comparison between Flint Faience and their chief competitors, which they list as American Encaustic Tiling Company, Mosaic Tile Company, Franklin Pottery, and Architectural Tile.

This "Suggested Sales Plan & Policy" also elaborated on the types of materials that should be available for the trade and salesmen, included special sketches, a booklet regarding stock tile, and sample color boards. Page 11 advises against advertising in any of the "regular" publications such as *House and Garden* and *Home Beautiful*, but rather recommends a "small booklet be designed which could be used in connection with a nicely prepared letter and either sent out by the Flint Faience Tile Company, direct to the architect and prospective customers – or – by the special dealer accounts that would be established or the manufacturers' agents wherever they are established."

Sweet's Architectural Catalogues, Volume B 1931, published a listing of Flint Faience & Tile Company literature, available on request, including: A-303 Folder on Faience for Bathrooms; A-304 Folder on Faience for the Home; A-317 General Faience Catalog, Series "G;" A-318 Architectural Brochure on Faience with color palette; A-322 Folder on Vitrocraft (unglazed) Tile; A-343 Flint Faience & Tile Co. Color Palette; and A-363 Folder on Flintcraft (machine-made Faience) Tile. *Catalog "G"* is available for purchase on the Internet from the Tile Heritage Foundation in Healdsburg, California (www.tileheritage.org).

Salesman's sample box. 9" x 9". *Courtesy of www.BungalowBill.com.*

Masonic Temples

see also Theatres

The Warwick Masonic Lodge, located on Main Street in Warwick, New York, occupies a building which dates to the late 1800s. However, the April 1929 issue of *AC Sparks* lists the Warwick Masonic Temple as having a recent installation of Flint Faience tiles. Apparently the Masons bought the building in 1928 and added a triangular shaped addition to it. Flint Faience field tiles can still be seen in the entranceways to the many shops that line the periphery of the building today. Additionally, the owner of the building believes that the Masonic Temple sign on the building is composed of Flint Faience tiles.

• • • • • • • • • • • • • • • • • •

Melville Shoe Corporation

see Signage

• • • • • • • • • • • • • • • • • •

Mother, To My

Tile plaques inscribed "To My Mother" form another genre of Flint Faience tile products. Rather than being mass produced for the general public, these should be viewed as personal gifts from some of decorators to their mothers. One 9" x 12" tile plaque decorated, signed, and dated by Eula (Irish) in May 1929 is inscribed "To My Mother / It's the million things you've done to help me that makes you mean the world to me." It is now in the collection of Ken Galvas. An almost identical plaque is signed by "Marjorie" (Milloy). A 9" x 6" plaque signed "Eula," which is actually the top portion of the standard "To My Mother" plaque, is also in the Galvas collection.

"To My Mother" tile, measuring 9" x 6". $800-1000.

"To My Mother" plaque, measuring 9" x 12". $1500+.

"To My Mother" plaque, measuring 9" x 12". $1500+.

Movies

see also Theatres

Believe it or not, there have been movies produced that show Flint Faience tiles in various scenes. You can rent *Under Suspicion* with Gene Hackman and Morgan Freeman and see the tiles found in the U.S. Customs House in San Juan, Puerto Rico.

Nursery Rhymes

see Children's Nursery Rhymes and Stories

Paperweights

see Bookends, Paperweights, Ashtrays, and Penholders

Park Gables

see Apartment Houses

Plants

see Botanicals

Presidential Palaces

see Bathrooms

Radiator Grills

Even the radiator grills seen in sunrooms and bathrooms could be ordered from the stock designs available in *Catalog "G."* No. 7007, a 10" x 10" ceramic tile grill, is found on page 12 of *Catalog "G."* A 4.25" square version of this same ceramic tile radiator grill can be seen installed in two different rooms within the former Prosper Champion home, constructed in 1928 and located in Flint, Michigan. The sunroom on the main floor contains a radiator grill comprised of more than five conjoined radiator grill tiles in green and amber hues, while the upstairs bathroom contained a row of Flint Faience tiled radiator grills in stylish pinkish-lavender hues. Each of these five bathroom radiator grills is 4" square.

FLINT FAIENCE TILE COMPANY, FLINT, MICHIGAN.
STOCK DESIGNS IN APPROPRIATE COLORS

6222 6221 6201 6212 6210
Individual tiles 6x6 in.

6208
Size 12x12 in.

7007
Radiator Grill.
Size 10x10 in.

6209
Size 9x9 in.

6205
Size 15x15 in.

6207 6211
Size 15x10 in.

All designs embossed process with ornaments in ⅜ in. relief.

[12]

Page 12 of *Catalog "G,"* illustrating radiator grills.

Radiator grill in the sunroom of the former home of Prosper Champion, Flint, Michigan. *Courtesy of Jim Fitzell and Jessica Higgins.*

Radiator grill in the upstairs bathroom of the former home of Prosper Champion, c. 1928. Tiles are 4" x 4". *Courtesy of Jim Fitzell and Jessica Higgins.*

Raised Line

According to company records in the form of large index cards now in the permanent collection of the Sloan Museum in Flint, Michigan, 'raised line' is:

> "a technic [sic] used to outline a design on a bisque (unglazed, once-fired) tile surface. The design is sketched free-hand as with pencil, or is transferred to the tile's dampened surface by dusting fine carbon or graphite from a small cloth bag through pin holes pricked along the lines of the design as drawn on thin 'waxes' paper such as draftsman's tracing paper. The 'raised line' paste is applied along the lines of the design, by forcing it in a more or less continuous ribbon from the small tip (about .03" dia. Opening) of a nozzle screwed or attached to the end of a collapsible tube about the size of those used to contain toothpaste. Such tubes with caps (into which the inch-long nozzle is built) and open bottom ends may be purchased from Michigan Collapsible Tube Company, 14626 Houston Ave., Detroit 5. After the 'raised line' paste has dried, glazes of various colors are applied by brush or syringe and are confined in proper place by the 'raised line.'"

The same large index card provided the formulas for the tubing paste base and batch.

There are few vintage examples of these pierced sketches and the resulting tiles. These would include the charming watercolor depiction of an elephant (possibly favorite storybook character Babar), a giraffe and a mouse, complete with piercings and colors softly noted in pencil on the paper surface. The piercings can clearly be seen in the accompanying photograph of the back of the pierced sketch. The perforated sketch measures 11.625" x 10" and is in the Galvas collection. The Galvas collection also includes the 9" Flint Faience tile created in raised line decoration with this perforated watercolor sketch. A similar elephant tile can be seen in the collection currently on loan at the Western Reserve Historical Society in Cleveland. They were originally installed in the Juvenile Court Building in downtown Cleveland.

Original elephant watercolor sketch and stencil.

Reverse side of the original elephant watercolor sketch and stencil.

Elephant tile, measuring 9" x 9". $1500-2000.

Original watercolor and stencil for "Dutch Boy and Geese."

One more example of the perforated stencil used to design these raised line tiles is also in the Galvas collection. Measuring 10" x 7.375", this watercolor features a Dutch boy with three white geese. The perforations can be seen, once again, on the back of the paper sketch. And finally there is the 6" Flint Faience raised line tile (on the right) with the little Dutch boy and geese shown next to a 5.25" Empire tile of the same design (on the left).

Reverse side of the "Dutch Boy and Geese" watercolor and stencil.

"Dutch Boy and Geese" tiles. Left: Empire Tile Company, measuring 5.25" x 5.25". Right: Flint Faience tile measuring 6" x 6". $700-800.

Looking closely at the raised line process without viewing a few more examples would be a lost opportunity. Many handsome tile designs were created using this raised line process, including mundane subjects such as stock design no. 6800 featuring a 6" x 6" artist's palette, stock design no. 6805 depicting a music lyre on an 8" tile, stock design no. 6828 with a decoration of a helmet armor on an 8" tile, an inkwell on a 4.25" tile, and a court jester also on a 4.25" tile. Some raised line designs were classical in style, such as the 14.75" diameter tile featuring "Architecture," now in the permanent collection of the Sloan Museum in Flint, Michigan. Many of these decorations can be seen as stock designs in *Catalog "G."*

Helmet tile in raised line, stock design no. 6828, measuring 8" x 8". $700-900.

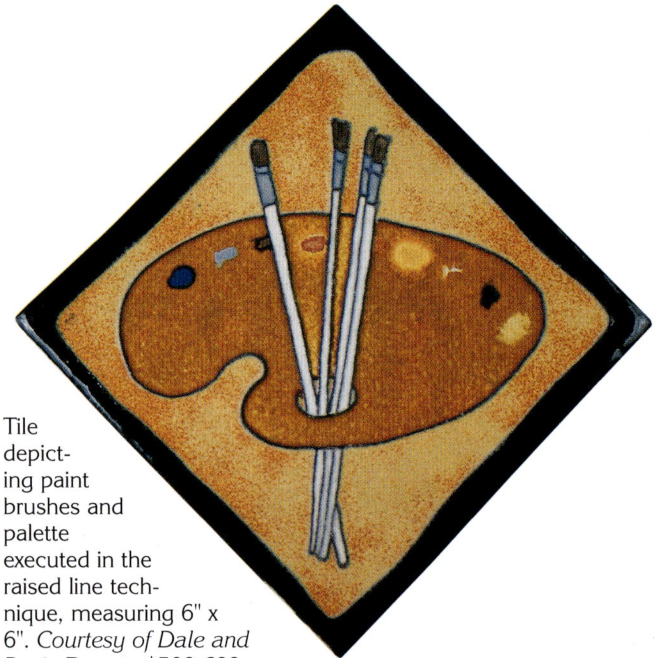

Tile depicting paint brushes and palette executed in the raised line technique, measuring 6" x 6". *Courtesy of Dale and Doris Barrett.* $500-600.

Molded inkwell tile, measuring 4.25" x 4.25". $125-150.

Lyre tile in raised line, stock design no. 6805, measuring 8" x 8". $700-900.

Jester tile executed in raised line design, measuring 4.25" x 4.25". $350-450.

"Architecture" tile executed in raised line, diameter 14.75". *Courtesy of the Alfred P. Sloan Museum.*

Details from page 20 of *Catalog "G,"* illustrating stock designs for the lyre, paint brush and palette, and inkwell tiles.

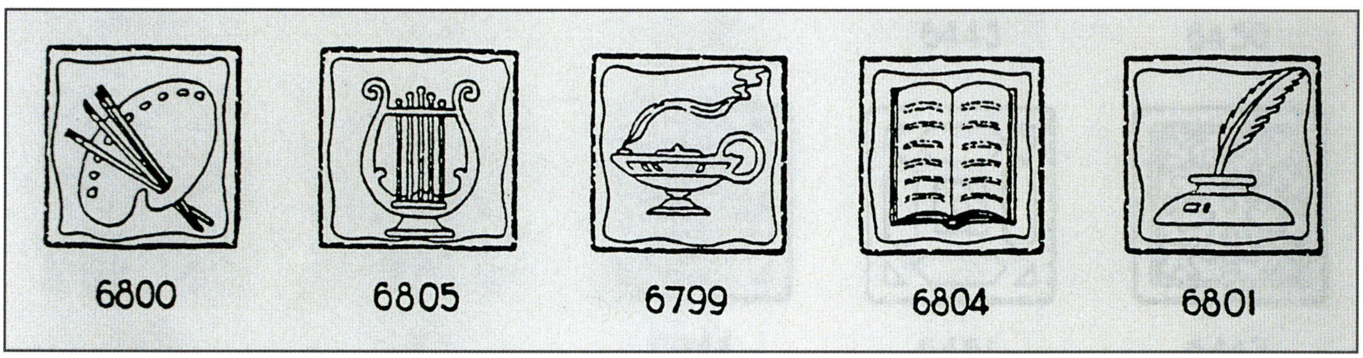

Religious Themes

see also Schools and Churches

It is no surprise that religious themes can be seen in the numerous churches with Flint Faience tile installations, as well as in several elementary schools. St. Paul's Catholic School, located in Grosse Pointe Farms, Michigan, circa 1927, contains a fireplace and a recess for a drinking fountain, each decorated with religious themes using the raised line process. They include the Three Wisemen (9" x 13.25"), Jacob and the Ladder (9" x 13.25"), Joseph in the Well (8.65" x 13.25"), and smaller 4.25" square tiles of a ladder and spears, chi-rho monogram, St. Matthew, crown with a cross and whipping post, nails and pliers and three fishes. Two individual tiles in the collection of Ken Galvas are the same designs as the chi-rho monogram and cross in crown motifs located at St. Paul's Catholic School.

The border tiles along the fireplace (4.25" square) and former drinking fountain (6" square) were also notable. The drinking fountain façade includes tiles representing a pelican with chicks, INRI, St. Mark, chalice and host, St. John, a pomegranate, and St. Luke. The border tile along the drinking fountain includes stock designs nos. 6849 and 6850 from *Catalog "G."* Individual 6" square tiles matching these border tile patterns can be seen in the private collections of Norman Karlson and Ken Galvas. The fireplace border tiles at St. Paul's are illustrated as stock design no. 6776 on page 13 of *Catalog "G."*

"The Three Wisemen" panel, measuring 9" x 13.25", from the fireplace in St. Paul's Catholic Church Elementary School.

Fireplace in St. Paul's Catholic Church Elementary School, in Grosse Pointe Farms, Michigan.

"Jacob and the Ladder" panel, measuring 9" x 13.25", from the fireplace in St. Paul's Catholic Church Elementary School.

"Joseph in the Well" panel, measuring 8.65" x 13.25", from the fireplace in St. Paul's Catholic Elementary School.

Ladder and spears motif tile, measuring 4.25" x 4.25", from the fireplace in St. Paul's Catholic Elementary School.

Chi-rho monogram and symbol for St. Matthew tiles, measuring 4.25" x 4.25" each, from the fireplace in St. Paul's Catholic Elementary School.

Crown with cross and whipping post tiles, measuring 4.25" x 4.25" each, from the fireplace in St. Paul's Catholic Elementary School.

Three fishes, pliers and nails tiles, measuring 4.25" x 4.25" each, from the fireplace in St. Paul's Catholic Elementary School.

Chi-rho monogram and crown with cross tiles, 4.25" x 4.25". $120-150 each.

St. Mark symbol tile, measuring 4.25" x 4.25", from the drinking fountain at St. Paul's Catholic Elementary School.

Pelican and chicks tile motif, measuring 4.25" x 4.25", from the drinking fountain at St. Paul's Catholic Elementary School.

Chalice and host tile, measuring 4.25" x 4.25", from the drinking fountain at St. Paul's Catholic Elementary School.

"INRI" tile, measuring 4.25" x 4.25", from the drinking fountain at St. Paul's Catholic Elementary School.

St. John symbol tile, measuring 4.25" x 4.25", from the drinking fountain at St. Paul's Catholic Elementary School.

St. Luke symbol tile, measuring 4.25" x 4.25", from the drinking fountain at St. Paul's Catholic Elementary School.

Pomegranate tile, measuring 4.25" x 4.25", from the drinking fountain at St. Paul's Catholic Elementary School.

Border tiles from the drinking fountain at St. Paul's Catholic Elementary School., measuring 6" x 6".

Detail from page 20 of *Catalog "G,"* illustrating stock designs nos. 6849 and 6850, both patterns seen in church installations.

Raised line tile, stock design no. 6850, measuring 6" x 6". $275-375.

Raised line tiles, stock design no. 6849-2, measuring 6" x 6". $350-400 each.

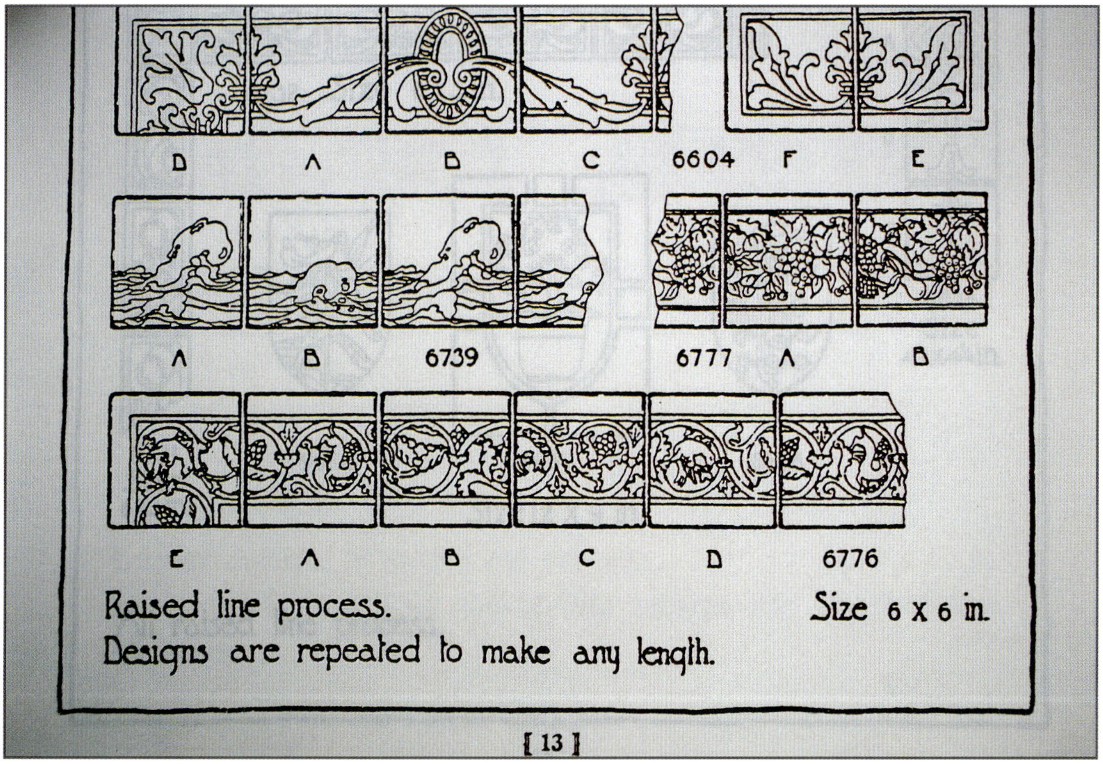

D A B C 6604 F E

A B 6739 6777 A B

E A B C D 6776

Raised line process. Size 6 X 6 in.
Designs are repeated to make any length.

[13]

Page 13 of *Catalog "G,"* illustrating stock design fireplace border tiles.

Raised line fireplace border in the classroom at St. Paul's Catholic Elementary School.

Reptiles and Amphibians

Considering how popular tiled fireplaces, sand boxes, drinking fountains, and sinks were in elementary schools of the late 1920s and early 1930s, and considering how much children have always enjoyed snakes, lizards, and frogs, it should come as no surprise that these creatures were found illustrated among the tile designs in school rooms. Some have now found their way into both public and private collections. 4.25" square tiles depicting a green lizard, splendidly depicted using the raised line process, are in the collection of Roger Ellingsworth and the Sloan Museum, and a tan turtle also executed with the raised line process is in the collection of Rob Rozycki. These were stock designs available through *Catalog "G."* As the catalog noted "any color combination" was available. Another turtle tile, this one framed 6" square and in the collection of Roger Ellingsworth, shows another glaze color variance.

Raised line lizard tile, stock design no. 6763, measuring 4.25" x 4.25". *Courtesy of the Alfred P. Sloan Museum.*

Raised line lizard tile, stock design no. 6763, measuring 4.25" x 4.25". *Courtesy of Roger Ellingsworth.* $250-300.

Turtle in raised line, stock design no. 6742, measuring 6" x 6". *Courtesy of Robert Rozycki.* $400-500.

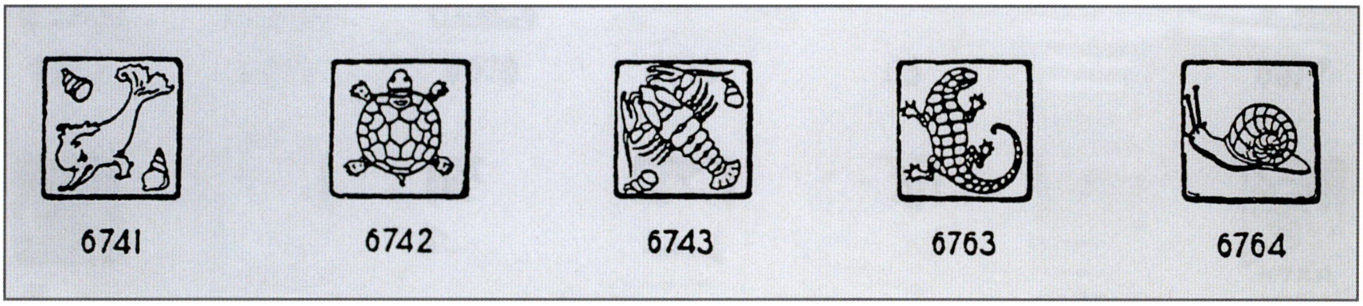

Detail of reptiles and amphibians from page 22 of *Catalog "G."*

Turtle tile in raised line, stock design no. 6742, measuring 6" x 6". *Courtesy of Roger Ellingsworth.* $400-500.

Turtle tile installed at the John Marshall Elementary School, c. 1928. *Courtesy of the John Marshall Elementary School.*

The John Marshall Elementary School in Detroit, constructed in 1928, has several similar 6" square turtle tiles installed in the charming drinking fountain/sink and sandbox in one of the classrooms. These turtles can be seen alongside animals such as lions, deer, elephants, giraffes, bears, horses, and ducks, plus one amazing large tile panel depicting trees in an Arts & Crafts style. The animals and aquatic creatures such as fish and a lobster adorn the once-functional architectural features in the room, and the long-term use of these facilities can be seen in the worn images of the animal tiles where children have climbed in and out of the sandbox over the years.

A comparatively delicate raised line design of a frog on a lily pad can be found on a 4.25" square tile in the collection of Ken Galvas. The frog looks almost wistful.

Frog on lily pad tile, measuring 4.25" x 4.25". $350-400.

Restaurants and Cafeterias

see also Fort Shelby Hotel Restaurant and Art Deco

Restaurant interiors and exteriors were a perfect location for Flint Faience tiles, as they could handle heavy public traffic, be kept clean and sanitary, and provide an attractive and distinctive decorative element. Halo Burger, located on Saginaw Street in Flint, Michigan, the original home of Vernor's Headquarters, is a perfect example. Constructed between 1928-30, both the interior and exterior of the Spanish-style building contain Flint Faience tiles, with glazed insert tiles randomly placed among unglazed Vitrocraft floor tiles. The building has easily withstood over seventy years of heavy traffic with little sign of wear. Floor inserts include no. 6536, 2" square tiles decorated utilizing the inlay process, as shown in *Catalog "G."* Exterior tiles, measuring 4.25" x 4.25", are largely monochromatic with matte blue glazes in various hues, but also include an occasional embossed design.

Other restaurants have been detailed elsewhere, and include the Fisher Building Cafeteria in Detroit; the Fort Shelby Hotel Restaurant, also in Detroit; and the cafeteria at the Minck Hotel, Tulsa, Oklahoma.

Halo Burger Restaurant in Flint, Michigan. *Courtesy of Bill Thomas Halo Burger.*

Halo Burger Restaurant in Flint, Michigan, showing Flint Faience tiles installed on building exterior. *Courtesy of Bill Thomas Halo Burger.*

Interior tile floor detail in the Halo Burger Restaurant in Flint, Michigan. *Courtesy Bill Thomas Halo Burger.*

Rockefeller Playhouse at Kykuit

A visit to Kykuit, the Rockefeller family estate located in Pocantico Hills, near Sleepy Hollow in the Hudson River Valley region of New York State, will allow one to view magnificent scenery, the mansion, and an incredible art collection owned by the Rockefellers. However, it will not provide even one glimpse of the breathtakingly tiled swimming pool created by Flint Faience Tile Company for the Rockefeller Playhouse, which was built by John D. Rockefeller, Jr. between 1925-27. Part of the year the Rockefeller family still occupies this area of the estate and it is off limits to tourists and tile lovers. It was built and remains as a place of recreation for the whole Rockefeller family and their friends. The building was designed in English-Norman style by architect Duncan Candler (1874-1949). In addition to the swimming pool, there is a bowling alley, a pool room, a gymnasium, a card room and a two-story living room all located within the Playhouse at Kykuit.

The wonderful book about Kykuit titled *The Rockefeller Family Home, Kykuit*, published in 1998 by Abbeville Press, contains several beautiful photographs of these areas of the Playhouse today. There are no archival records that have been located regarding the use of Flint Faience tile in these areas, the source concerning this installation being a 1929 publication produced by Flint Faience Tile Company, *AC Sparks*, which listed this site as a recent installation.

Exterior view of Rockefeller Playhouse at Kykuit, Poncantico Hills, New York, c. 1927. *Courtesy of The Rockefeller Archive Center.*

Interior of pool area in the Rockefeller Playhouse at Kykuit, c. 1927. *Courtesy of The Rockefeller Archive Center.*

Tiled deck area of the Rockefeller Playhouse swimming pool, c. 1927. *Courtesy of The Rockefeller Archive Center.*

Sandboxes

Sandboxes were one special genre of creatively tiled furniture placed in several of the elementary school kindergarten rooms in the late 1920s to early 1930s utilizing Flint Faience tiles. The John Marshall School, built in 1928 in Detroit, has a wonderful example of a combination sandbox, drinking fountain, and sink all adorned with animals and sea life and an Arts & Crafts style panel with trees and clouds on one side. The animal tiles are faded and worn on the edges of the sandboxes where little feet have climbed in and out over the decades and scratched the images with sand and dirt. The kindergarten room in the Washington School in Wyandotte, Michigan contains its original, captivating tiled installation of a combination sandbox with working terrarium and working drinking fountain. The background installation tiles are rich shades of green and the 4.25" raised line decorated tiles illustrate fantasy tales of witches, Dutch boys and girls, pirate ships, windmills, scary masks, court jesters, and more. These types of installations were important enough to be illustrated in the leading trade journal of the day in which Flint Faience tiles were advertised – the *Keramic Tile Journal* (*Keramic Tile Journal*, June 1931, 3). The sandboxes in both the John Marshall School and the Washington School were illustrated in the same advertisement for Flint Faience tile.

Combination drinking fountain, sink, and sandbox at the John Marshall Elementary School, Detroit, c. 1928. *Courtesy of the John Marshall Elementary School.*

Lobster tile from the kindergarten installation at the John Marshall Elementary School, measuring 6" x 6", c. 1928. *Courtesy of the John Marshall Elementary School.*

Duck silhouette tile from the kindergarten installation at the John Marshall Elementary School, measuring 6" x 6", c. 1928. *Courtesy of the John Marshall Elementary School.*

Side view of the sandbox in the kindergarten room at the Washington Elementary School, Wyandotte, Michigan. *Courtesy of Washington Elementary School.*

Well loved and much worn 6" x 6" horse tile from the sandbox edge in the kindergarten room at the John Marshall Elementary School. *Courtesy of the John Marshall Elementary School.*

Jolly Roger and Dutch girl tiles, measuring 4.25" x 4.25" each, from the sandbox in the kindergarten room at the Washington Elementary School, Wyandotte, Michigan. *Courtesy of Washington Elementary School.*

Dutch boy and windmill tiles, measuring 4.25" x 4.25" each, from the sandbox in the kindergarten room at the Washington Elementary School, Wyandotte, Michigan. *Courtesy of Washington Elementary School.*

Mask and jester tiles, measuring 4.25" x 4.25" each, from the sandbox in the kindergarten room at the Washington Elementary School, Wyandotte, Michigan. *Courtesy of Washington Elementary School.*

Flint Handmade Faïence

finds interesting new uses in

KINDERGARTENS

There is practically no limit to the variety and interest of designs that can be reproduced in Flint Handmade Faience. Gay Mother Goose characters, clowns and cats and fish, turtles and squirrels and giraffes—all the delightful little peoples that make up the storybook world of kindergartners—are reproduced in colors and incorporated in the sandboxes and fireplace illustrated here.

We have a wealth of practical suggestions for interesting new uses of tile. We also maintain a designing staff of professional calibre, to work with you in creating new designs for special jobs. Write to our sketch service department. Catalogs of Flint Handmade Faience, Flintcraft (the machine-made tile of faience appearance), and Vitrocraft, the non-slip unglazed floor tile, on request.

Above—Sandbox and fountain in Washington School, Wyandotte, Mich. Architect—B. C. Wetzel Co., Detroit, Mich. Tile Contractor—Venetian Marble Mosaic Art Co., Detroit, Mich.

Below—Sandbox and fountain in John Marshall School, Detroit, Mich. Architect—N. Chester Sorenson Co., Detroit, Mich. Tile Contractor—Detroit Tile & Mosaic Co., Detroit, Mich.

Above—Fireplace in Barnum School, Birmingham, Michigan. Note detail of decorative tile in raised Flint Handmade Faience. Architect—Frederick P. Madison, Inc., Royal Oak, Michigan. Tile Contractor—Detroit Tile & Mosaic Co., Detroit, Michigan.

FLINT FAÏENCE AND TILE CO.

FLINT - - MICHIGAN

3

Illustrations of two sandboxes in elementary schools from the *Keramic Tile Journal,* Volume 3, Number 6, 1931, page 3.

The sandbox located in room 103 of the Garfield School in Wyandotte, Michigan was part of the original 1932 building design. The 6" square tiles, set on point, are decorated with undersea fish, parrots, and one mean looking bird. This is the same room that contains an amazing fireplace illustrated with the nursery rhyme Humpty Dumpty. The kindergarten room at the same school, room 109, contains a marvelous installation of the Story of Little Black Sambo on a fireplace facing. In that same kindergarten room is a sandbox with a working terrarium (complete with lizard) and working drinking fountain. This combination sandbox and drinking fountain measures 87" x 50.5" x 27.5". The background tiles are an undecorated beige glaze color and the 6" square decorated tiles show clever designs of puppies, birds, Miss Muffet, a Dutch boy, the goose girl, and more, all installed on point.

Detail of three 6" tiles from the sandbox in Room 103 at the Garfield Elementary School, Wyandotte, Michigan. *Courtesy of Mary Wharton Thorson.*

Sandbox in the kindergarten room of the Garfield Elementary School, Wyandotte, Michigan. Overall dimensions 87" x 50.5" x 27.5". *Courtesy of Mary Wharton Thorson.*

Dutch boy and Little Miss Muffet tiles, each 6" x 6", installed in the sandbox at the Garfield Elementary School, Wyandotte, Michigan. *Courtesy of Mary Wharton Thorson.*

Old King Cole, bird, and dog tiles, each 6" x 6", installed in the sandbox at the Garfield Elementary School, Wyandotte, Michigan. *Courtesy of Mary Wharton Thorson.*

Goose girl and servant with turkey tiles, each 6" x 6", installed in the sandbox at the Garfield Elementary School, Wyandotte, Michigan. *Courtesy of Mary Wharton Thorson.*

Schools

see also Fireplaces, Sandboxes, Religious Themes, Fountains, Signage, Animals

Schools, both elementary and university level, were frequent sites of Flint Faience tile installations. Many of the elementary schools known to have utilized Flint Faience tiles in classroom fireplaces, fountains, drinking fountains, sandboxes, sinks, and building exteriors appear to be clustered in the Flint and Detroit, Michigan areas. All were constructed between 1925 and 1932. A brief listing of these would include, in Flint, the Garfield School (1928) with exterior tiles and signage, and the Pierson School with similar exterior tiles and signage. St. Paul's Catholic School in Grosse Pointe Farms, Michigan, circa 1927, includes an unusual fireplace with tiles recording religious themes, such as Moses and the Burning Bush (8.75" square), Daniel and the Lions (8.75" x 13.75"), and David and Goliath (8.75" square), as well as a tiled architectural feature that used to house a drinking fountain with additional religious symbols such as Trinity Rings (4.25" square). Another school with important Flint Faience installations is the Barnum School, located at 746 Purdy in Birmingham, Michigan (now the Beaumont Rehabilitation and Health Center) with the 1928-29 addition to the original 1912 structure containing classrooms for younger children (the school was named for Horace Barnum, a village farmer and blacksmith who donated the land for the school). Additionally, there is the Brookside School Library at Cranbrook, circa 1925, located in Bloomfield Hills, Michigan, with a large 95" x 36.25" tiled fountain (see photo on page 124), and the Henry Ford Elementary School in Dearborn, Michigan, with a magnificent installation in the kindergarten room featuring thirty-two insert tiles of birds and animals on the fireplace facing and Art Deco style drinking fountains in the hallways. The Washington School in Wyandotte, Michigan, has a reinstalled fireplace with a tiled panel depicting ships at sea in the library; another fireplace in the kindergarten room with Arts & Crafts flavored tiled panels depicting an owl and the moon, a duck and chicken, and a rooster; and a sandbox with a built in terrarium, also in a kindergarten room. Last but certainly not least, is the Garfield School, also located in Wyandotte, Michigan, circa 1932, where the fireplace in room 103 features the Humpty Dumpty nursery rhyme; another fireplace facing in room 109 features the Story of Little Black Sambo; and in the same room is a tiled sandbox, complete with an iguana named Max. The Garfield School also has four tiled drinking fountains in the hallways, all with carp motifs, and still another beautiful fireplace in the second floor library, with an Art Deco style design of ships at sea in 6" tiles.

Exterior panel installed at the Garfield Elementary School in Flint, Michigan, c. 1928. Identical panels exist on the Pierson Elementary School, also located in Flint, Michigan.

Moses and the burning bush tile panel executed in raised line design, measuring 8.75" x 8.75", located in the fireplace installation at St. Paul's Catholic Elementary School, Grosse Pointe Farms, Michigan.

Daniel and the Lions tile in raised line design, measuring 8.75" x 8.75", located in the fireplace installation at St. Paul's Catholic Elementary School.

David and Goliath tile in raised line design, measuring 8.75" x 8.75", located in the fireplace installation at St. Paul's Catholic Elementary School.

Trinity rings tile, measuring 4.25" x 4.25", located in the drinking fountain at St. Paul's Catholic Elementary School.

Barnum School library fireplace, Birmingham, Michigan. *Courtesy of the City of Birmingham, Michigan.*

Detail of "Crooked Old Man" panel, from the Barnum School library fireplace. *Courtesy of the City of Birmingham, Michigan.*

Other schools besides the Garfield and Pierson Schools in Flint have extensive Flint Faience tile work on the school building exterior. Another school with plentiful tile work is the John Marshall School, constructed in 1928, located in Detroit. The façade has hundreds of 5" square tiles with modeled geometric and floral motifs and smaller border tiles surrounding these. The contrast between these colorful tiles and the red bricks is beautiful to behold.

Exterior tiles on the John Marshall Elementary School in Detroit, Michigan. *Courtesy of the John Marshall Elementary School.*

Upper tile panels on the John Marshall Elementary School in Detroit, Michigan. *Courtesy of the John Marshall Elementary School.*

Upper panel of the John Marshall Elementary School in Detroit, Michigan. *Courtesy of the John Marshall Elementary School.*

Detail of tiles on the John Marshall Elementary School in Detroit, Michigan. *Courtesy of the John Marshall Elementary School.*

Molded tile details, each measuring 5" x 5", from the John Marshall Elementary School in Detroit, Michigan. *Courtesy of the John Marshall Elementary School.*

Ships

see also U.S. Customs House, San Juan, Puerto Rico

Tile decorated with ships at sea are a passion for all tile collectors, whether it be Flint Faience, Marblehead, Mosaic, or Rookwood. Individual Flint Faience tiles can be found in many collections, and there are also large splendid tiled panels depicting ships, which are common in fireplace installations in schools and libraries. Tiled panels including ships and windmills were among the stock mantel designs illustrated and available through Flint Faience Tile Company's *Catalog "G."* A circa 1929 photograph of the designing and decorating room at Flint Faience & Tile Co. shows one staff member working from a large pattern of ships in full sail. One example of a Flint Faience tile mural created from this design was salvaged from the Jefferson Hotel in Atlantic City, New Jersey and is now in a private collection. It consists of forty-four full or partial tiles, depicting Christopher Columbus' three ships about to land on a Caribbean Island.

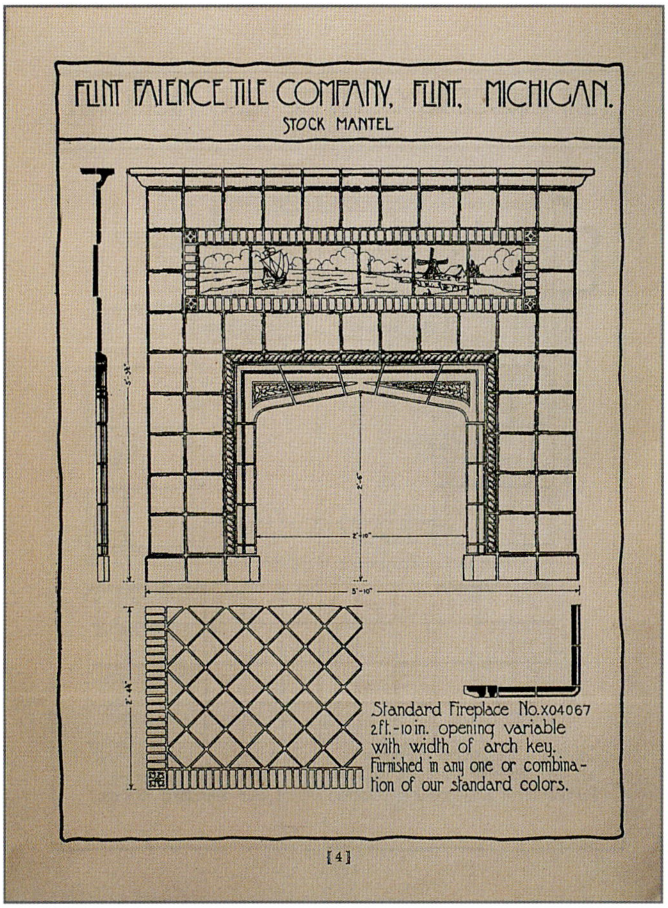

Page 4 of *Catalog "G,"* illustrating stock mantel design with depiction of ship and windmill tiled mural.

Decorators applying the raised line design material to tiles, c. 1929. Note the large ship watercolor, which came to life on panels installed in the U.S. Customs House in San Juan, Puerto Rico; the Jefferson Hotel, in Atlantic City, New Jersey; and the Garfield School in Wyandotte, Michigan. *Courtesy of the* Flint Journal.

Ship mural salvaged from the Jefferson Hotel in Atlantic City, New Jersey, measuring approximately 66" x 34". *Courtesy of Philip Henius.*

The fireplace in the library at the Washington Elementary School in Wyandotte, Michigan, not only has an elaborate panel of twelve 6" tiles depicting three ships in full sail at sea (see Fish and Sea Life entry), but that same panel is flanked by two 12" square tiles of ships. Those two separate 12" panels are identical to *Catalog "G"* stock design no. 6651. The fireplace was moved from the second floor to the first floor, and none of the tiles surrounding the panels are vintage.

Detail of stock design ship tile no. 6651, illustrated on page 19 of *Catalog "G."*

Ship in raised line design, measuring 12" x 12", located in the fireplace in the library at Washington Elementary School, Wyandotte, Michigan. *Courtesy of Washington Elementary School.*

Another fireplace in Wyandotte, Michigan contains a somewhat Art Deco style fireplace with a scene of three ships in full sail on the high seas. The Garfield School second floor library, dating circa 1932, is not to be missed if sleuthing out remarkable tile panels in Flint Faience. The subtle treatment of the whitecaps on the waves and the sky gradations of blues are simply amazing. The fireplace measures 81.5" wide and 68.5" high. All tiles in the panels are 6" square. It is nearly identical to one of the four tiled lunettes created by Flint Faience chief designer Julio Haro for the United States Customs House in San Juan, Puerto Rico, circa 1929. See U.S. Customs House entry for a description and illustrations.

Ship at sea tile mural installation in the library of the Garfield Elementary School in Wyandotte. Michigan. *Courtesy of Mary Wharton Thorson.*

Detail of the ship at sea tile mural installation in the library in the Garfield Elementary School Library. *Courtesy of Mary Wharton Thorson.*

It is interesting to compare the various individual tiles depicting ships in private collections. Sometimes one can tell that the same stencil or sketch was used as the template for more than one tile, even though the resulting tiles are not identical. For instance, one can see that stock design no. 6819 from *Catalog "G"* was used to create five separate tiles with ship motifs that are remarkably similar, even though the tile size or shape or even glazing may vary somewhat.

Detail of stock design ship tile no. 6819 from page 20 of *Catalog "G."*

Sailboat tile, stock design no. 6819, measuring 6" x 6". $400-500. *Courtesy of Ruth Hylen.*

Sailboat tile, stock design no. 6819, measuring 5" x 5". *Courtesy of Dale and Doris Barrett*. $400-500.

Pair of raised line sailboats, stock design no. 6819, each measuring 6" x 6". $400-500 each.

Sailboat tile on window shape based on stock design no. 6819, measuring 5" x 6.75". *Courtesy of Dale and Doris Barrett.* $400-500.

Art Deco ship on rough seas, measuring 9" x 12". *Courtesy of Dale and Doris Barrett.* $1500-2000.

Viking ship in raised line design, measuring 8.25" x 8.25". *Courtesy of Dale and Doris Barrett.* $900-1200.

Other sailing ships depicted on Flint Faience tiles do not seem to match any of the stock designs found in *Catalog "G,"* even though it is possible that there were other stock designs. There are Art Deco style ship tiles such as the magnificent 9" x 12" tile of a ship with orange sails and spinnaker and fantastic waves in the Barrett collection. A Viking ship is portrayed in a 8.25" square tile also in the Barrett collection. A small ship in full sail, riding the waves, is depicted on a 6" round tile in the Ken Galvas collection. Another 6" diameter tile with almost a silhouette effect is located in the Roger Ellingsworth collection. A precious 6" square tile depicting a ship with one sail is included among the decorated tiles installed on point in the sandbox in the Humpty Dumpty fireplace room at the Garfield School in Wyandotte, Michigan. A rather foreboding black glazed silhouette of a sailing vessel is depicted on a 6" square tile in the Ken Galvas collection. And finally, a charming 4.25" tile decorated with a wooden vessel that resembles a pirate ship in full sail, with no details such as sea water or waves, is located in the Ken Galvas collection.

Ship riding a large wave, measuring 6" in diameter. $500-700.

6" x 6" ship tile installed on the sandbox in the Garfield Elementary School in Wyandotte, Michigan. *Courtesy of Mary Wharton Thorson.*

Sailboat silhouette design on 6" round tile. $500-700. *Courtesy of Roger Ellingsworth.*

Black silhouette Viking ship, measuring 6" x 6". $400-500.

Pirate ship in raised line design, measuring 4.25" x 4.25". $300-400.

S. S. *Washington* postcard. *Courtesy Ken Galvas.*

First Day Cover mailed from the S. S. *Manhattan*, August 10, 1932. *Courtesy Ken Galvas.*

While ships depicted *on* tiles are a category in themselves, ships with Flint Faience tiles *inside* are another matter. At least two ships, the S.S. *Manhattan* and the S.S. *Washington*, had gigantic tiled swimming pools on board. The *Manhattan* was a 24,289-ton ship, 705' in length, and at the time it was said to be the largest merchant vessel ever built in the United States. Not surprisingly then, at the time of its creation, the tile for this swimming pool was believed to be the most elaborate in the world. The *Manhattan* was launched December 5, 1931 by Mrs. Edith Kermit Roosevelt. Her maiden voyage took place in August 1932. The S.S. *Washington* entered service in May 1933. Both ships were built for the United States Lines by the New York Shipbuilding Corporation. The S.S. *Manhattan* was the first ship owned by the United States Lines that was constructed strictly for passenger use.

S. S. *Manhattan* postcard. *Courtesy Ken Galvas.*

The whereabouts of the tile from these decommissioned vessels is not currently known, (both the S.S. *Manhattan* and S.S. *Washington* were sold for scrapping in 1964), but there is much documentation about these major tile installations. A sea scene was the design for the side walls of the swimming pool or natatorium of the S.S. *Manhattan*, with blue sky, green sea, and soft golden sand. The sky was described as full of sea gulls and white clouds. Fish are seen leaping out of the sea among tinted bubbles. Starfish and sea shells adorn the beach. On the pool ends are designs of dolphins and seaweed. There are plain tiles on the floor of the pool with insets of lobsters, sea anemones, and exotic deep sea designs. Two columns decorated with seaweed and plants were situated at one end of the pool. It is known that all the tiles were made by hand under the supervision of Julio Haro at Flint Faience and Tile Company. There were 4,400 individual tiles which had to be hand-decorated with stencil patterns to complete this project for the S.S. *Manhattan*, and each tile was numbered to record the position of each tile during installation on the ship's pool area. The installation was supervised by Ballard & Company, interior decorators, of New York. One individual 6" square tile, now in the Ken Galvas collection, reflects the beauty of that swimming pool area. It has raised line designs of seaweed and plants.

Flint Faience & Tile Company workers assembling a panel for the S. S. *Manhattan* before numbering and shipping tiles. *Courtesy of the Alfred P. Sloan Museum.*

Panel to be installed in the S. S. *Manhattan*. *Courtesy of the Alfred P. Sloan Museum.*

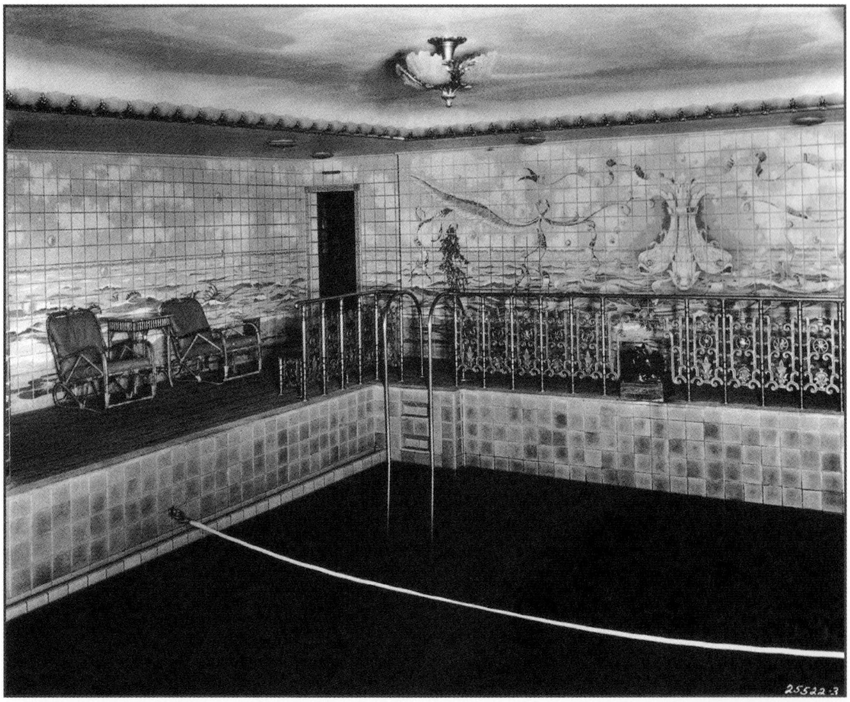

Installed marine scene on the S. S. *Manhattan*. *Courtesy of the Alfred P. Sloan Museum.*

Marine scene in the S. S. *Manhattan*. *Courtesy of the Alfred P. Sloan Museum*.

Deck detail on the S. S. *Manhattan*. Note the sand dune flooring effect. *Courtesy of the Alfred P. Sloan Museum*.

Tile depicting seaweed section, measuring 6" x 6". Possibly the only piece left of the S. S. *Manhattan* panels.

Signage

see also Arrowhead, Flint

Signage created from Flint Faience tiles range from the signs created to advertise their own tile plants to special order signs executed for major companies during their heyday. Flint Faience plant signs include one that is still present on the exterior of the old Flint Faience factory on the corner of Dort Highway and Davison Road in Flint, and the old "AC" plant red and black tiled sign now in the collection of the Sloan Museum in Flint. The old AC plant on Industrial Highway with visible catwalks between buildings where the AC sign was installed has since been demolished. A "Body by Fisher" sign with an antique carriage is also in the permanent collection of the Sloan Museum. Exterior signage on elementary school buildings in the Flint and Detroit, Michigan areas can be seen on the Garfield School in Flint, where there are tiles surrounding the "Garfield School A.D. 1928" sign as well as ceramic plaques with "GS" for Garfield School also adorning the building's exterior.

Exterior sign above the Flint Faience Tile Company entrance on Dort Highway and Davison Road. *Courtesy of the Delphi Corporation, Flint, Michigan.*

Old "AC" sign now in the Alfred P. Sloan Museum, Flint Michigan. *Courtesy of the Alfred P. Sloan Museum.*

Aerial view of the Industrial Avenue Plant, illustrating catwalks where the old "AC" sign was originally installed. *Courtesy of the Alfred P. Sloan Museum.*

Postcard showing aerial view of the Fisher Body plant in Flint, Michigan. *Courtesy of Margaret Carney.*

Exterior tile signage at Garfield School, Flint, Michigan, c. 1928.

Molded "Body by Fisher" sign, measuring 27.5" x 19.25". *Courtesy of the Alfred P. Sloan Museum.*

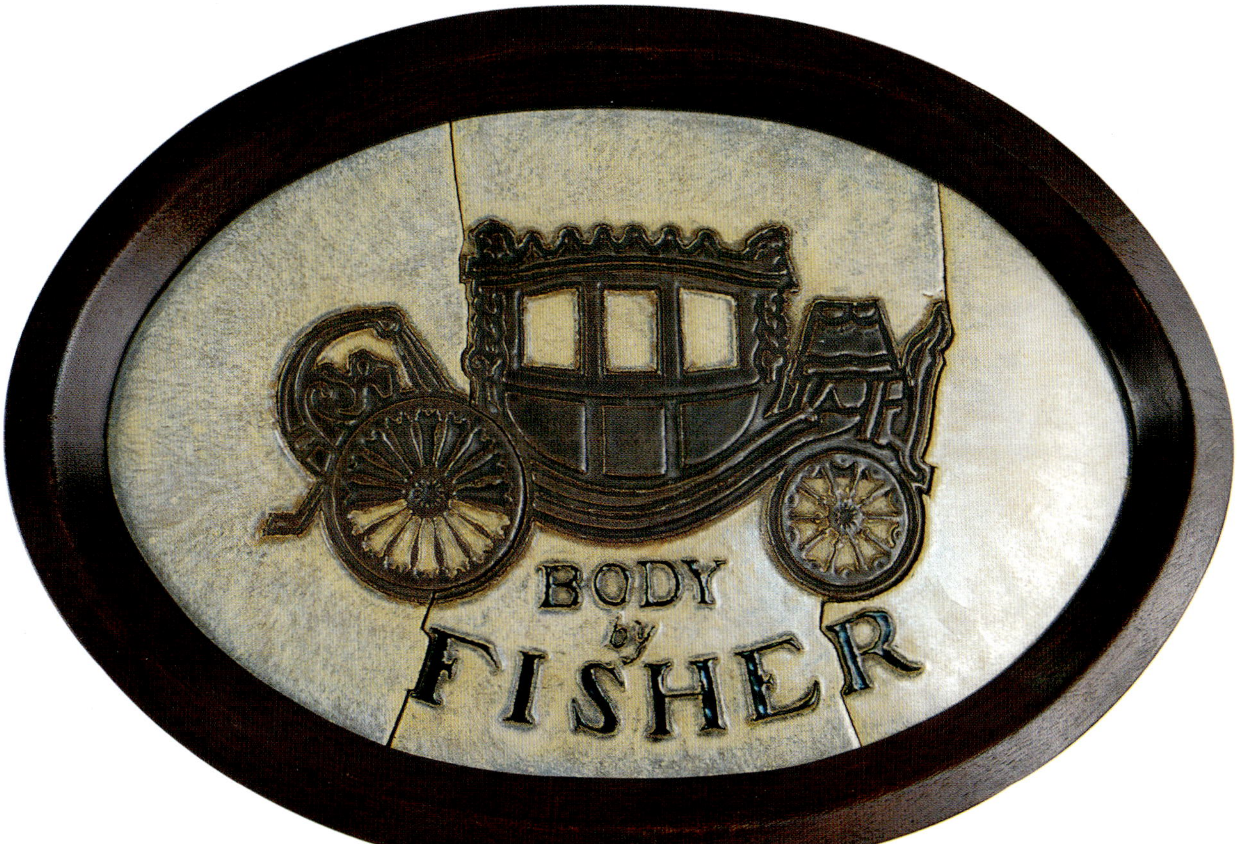

"Flint Faience Tiles A General Motors Product," sign measuring 24" x 14" now installed in the ceramics laboratory at the Delphi Corporation. *Courtesy of the Delphi Corporation, Flint, Michigan.*

It seems that many of the signs designed out of Flint Faience tiles advertise businesses that are no longer active, such as the E&B Brewery in Detroit and the Melville Shoe Corporation in Worcester, Massachusetts. The Melville Corporation can be traced back to 1892, when a gentleman named Frank Melville, a shoe jobber, took over three stores that were all but abandoned when his heavily debt-ridden employer left town. Bringing his son, John Ward Melville, into the business in 1909 aided in the longevity of a Melville being at the head of the organization until 1977. Under the same ownership, discount shoes such as Thom McAn, which first opened in 1922, earned the Melville Shoe Corporation (also incorporated in 1922) a fortune over the years. This same corporation can be linked with other profitable chain discount stores over the years, including CVS, Chess King, Kay-Bee Toys, Linen 'n Things, People's Drug Stores, and others. By 1927, the Thom McAn chain had proved so successful that the Nashua, New Hampshire plant could no longer handle all the production demand and a new factory was acquired in Worcester, Massachusetts. Hence, the building one sees today at 44 Hammond Street with the marvelous Flint Faience tile sign above the entranceway.

The Melville Shoe Corporation sign adorns a building that as of this writing is currently for sale at 44 Hammond Street. One of the most charming of all Flint Faience tile signs, the mural depicts a satisfied customer being fitted with shoes. Surrounding this image is a decorative motif of heel lifts. A cropped image of the Melville Shoe corporation entranceway sign was illustrated in the 1929 trade publication *Architectural Faience: An Introduction*. The full sign measures approximately 13 feet by 7 feet, utilizes Flint Faience tiles named "opus Sectile," and was designed by the New York Architectural Department of Flint Faience & Tile Company in collaboration with noted muralist Ezra Winter. The building architect was Aberthaw Company of Boston and the tiling contractor was Galassi Mosaic & Tile Co., also of Boston. Vivid colors are employed throughout, including shades of green, tinted white, yellows, browns, and cream. The two fish (sometimes not seen in cropped images which have been reproduced in several publications) apparently represent the trademark of one of the Melville Shoe Corporation's subsidiary companies, signifying that neither fish nor the public wearing the company's shoes have any foot problems! (*Journal of the Tile and Mantel Contractors Association of America,* 1928, 33)

Flint Faience tile sign hanging at the American Ceramic Society headquarters in 1930. *Photo from the* Bulletin of the American Ceramic Society.

Another Flint Faience & Tile Co. sign can be seen today in the Materials Technology Laboratories Technical Center, part of the Delphi facility in Flint, Michigan. This two-piece 24" x 14" (tiles only) sign is framed in oak and reads "Flint Faience Tiles" above "A General Motors Product." This sign, along with one version of the allegorical mural titled "Agriculture – Egypt," were temporarily located at the American Ceramic Society headquarters in Columbus, Ohio in 1930.

Exterior signage at E&B Brewery in Detroit, Michigan.

Details of exterior signage on the E&B Brewery in Detroit, Michigan.

Architectural Faience: An Introduction, page 14, with an illustration of the tiled Melville Shoe Company sign in Worcester, Massachusetts. *Courtesy of Jim Graham.*

Melville Shoe Corporation sign, Worcester, Massachusetts. *Photograph courtesy of Ruth Pyne.*

Lorch Hall, located on the central campus of the University of Michigan, Ann Arbor, is a 1927-era building constructed principally of limestone with bas reliefs. It has a decorative tiled Flint Faience floor roundel in the first floor main lobby, noting the original usage of the building, to house the College of Architecture. This signage, in earthy field tiles and blue and amber hues, includes a representation of the University's seal which notes the year 1837 – this is the date the University of Michigan was moved to Ann Arbor from Detroit, not the date that the University was originally founded, which was 1817. Lorch Hall was designed by Emil Lorch, the first dean of the College of Architecture.

Sign in the entrance of Reilly Hall, University of Detroit Mercy. *Courtesy of the Jesuits at the University of Detroit Mercy.*

University of Michigan logo, measuring 46.5" in diameter, in Lorch Hall, Ann Arbor, Michigan.

"Pipeman Flint Fire Department" 6" x 6" tile, thought to be an award tile. The "Pipeman" was the firefighter who was responsible for getting the hoses connected to the water hydrants at the scene of a fire. $700-800.

A few more Flint Faience signs are worthy of note. The University of Detroit Mercy, with a major entry under Universities, has a wonderful tiled sign dating from 1926 in the old (original) entranceway foyer of its Faculty Building. The handsome dedication sign, 27.25" x 18.5", with scrolled border tiles in amber and relief lettering in the same glaze, reads: "To Cornelius J. Reilly and Lansing Reilly From Manette Reilly and Marie Lansing." Also, one impeccably designed 6" square tile in beige and blue glazes with symbols of crossed fire hoses and fire hat is inscribed utilizing raised line techniques "Pipe Man Flint Fire Department." It is oriented on point. Whether or not this was a small sign, or perhaps an award, is unknown.

Finally, the old Flint Faience plant located on the corner of Dort Highway and Davison Road had still another sign advertising the location of the factory. This tile sign was installed among other beautiful exterior tiles, and noted simply FFT&Co in a modified heraldic emblem.

Signage above the employees' entrance at the old Flint Faience Tile Company plant on Davison Road, Flint, Michigan. *Courtesy of the Delphi Corporation, Flint, Michigan.*

Sizes and Shapes

The sizes of standard tiles were illustrated on page 26 of the Flint Faience Tile Company's 1926 *Catalog "G"*. The largest size they claimed to manufacture was square or rectangular or specially cut tiles with a maximum dimension limited to 15" with a thickness of 15/16". Standard tile sizes were 6 x 6, 6 x 3, 6 x 2, 6 x 1-1/2, 6 x 1, 3 x 3, 3 x 1-1/2, 1-1/2 x 1-1/2, 1 x 1, 4-1/4 x 4-1/4, 4-1/2 x 2, 2 x 2, and diagonally cut tiles.

While it is easy to see from the above listed tile sizes that most tiles were square or rectangular in shape, many interesting tiles were round or hexagonal, too. Some had arched ends or were cut in the shape of the design. Unusual floor tile shapes can be seen in the illustration included in the Flint Faience & Tile Co. booklet *Architectural Faience: An Introduction*, where a box design floor is shown in a vestibule. The former E.T. Strong/Hamady house in Flint, Michigan, had a particularly large number of hexagonally shaped tiles in several rooms.

Cut out dog tile, measuring 4" x 4". $350-450.

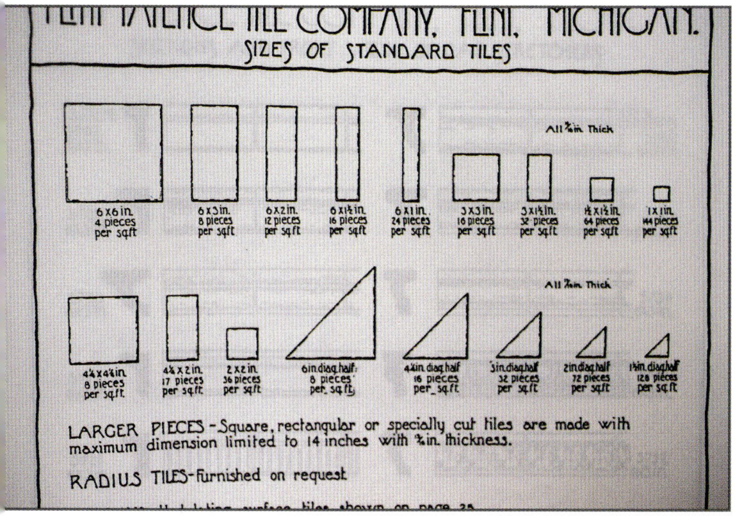

FLINT FAIENCE TILE COMPANY, FLINT, MICHIGAN.
SIZES OF STANDARD TILES

All ¾in. Thick

6x6in. 4 pieces per sq.ft — 6x3in. 8 pieces per sq.ft — 6x2in. 12 pieces per sq.ft — 6x1½in. 16 pieces per sq.ft — 6x1in. 24 pieces per sq.ft — 3x3in. 16 pieces per sq.ft — 3x1½in. 32 pieces per sq.ft — 1½x1½in. 64 pieces per sq.ft — 1x1in. 144 pieces per sq.ft

All ¾in. Thick

4¼x4¼in. 8 pieces per sq.ft — 4¼x2in. 17 pieces per sq.ft — 2x2in. 36 pieces per sq.ft — 6in. diag. half 8 pieces per sq.ft — 4¼in. diag. half 16 pieces per sq.ft — 3in. diag. half 32 pieces per sq.ft — 2in. diag. half 72 pieces per sq.ft — 1½in. diag. half 128 pieces per sq.ft

LARGER PIECES - Square, rectangular or specially cut tiles are made with maximum dimension limited to 14 inches with ¾in. thickness.

RADIUS TILES - Furnished on request.

Detail illustrating standard tile sizes from page 26 of *Catalog "G."*

Vestibule Floor; Box Design in Flint Faience

Illustration of "Box Design," from page 12, *Architectural Faience: An Introduction. Courtesy of Jim Graham.*

Round architectural tile. This tile was incised so that it would appear to be made up of nine tiles after it was grouted. 8.25". $125-150.

Hexagonal shaped tiles from a bathroom in the former E. T. Strong home. Insert tile measures 3.5". *Courtesy of the Hamady Estate.*

Hexagonal tiles installed in the conservatory in the former E. T. Strong home, Flint, Michigan. Tiles measure 5.125". *Courtesy of the Hamady Estate.*

Spark Plugs

There are probably no other American tile companies that owe their entrance and exit to spark plugs. Not only was Flint Faience and Tile Company founded by the "Father of American Spark Plugs," Albert Champion, but tile manufacturing began at the AC Spark Plug Company in 1921, when company leaders decided they should make fuller use of the spark plug tunnel kilns that were idle during part of the spark plug manufacturing process. With the advent Flint Faience tile production, the spark plugs and tile firings kept the kilns busy around the clock. Flint Faience tiles were even comprised of spent spark plug refractories which appeared in the form of grog for the tiles. In 1933, even though the faience tile business was still strong, it was determined that more room was needed in the kilns for firing spark plugs, and the tile business was formally closed. The almost-legendary link between the spark plugs and tiles can be seen in a 1971 obituary for AC artist and designer, Julio Haro, which reads, "Faience tile, a byproduct of the early spark plug..."

Even the retirement plaques handed out to long term employees – a handsome 6" x 4.25" Flint Faience tile with raised line decoration, mounted on wood – depicts a sparkplug and the AC logo among other designs. A 1927 historic black and white photograph taken in the AC Sparkplug/Flint Faience showroom shows AC employees standing next to a giant sparkplug and also holding their sparkplug products. For more information and an illustration, see entry for Amelia Earhart.

Spark plugs warrant a brief history in themselves. The invention of the first spark plug is credited to Edmond Berger on February 2, 1839. It is sufficient to note that France dominated the spark plug market in the early 1900s with expensive and unreliable products.

Retirement plaque comprised of a Flint Faience tile. This tile is one of many that were salvaged from the original Flint Faience Tile, Harriet Street plant. The Harriet Street plant was torn down in the late 1950s. These tiles were used to decorate the stair risers near the plant entrance. AC Spark Plug personnel salvaged these riser tiles and mounted them into walnut bases, then awarded them to select retirees upon their retirement dates. *Courtesy of Richard J. Rademacher.*

Detail of retirement tile, measuring 6" x 4.25". *Courtesy of Richard J. Rademacher*. $500-700.

Sports

see Athletics

S.S. *Manhattan*

see Ships and Swimming Pools

Stairs and Risers

see also Dryden Hotel

Ceramic tile stairs and risers provide a clear sense of drama and elegance in a home or business. While only fragments of the stair risers remain in the Dryden Hotel in New York City, some homeowners have allowed their stair risers to remain a focal point in their residences.

Stair treatments with variable tread and risers were fully illustrated and described on page 32 of the 1926 Flint Faience publication *Catalog "G."* Similarly, an article in the July 1930, Vol. II, no. 7 issue of *Keramic Tile Journal*, used a photograph of stair risers in a Cleveland home to make a point about faience tiles.

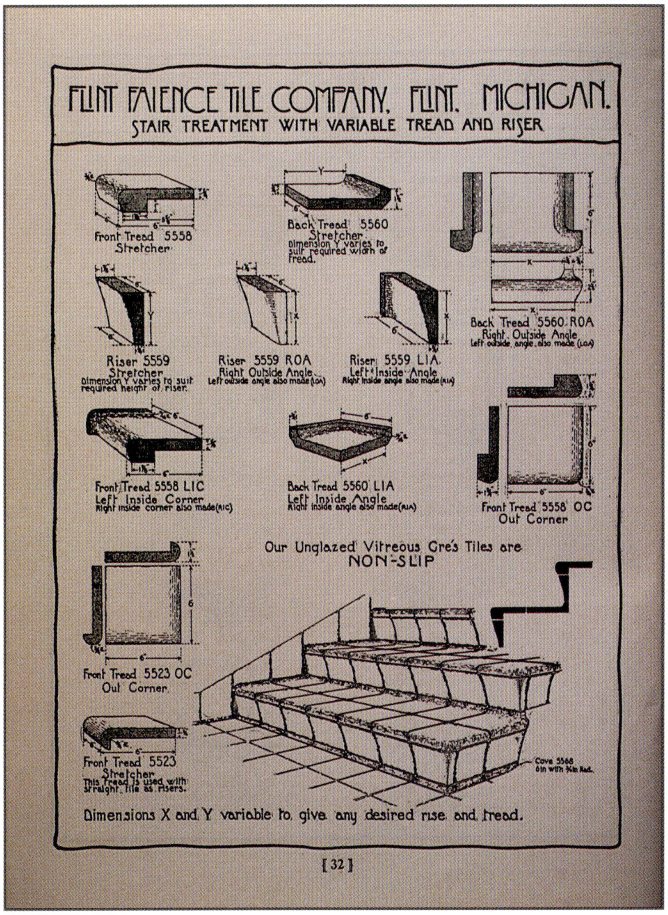

Page 32 of *Catalog "G,"* illustrating stair treatment with variable tread and riser.

Illustration of dramatic stair risers in a Cleveland home, from *Keramic Tile Journal*, Volume 2, no. 7, July 1930, page 26.

Kevin and Cynthia Godin now own the elegant home originally built by Bertha Richards in 1928, located in Flint, Michigan. In 1928 or 1929 Bertha Richards married Arthur Freeman, and historically this home is often referred to as the Freeman home. Although the home has many remarkable features, chief amongst these would be the dramatic staircase with 5" x 6" Flint Faience stair risers (the riser end tiles are 5.25" x 3.875"). One of the 5" x 6" riser tiles with four fleur-de-lis and double loops is identical to *Catalog "G"* stock design no. 6765, illustrated on page 22 of the catalog, except that the *Catalog "G"* example is described as being only 4.25" square, not stair riser size. The other riser tile on their stairwell has a matching tile in the collection of Ken Galvas.

Stairwell with stunning Flint Faience tile risers in the former Bertha Richards home, c. 1928, Flint, Michigan. *Courtesy of Kevin and Cynthia Godin.*

Raised line riser tiles in the former Bertha Richards home, measuring 5" x 6". *Courtesy of Kevin and Cynthia Godin.*

Detail of raised line riser tile, measuring 5" x 6", stock design no. 6765, in the former Bertha Richards home, Flint, Michigan. *Courtesy of Kevin and Cynthia Godin.*

Detail of raised line riser tile, measuring 5" x 6", stock design no. 6851, in the former Bertha Richards home, Flint, Michigan. *Courtesy of Kevin and Cynthia Godin.*

View of end risers in the stairwell of the former Bertha Richards home, Flint, Michigan. *Courtesy of Kevin and Cynthia Godin.*

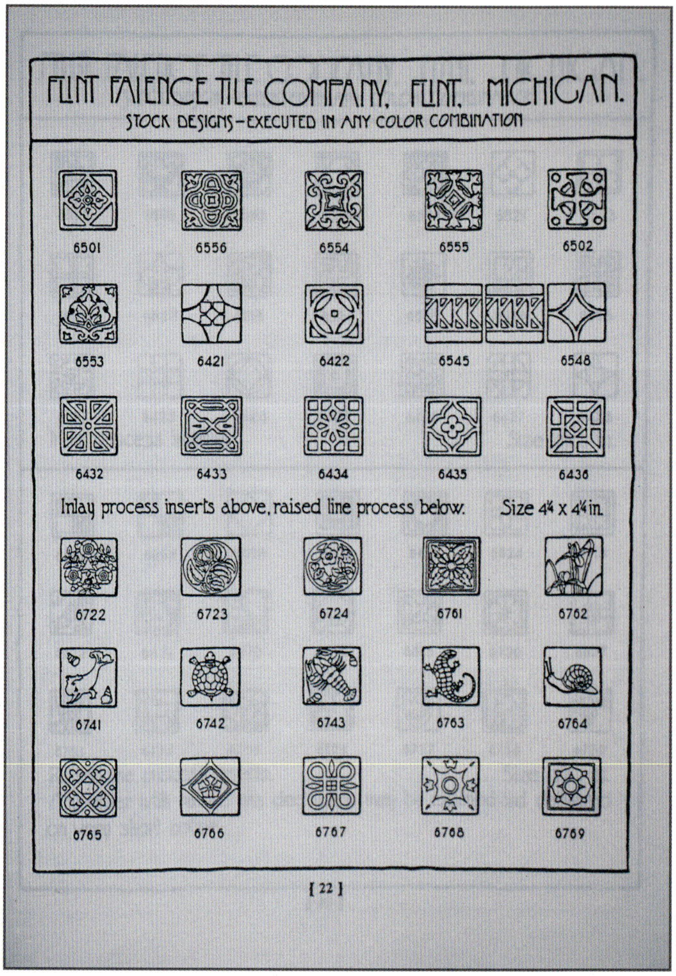

FLINT FAIENCE TILE COMPANY, FLINT, MICHIGAN.
STOCK DESIGNS–EXECUTED IN ANY COLOR COMBINATION

6501 6556 6554 6555 6502
6553 6421 6422 6545 6548
6432 6433 6434 6435 6436

Inlay process inserts above, raised line process below. Size 4¼ x 4¼ in.

6722 6723 6724 6761 6762
6741 6742 6743 6763 6764
6765 6766 6767 6768 6769

[22]

Examples of tiles used as risers from page 22 of *Catalog "G."*

Detail of end risers, measuring 5.25" x 3.875", in the stairwell of the former Bertha Richards home, Flint, Michigan. *Courtesy of Kevin and Cynthia Godin.*

Example of raised line riser tile, measuring 5" x 6". $150-175.

Another private residence with beautifully tiled stair risers is the former E.T. Strong home in Flint, Michigan. The tiled conservatory, complete with fountain and all the accoutrements, also has one exit via either of two tiled stairways rising from the luscious green hexagonal tile floor. The one illustrated here includes stock designs nos. 6765 and 6768, in brilliant contrasting blues and orange hues. Two examples of stock design no. 6768 with different glazes can be seen in the Barrett and Galvas collections, the first tile 6" x 6" and the second 4.25" x 4.25". The Galvas collection also contains a 4.125" square example of stock design no. 6765, installed in the former E.T. Strong residence stair risers.

Stairway in the conservatory of the former home of E. T. Strong. *Courtesy of the Hamady Estate.*

Four crowns raised line tile, stock design no. 6768, measuring 6" x 6". *Courtesy of Dale and Doris Barrett.* $150-175.

Center right:
Four crowns raised line tile, stock design no. 6768, measuring 4.25" x 4.25". $125-150.

Bottom right:
Raised line tile, stock design no. 6765, measuring 4.125" x 4.125". $125-175.

Tiled stairs and risers were not just for the home, but also for public buildings such as the Faculty Building (Reilly Hall) at the University of Detroit Mercy. Constructed in 1926, the stairs and risers in Flint Faience tile form a memorable exit from the chapel into the main hallway of the building. The stairway, wall tiles, and individual risers are jewel-like in their designs, all with a Spanish or Southwestern flavor, whether containing abstract or simple geometric floral forms. The risers are 6" square in one pattern and two glaze palettes.

Riser tiles in Faculty Building (Reilly Hall). *Courtesy of the Jesuit Community at the University of Detroit Mercy.*

Stairwell in Faculty Building (Reilly Hall), University of Detroit Mercy, c. 1926. *Courtesy of the Jesuit Community at the University of Detroit Mercy.*

Wall tiles in the stairwell at Faculty Building (Reilly Hall). *Courtesy of the Jesuit Community at the University of Detroit Mercy.*

Raised line riser detail in Faculty Building (Reilly Hall), each riser 6" x 6". *Courtesy of the Jesuit Community at the University of Detroit Mercy.*

Riser detail in Faculty Building (Reilly Hall), each riser 6" x 6". *Courtesy of the Jesuit Community at the University of Detroit Mercy.*

Wall tile border detail in raised line design at Faculty Building (Reilly Hall), c. 1926. *Courtesy of the Jesuit Community at the University of Detroit Mercy.*

Sunrooms, Solariums or Breakfast Rooms

Flint Faience literature describes the sunroom as "the connecting note between outdoors and in." (Flint Faience & Tile Company, *Bathroom Flyer A-303*, 1929, n.p.) Sunrooms or solariums, with floors comprised generally of earthy field tiles made by Flint Faience juxtaposed with colorful and imaginative insert tiles, form the core of many splendid installations in homes of the wealthy during the late 1920s. These cheerful rooms must have contained many a breakfast feast or leisurely perusal of the Sunday newspaper, accompanied by several cups of aromatic coffee. Notable among them would be the sunroom located in the Samuel Stewart home in Flint, Michigan, which measures 128" x 162" overall. Construction of this fine home was begun in 1929 and completed in 1932. Here, inserted among the field tiles, were some 3" x 2.75" and some 6" x 6" larger tiles in dramatic crystalline glazes and fleur-de-lis, key fret, and endless knot patterns.

Sunroom as illustrated in a Flint Faience & Tile Company promotional publication, *Flyer A-303*. *Courtesy the Archives, New York State College of Ceramics at Alfred University.*

Insert tile, measuring 6", stock design no. 6532 in the sunroom of the former Samuel Stewart home, Flint, Michigan, c. 1929-32. *Courtesy of Stephen and Rosanne Heddy.*

Sunroom in the former Samuel Stewart home. *Courtesy of Stephen and Rosanne Heddy.*

Insert tile, measuring 6", stock design no. 6453 in the sunroom of the former Samuel Stewart home, Flint, Michigan. *Courtesy of Stephen and Rosanne Heddy.*

The home of Prosper Champion (the brother of Albert Champion), built in Flint, Michigan in 1928, also contains a charming sunroom with field tiles that vary in dimensions from 2.75" square, to 6" square, to 9" square, to 2.75" x 6", and 1.25" square. Carefully placed among this variety of field tiles are inserts measuring 2.75" square.

E.T. Strong, President of Buick Motor Co. in Flint, Michigan, had an impressive home constructed in 1929. It contained a beautiful breakfast room with a floor of reddish-yellow handmade Flint Faience with 2.75" inserts in contrasting colors. Similar insert tiles such as stock design no. 6525 can also be seen in private collections.

Breakfast nook in the former home of E. T. Strong, Flint, Michigan, c. 1929. *Courtesy of the Hamady Estate.*

Left and below: Overview of the sunroom in the former Prosper Champion home, Flint, Michigan, c. 1928. *Courtesy of Jim Fitzell and Jessica Higgins.*

Insert tile, measuring 2.75" x 2.75", stock design no. 6425, in the breakfast nook floor of the former E.T. Strong home, Flint, Michigan, c. 1929. *Courtesy of the Hamady Estate.*

Insert tile, measuring 2.75" x 2.75", installed in the breakfast nook floor of the former E.T. Strong home, Flint, Michigan. *Courtesy of the Hamady Estate.*

Insert tile measuring 2.85" x 2.85", stock design no. 6525. $50-75.

Insert tile, measuring 2.75" x 2.75", stock design no. 6525, installed in the breakfast nook floor of the former E.T. Strong home, Flint, Michigan. *Courtesy of the Hamady Estate.*

Swimming Pools

see also Rockefeller Playhouse, Apartment Houses, Ships

Swimming pools and tiles are virtually inseparable in terms of functionality. Beautiful swimming pool tile installations were one hallmark of Flint Faience and Tile Company, having gained prestige after the company executed the indoor pool at the Rockefeller Playhouse at Kykuit, Pocantico Hills, near Sleepy Hollow, New York. The swimming pool installation created for the Park Gables Apartments in Chicago is still another example of the Flint Faience success in this genre. Both are detailed and illustrated in separate entries, Rockefeller Playhouse and Apartments.

Although it seems that few have survived until today and none have been positively identified, it is known that Flint Faience tiles were used at least in the swimming pools of south-central Michigan Y.M.C.A.'s. Not only can this be verified through the stock designs available in *Catalog "G"* in 1926 (which, on page 24, illustrates a small 2.75" square insert tile, no. 6414 bearing the "YMCA" insignia, for wall and floor installations), but also through a listing of recent Flint Faience tile installations in the April 1929 issue of *AC Sparks*, which includes, right alongside that of John D. Rockefeller's swimming pool in Pocantico Hills, a Y.M.C.A. in Detroit and also the lobby floor of a Y.M.C.A. in Flint, Michigan.

In addition, at least two major swimming pool installations were included and well-documented on U.S. passenger steamliners. One was on the S.S. *Manhattan* and the other the S.S. *Washington*. See Ships entry for more information and photographs.

Detail illustrating the special Y.M.C.A. stock design insert tile from page 24 of *Catalog "G."*

Postcard of a Y.W.C.A. tiled swimming pool. Detroit, Michigan. *Courtesy of Margaret Carney.*

Theatres

While Flint Faience tiles were popular in many residential settings such as bathrooms, foyers, kitchens, and fountains, public spaces such as theatres often used tiles for more than just embellishment. One example is the Warner Theatre in downtown Erie, Pennsylvania. The theatre, located at 811 State Street, was commissioned by Warner Brothers in 1929, with a goal to create a luxury movie palace. The architects for the theatre, which was built in 1931, were Cornelius Ward Rapp and George Leslie Rapp, brothers who were well-known designers of splendid movie palaces. The interior, recently renovated, is stunning in its opulent use of gold gilding, rich tapestries, French mirrors, and Czechoslovakian glass and crystal chandeliers. Equally stunning is the use of ceramic tile in significant installations in the form of fountains, fireplaces, and panels. While the pair of dramatic fountains in the Warner Theatre are Batchelder, and the Smoker panel is Mueller Mosaic Company of Trenton, New Jersey (Reed, n.d., 19), the fireplace facings are Flint Faience. One features nine 6" x 6" tiles similar to stock design no. 6456 identifiable in the 1926 Flint Faience Tile Company *Catalog "G,"* page 21. These same motifs, with four crowns and crescent moons, were also used in the Winchester Hospital in Flint, Michigan and the U.S. Customs House in San Juan, Puerto Rico.

Exterior view of the Warner Theatre, Erie, Pennsylvania. *Courtesy of the Warner Theatre, Erie, Pennsylvania.*

Fireplace detail, Warner Theatre, Erie, Pennsylvania. Note the electric outlet in the fireplace interior. *Courtesy of the Warner Theatre, Erie Pennsylvania.*

Flint Faience tile fireplace in the Warner Theatre, Erie, Pennsylvania. *Courtesy of the Warner Theatre, Erie, Pennsylvania.*

Tile installation in the second floor men's room, Warner Theatre, Erie Pennsylvania. *Courtesy of the Warner Theatre, Erie Pennsylvania.*

Stock design no. 6456, featured on page 21 of *Catalog "G."*

Molded tile, stock design no. 6456, measuring 6" x 6". $100-150.

One of the most used advertisements for Flint Faience tiles featured photographs of the tile installations from the Fox Theatre in the Islamic and Egyptian-inspired Yaarab Temple in Atlanta, Georgia. Many issues of the leading tile trade publication, *Keramic Tile Journal*, were illustrated with a photograph or two of this tiled wonder. It was designed by the architectural firm of Marye, Alger, Vinour & Armistead in Atlanta and the tiling contractors were Carmichael Tile Co. and Eubank Mantel & Tile Co. This installation included a glorious fountain "in a rich, yet harmonious combination of Flint designs." The tiles for this particular fountain were 4.25" square with raised line process designs. Advertisements from 1931 also illustrate one mantel in the Egyptian room which contains a scarab motif in Flint Faience design and another fountain in "graceful floral pattern."

Today, the restored Fox Theatre, referred to as "The Fabulous Fox," is considered one of the most ornate movie palaces in the United States. According to one Internet web site devoted to the Fox Theatre, its architectural style can be described as more of the fantasy type than typical Neo-Mideastern Eclectic, Neo-Mideastern Exotic, or Islamic Revival. Opening on Christmas Day, 1929, the building (250,000 square feet) was originally planned and designed to be the new headquarters for the Shriners of Atlanta, with the Fox Theatre occupying (leasing) the 5,000 seat auditorium planned for the Shriner's new mosque, the Yaarab Temple. However, the economic collapse that came with the Great Depression forced the Fox Theatre to close only 125 weeks after it had opened, while at the same time the members of the Yaarab Temple could not meet their pledges. The mortgage was foreclosed and prosperous times did not reappear until a new partnership, Mosque Inc., acquired the Fox Theatre. It was operated as a fine movie palace between the 1940s and the 1960s. Eventually, after several decades that included threatened demolition and a "save the Fox" campaign, the Fox Theatre became a successful multi-purpose performing arts center owned by Atlanta Landmarks. It has been restored and was designated a National Historic Landmark in 1976. It is located at 6660 Peachtree St., N.E.

Postcard of the Shrine Mosque and Fox Theatre, Atlanta, Georgia. *Courtesy of Ken Galvas.*

Flint Handmade Faïence

in the

Fox Theatre

in Yaarab Temple

Atlanta, Georgia

Marye, Alger, Vinour & Armistead
Architects—Atlanta

Carmichael Tile Co., and Eubank Mantel & Tile Co.
Tiling Contractors—Atlanta

Left: Mantel in Egyptian room. Note scarab motif in Flint Faience tile design

Below: Fountain, in Flint Faience tile of graceful floral pattern

Above: Fountain, in a rich, yet harmonious combination of Flint designs. Panel specially designed, and executed in 4¼" x 4¼" handmade tile in raised line

With a rich variety of over 150 colors to choose from—with a sketch service ready to co-operate in creating original designs to carry out any decorative motif—with delivery service noted for its promptness—

—It is only natural that theatre architects like to work with Flint Handmade Faience. The Fox Theatre is one of many notable installations.

Write for catalogs of Flint tile designs—in Handmade Faience—non-slip, unglazed Vitrocraft—and Flintcraft, the machine-made, all-purpose tile.

FLINT FAÏENCE AND TILE CO.
FLINT MICHIGAN

3

Keramic Tile Journal, Volume 3, no. 4, 1931, page 3, illustrating the Fox Theatre, Atlanta, Georgia.

Tiled fountain executed in raised line design, part of the Fox Theatre, Atlanta, Georgia. *Courtesy of the Fox Theatre, Atlanta, Georgia.*

Trim detail in the Fox Theatre, Atlanta. *Courtesy of the Fox Theatre, Atlanta, Georgia.*

Fountain detail from the Fox Theatre, Atlanta. *Courtesy of the Fox Theatre. Atlanta, Georgia.*

Raised line tiles in the Fox Theatre, Atlanta. *Courtesy of the Fox Theatre, Atlanta, Georgia.*

One example of a 4.25" round raised line insert tile from the Fox Theatre is part of the collection of Ken Galvas. The brilliant Islamic-type motifs and color scheme in vivid red, blue, gold, and white are boldly evident on this particular tile.

Brilliantly glazed insert tile typical of the Fox Theatre, with a diameter of 4.25". $150-200.

Tree of Life

In the decorative arts, the tree of life design has been described as symbolizing the creative force of the universe. Several large tile murals of Flint Faience have been referred to as the *Tree of Life*. One of these, in the collection of the Sloan Museum in Flint, Michigan, is the only mural signed by any Flint Faience employee. It is signed "C. Bergma..." in the bottom right corner on the edge of the face of the mural, with the last letters lost to chipping of the tile surface. It is comprised of 24 tiles, each 8" square. This mural is a spectacular creation done in raised line process and breathtaking glaze colors and looks like one-of-a-kind until one has the opportunity to view two more in a neighboring city.

"Tree of Life" mural in the Sloan Museum, Flint, Michigan. *Courtesy of the Alfred P. Sloan Museum, Gift of Richard Pohrt.*

Detail showing Carl Bergmans's signature on the "Tree of Life" panel in the Alfred P. Sloan Museum. *Courtesy of the Alfred P. Sloan Museum, Gift of Richard Pohrt.*

Another pair of *Tree of Life* tiled panels, identical to the Sloan *Tree of Life* mural in every way except the size of the individual tiles comprising the panel, can be seen today in the General Motors Headquarters Building in Detroit. The pair flank both sides of a downstairs tunnel stairway, largely hidden from the general public today. Each measures 72" high x 36" wide and is comprised of forty whole or partial tiles in the central panel (58" high x 25" wide). The central panel depicts seven birds, mostly peacocks in full plumage, surrounded by border trim and a frame of brilliant blue tiles. The panels are stunningly executed, mysterious and beautiful, like Ming dynasty cloisonné. The double circle patterns on the tree trunk and branches and the fantastic flower shapes and colors all allude to the pattern on a rich Persian tapestry. Upon comparison, these two panels closely resemble the *Tree of Life* now in the Sloan Museum permanent collection, except for the overall shape of the panel (rectangular vs. sculpted) and the color palette.

One of two "Tree of Life" panels in the former General Motors World Headquarters, Detroit, Michigan.

Detail from the "Tree of Life" mural in the former General Motors World Headquarters, Detroit, Michigan.

Detail from the "Tree of Life" mural in the former General Motors World Headquarters, Detroit, Michigan.

The General Motors Building, originally called the Durant Building (headquarters of General Motors), is located at 3011 W. Grand Boulevard in Detroit and was once advertised as the largest office building in the world. It was designed by noted architect Albert Kahn. Completed in 1920, it originally housed 1,960 offices (each with outside windows), was served by thirty-one elevators, and contained nineteen bowling alleys, men's and women's swimming pools, a ballroom with the world's only "floating" floor, hotel suites for visiting GM officials and dignitaries, and a day hospital with a doctor and nurse for employees.

General Motors Building, Detroit, Michigan. *Courtesy of Margaret Carney.*

Trees

see Botanicals

Turtles

see Reptiles and Amphibians

Universities

see also Binns, Custom Designs, Signage and Stair Risers

Several universities in the United States utilized Flint Faience tiles in significant installations within the university setting. None are more notable than that at the University of Detroit Mercy, located in Detroit, Michigan. The Faculty Building (Reilly Hall) alone contains Flint Faience tiles throughout its original entranceway, hallway floors and wall, parlor, cafeteria, stairways, and chapel. Built in 1926, it may be one of the premiere uses of this remarkable tile. A 1931 issue of *Keramic Tile Journal* (*Keramic Tile Journal*, February 1931, 3) notes that the tiles for the facility were designed by Flint Faience and Tile Co., in cooperation with the Detroit architectural firm of Malcomson & Higginbotham and installed by the tiling contractor George R. Mehling, also of Detroit. The architectural style can be described as Spanish Renaissance or Spanish Mission. At the time, the Jesuits owned the University of Detroit. (Muller, 1976, 146)

Specific areas of the Faculty Building are worthy of more detailed description. In the Chapel, the altar arch, stunning in its use of vibrant colors and gold, is "completely executed in Flint Handmade Faience." The wall tile is of a "Renaissance" design, while the Chapel aisle is an "unusual combination of marble and Flint Handmade Faience." The decorative wall tiles in vibrant red, blue, gold, and green are 6", with 6" by 4.5" gold border tiles, while the sacristy utilized large 4-piece interlocking "IHS" tiles measuring 16.75" square within a larger 32" square. The adjoining tiles depicting grain and grapes are beautifully produced in high relief.

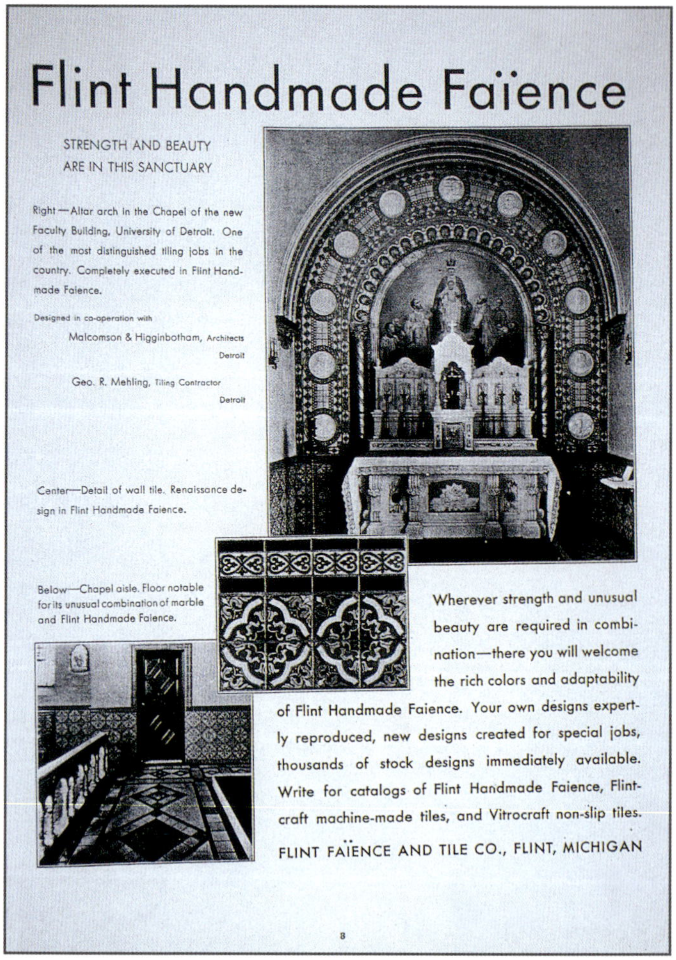

Flint Handmade Faïence

STRENGTH AND BEAUTY ARE IN THIS SANCTUARY

Right—Altar arch in the Chapel of the new Faculty Building, University of Detroit. One of the most distinguished tiling jobs in the country. Completely executed in Flint Handmade Faience.

Designed in co-operation with
Malcomson & Higginbotham, Architects, Detroit
Geo. R. Mehling, Tiling Contractor, Detroit

Center—Detail of wall tile. Renaissance design in Flint Handmade Faience.

Below—Chapel aisle. Floor notable for its unusual combination of marble and Flint Handmade Faience.

Wherever strength and unusual beauty are required in combination—there you will welcome the rich colors and adaptability of Flint Handmade Faience. Your own designs expertly reproduced, new designs created for special jobs, thousands of stock designs immediately available. Write for catalogs of Flint Handmade Faience, Flintcraft machine-made tiles, and Vitrocraft non-slip tiles.

FLINT FAÏENCE AND TILE CO., FLINT, MICHIGAN

3

The University of Detroit Faculty Building tile installations as illustrated in *Keramic Tile Journal*, Volume 3, no. 2, 1931, page 3.

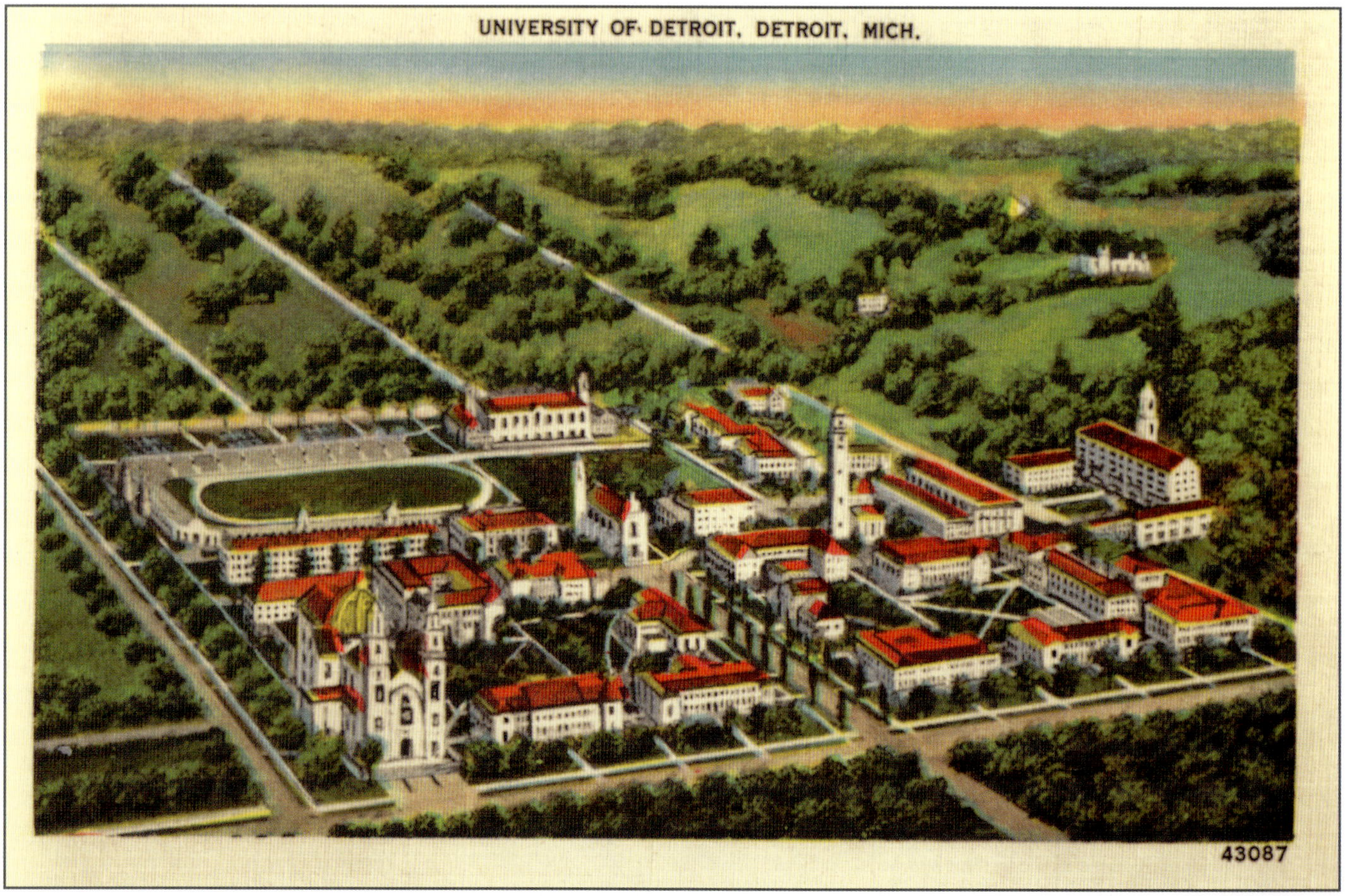

Vintage postcard of the University of Detroit. *Courtesy of Margaret Carney.*

Faculty Chapel at the University of Detroit Mercy. *Courtesy of the Jesuits at the University of Detroit Mercy.*

Chapel niche showcasing a statue of Mary, measuring 20.5" x 45". *Courtesy of the Jesuits at the University of Detroit Mercy.*

Wainscoting tile pattern executed in raised line design, located near the chapel niche at the University of Detroit Mercy. Tiles 6" x 6". *Courtesy of the Jesuits at the University of Detroit Mercy.*

Border tiles above the wainscoting, measuring 6" x 4.25", at the University of Detroit Mercy. *Courtesy of the Jesuits of at the University of Detroit Mercy.*

Bluebell border tiles in raised line design in the chapel, University of Detroit Mercy. *Courtesy of the Jesuits at the University of Detroit Mercy.*

"IHS" tile in front of the altar in the chapel at the University of Detroit Mercy, measuring 16.75" x 16.75". *Courtesy of the Jesuits at the University of Detroit Mercy.*

Carved wheat tile, measuring 7" x 7", located in the chapel, University of Detroit Mercy. *Courtesy of the Jesuits at the University of Detroit Mercy.*

Carved grape tile, measuring 7" x 7", in the chapel, University of Detroit Mercy. *Courtesy of the Jesuits at the University of Detroit Mercy.*

Insert tile, stock design no. 6449, used in the altar floor pattern in the chapel, University of Detroit Mercy. *Courtesy of the Jesuits at the University of Detroit Mercy*

Border cap tiles, measuring 6" x 5", similar to those at the University of Detroit Mercy. $10-20 each.

There are several related tiled areas in the University of Detroit Mercy Faculty Building, including the tile wall directly outside the chapel, leading to the stairway. These tiles have several patterns, one a very Art Deco zigzag border design in purple, pink, black, and turquoise, and the other a magnificent pattern, stock design no. 6911, which is illustrated in color in the Flint Faience & Tile Co. 1929 trade publication booklet *Architectural Faience: An Introduction.* (Flint Faience & Tile Company, *Architectural Faience: An Introduction*, 1929, 5) Additionally, an individual tile of this genre can be seen in the ceramics collection at Baggs Memorial Library at the Ohio State University in Columbus, Ohio.

Raised line design in the chapel doorway, University of Detroit Mercy. *Courtesy of the Jesuits at the University of Detroit Mercy.*

Stock design no. 6911, similar to some of the tile patterns at the University of Detroit Mercy, as illustrated on page 5 of *Architectural Faience: An Introduction. Courtesy of Jim Graham.*

Raised line tile, stock design no. 6911. *Courtesy of Baggs Memorial Library at the Ohio State University.*

While the use of Flint Faience tiles in stair risers and signage are detailed in other chapters, the use of Flint Faience field tile and inserts in the large parlor located down the hallway from the chapel in the Faculty Building, cannot be mentioned too often. The parlor floor has an intricate yet simple woven appeal with brightly glazed insert tiles creating a dramatic effect. The patterning of varying shapes and hues, alternating field tiles and inserts over such a large contiguous floor, is a joyful sight. Some individual tiles related to these University of Detroit Mercy installations have found their way into private collections. The pattern on the parlor's tiled walls is comprised of stunning 6" square tiles in a grouping of four tiles.

Overview of the parlor floor in Faculty Building (Reilly Hall), University of Detroit Mercy. *Courtesy of the Jesuits at the University of Detroit Mercy.*

Basket weave patterned tile parlor floor, University of Detroit Mercy. Large tiles are 6" x 12" and the inserts are 2.75" x 2.75". *Courtesy of the Jesuits at the University of Detroit Mercy.*

Insert tile, stock design no. 6417, installed in the parlor floor, University of Detroit Mercy. *Courtesy of the Jesuits at the University of Detroit Mercy.*

Insert tile, stock design no. 6591, installed in the parlor floor, University of Detroit Mercy. *Courtesy of the Jesuits at the University of Detroit Mercy.*

Insert tile, stock design no. 6416, installed in the parlor floor, University of Detroit Mercy. *Courtesy of the Jesuits at the University of Detroit Mercy.*

Insert tile, stock design no. 6591, measuring 2.75" x 2.75". $30-50.

Tiled wall pattern in the parlor at the University of Detroit Mercy. Individual tiles measure 6" x 6". *Courtesy of the Jesuits at the University of Detroit Mercy.*

Raised line tile with the same pattern used on wall tiles at the University of Detroit Mercy, measuring 6" x 6". *Courtesy of Ruth Hylen.*

Raised line border tile, measuring 6" x 3", installed in the parlor, University of Detroit Mercy. *Courtesy of the Jesuits at the University of Detroit Mercy.*

Before concluding with this magnificent tiled site, a few other areas of the building should be mentioned. Another tile pattern was featured in the original entranceway to the Faculty building. These 6" square tiles were meant to be installed in groupings of four tiles each. The Spanish style hallways are also covered with Flint Faience tiles, as are the cafeteria floors and pillars.

Tile installations at other universities would include the floor signage in the first floor lobby of Lorch Hall at the University of Michigan in Ann Arbor, the eight tiles designed by Charles Fergus Binns for the Alfred University Ceramics Building, and the Heifer sign that was moved from Crapo Farms near Flint to the University of Michigan, Flint campus in the 1980s. See also Signage, Binns, Custom Designs, and Stair Risers entries.

Entrance hallway of Faculty Building (Reilly Hall), University of Detroit Mercy. *Courtesy of the Jesuits at the University of Detroit Mercy.*

A four-tile wall design used in the foyer areas of Faculty Building (Reilly Hall), University of Detroit Mercy. Individual tiles measure 6" x 6". *Courtesy of the Jesuits at the University of Detroit Mercy.*

Tiled features within the faculty dining area in Faculty Building (Reilly Hall), University of Detroit Mercy. *Courtesy of the Jesuits at the University of Detroit Mercy.*

U.S. Customs House, San Juan, Puerto Rico

see also Julio Haro

Julio Haro, the chief designer at Flint Faience & Tile Co., created four tiled lunettes of Spanish galleons with full sails for the United States Customs House in San Juan, Puerto Rico, circa 1929. This feat was announced in the April 1929 issue of *AC Sparks*, a Flint Faience & Tile Co. publication. The cover of this issue illustrated one of the lunettes.

Postcard of the U.S. Customs House, San Juan, Puerto Rico. *Courtesy of Ken Galvas.*

Cover of the April 1929, issue of *AC Sparks,* illustrating one of the four tiled lunettes designed by Julio Haro for the U.S. Customs House, San Juan, Puerto Rico. *Courtesy of the Archives, New York State College of Ceramics at Alfred University.*

One of the four lunettes at the U.S. Customs House is nearly identical to the tiled ships installed above the fireplace at the Garfield School in Wyandotte, Michigan. The Garfield School mural dates several years after the one created for the Puerto Rico site. Three of the four lunettes can be seen in recent photographs of the U.S. Customs House. One of the three lunettes has the galleon and two smaller ships portrayed as black silhouettes against the sunset.

Large interior panels installed at the U.S. Customs House in San Juan, Puerto Rico. Designed by Julio Haro.

Lunette portraying a Columbus ship with palm trees panel in the U.S. Customs House, San Juan, Puerto Rico. Designed by Julio Haro.

Lunette portraying a Columbus ship at sea panel in the U.S. Customs House in San Juan, Puerto Rico. Designed by Julio Haro.

Lunette portraying a Columbus ship silhouetted against a sunset in the U.S. Customs House in San Juan Puerto Rico. Designed by Julio Haro.

Similar insert tile to those used in the U.S. Customs House in San Juan, Puerto Rico, stock design no. 6455, measuring 6" x 6". $100-150.

Detail from page 10 of *Catalog "G,"* illustrating stock design no. 6685 "Ceramics."

Occasionally an individual tile can be identified as matching those at the U.S. Customs House in San Juan. One example would be a geometric pattern, stock design no. 6455 in *Catalog "G,"* a 6" square tile with a rich selection of glazes in red, celadon, gold, and blue, and complex texturing in the surface of the design work. The decoration was created utilizing the inlay process. The U.S. Customs House exterior and interior can be seen in the movie *Under Suspicion*, starring Gene Hackman and Morgan Freeman.

Vases and Flowerpots

Vases and flowerpots were frequent themes on Flint Faience tiles. *Catalog "G"* illustrates many such stock designs on page 18, with nos. 6691 and 6694 Flowers all executed in the raised line process and 18" x 9". Perhaps the classic pattern was stock design no. 6685, titled "Ceramics," which illustrates the classical figure of a woman admiring a similarly classical vase. This tile can be seen in the collection of the Sloan Museum in Flint, Michigan.

"Ceramics" tile, stock design no. 6685, executed in raised line design, diameter 14.75". *Courtesy of the Alfred P. Sloan Museum, acc. no. 65.40.71.*

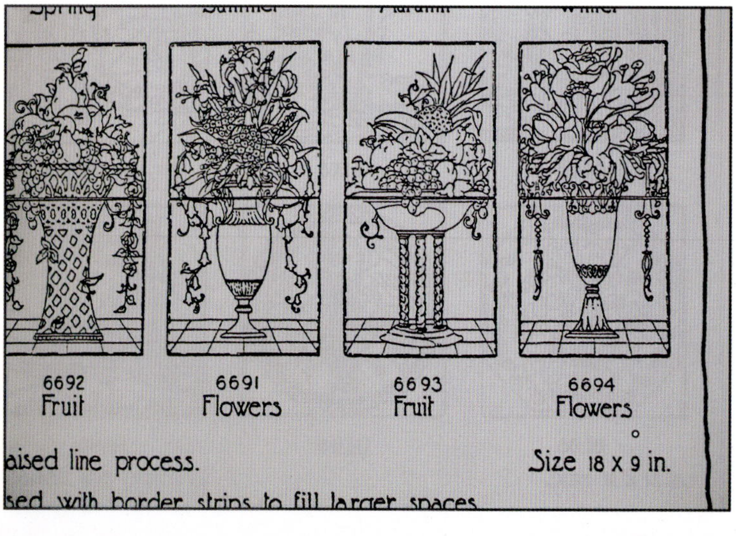

Detail from page 18 of *Catalog "G,"* illustrating stock designs of tiles with themes of vases and flowerpots, nos. 6691 and 6694, raised line process and 18" x 9".

Additionally, and significantly, functional and classically designed, unsigned vases and flower pots were created by several of the leading designers of Flint Faience tile. While some were strictly classical in form, others show the obvious connection with the Arts & Crafts Movement in the U.S. and Chinese porcelains of the Ming and Qing dynasties. Significant among these would be the stunning vase created by Flint Faience art director and architect, Howard B. Burton, now in the collection of his granddaughter, Kristine Burton. Some pieces were made into lamps. For more information, see entry under Howard B. Burton.

Crystalline glazed bud vase, height 8.5". $300-375.

12" vase with a yellow glaze. $300-400.

12" tall vase with a flowing green glaze. $550-650.

Lamp with crystalline glaze, body 11". $400-500.

Flowerpots were another subcategory of vases which could have included pieces the decorators made during their lunch hours for their own practice, experimentation, and fun. For instance, an 8-sided flowerpot, just 6-1/2" in diameter, was made by Marjorie Milloy and is now in the collection of Ken Galvas. Similarly, a 2" tall, 4.75" diameter bowl was created by the same decorator during her lunch breaks. The red and orange glazes create quite a contrast. She also made boxes, including one with a cover.

"Lunchtime" bowl from the estate of Marjorie Milloy, diameter 4.75". $30-50.

Flower pot by Flint Faience found in the estate of Flint decorator Marjorie Milloy, diameter 6.5". $100-125.

"Lunchtime" boxes from the estate of Marjorie Milloy. $30-50 each.

Vitrocraft

Vitrocraft was the name given to the Flint Faience & Tile Company unglazed tile, formerly known as vitreous grès. It was considered an all-purpose tile and was less expensive than their other types of tiles. These non-slip tiles were advertised in their 1929 trade booklet, *Architectural Faience: An Introduction*, with various patterns illustrated such as Octunis, Ranciez, Novarra, Seprova, and Decenza.

Vitrocraft was advertised not only as low-cost and non-slip, but additionally as frost-proof, non-absorbent, able to withstand public traffic, genuinely hand-made, both individual and artistic, with an interesting texture and dignified appearance, with four color ranges available, and stock floor patterns making possible immediate shipment. The four color ranges included dark range, light range, full range, and selected for uniform color. Their promotional material even recommended the selected light range type as particularly appropriate for banks, and lobbies of office and other public buildings because they believed it was in perfect architectural harmony with any wall treatment.

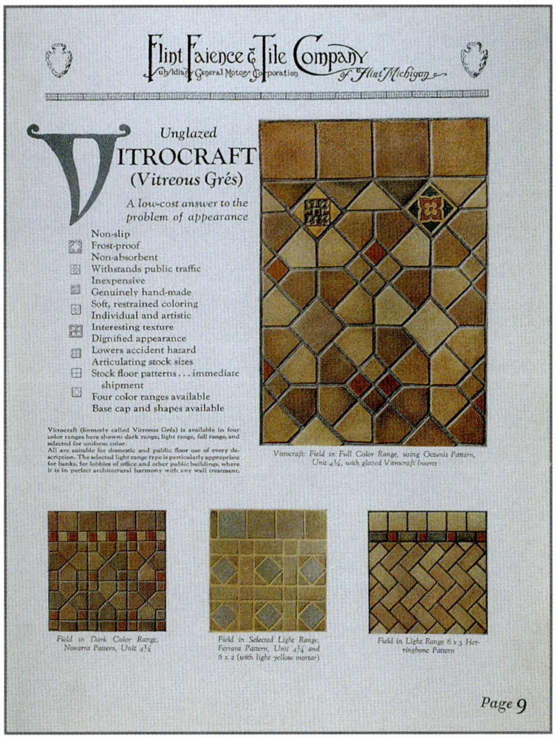
Flint Faience & Tile Company
Subsidiary General Motors Corporation of Flint Michigan

Unglazed
VITROCRAFT
(Vitreous Grés)

A low-cost answer to the problem of appearance

Non-slip
Frost-proof
Non-absorbent
Withstands public traffic
Inexpensive
Genuinely hand-made
Soft, restrained coloring
Individual and artistic
Interesting texture
Dignified appearance
Lowers accident hazard
Articulating stock sizes
Stock floor patterns . . . immediate shipment
Four color ranges available
Base cap and shapes available

Vitrocraft (formerly called Vitreous Grés) is available in four color ranges here shown: dark range, light range, full range, and selected for uniform color.
All are suitable for domestic and public floor use of every description. The selected light range type is particularly appropriate for banks, for lobbies of office and other public buildings, where it is in perfect architectural harmony with any wall treatment.

Vitrocraft: Field in Full Color Range, using Octunis Pattern, Unit 4¼, with glazed Vitrocraft Inserts

Field in Dark Color Range, Novarra Pattern, Unit 4¼

Field in Selected Light Range, Ferrara Pattern, Unit 4¼ and 6 x 2 (with light yellow mortar)

Field in Light Range 6 x 3 Herringbone Pattern

Page 9

Descriptions and illustrations of Vitrocraft floor and wall tiles from page 9 of *Architectural Faience: An Introduction. Courtesy of Jim Graham.*

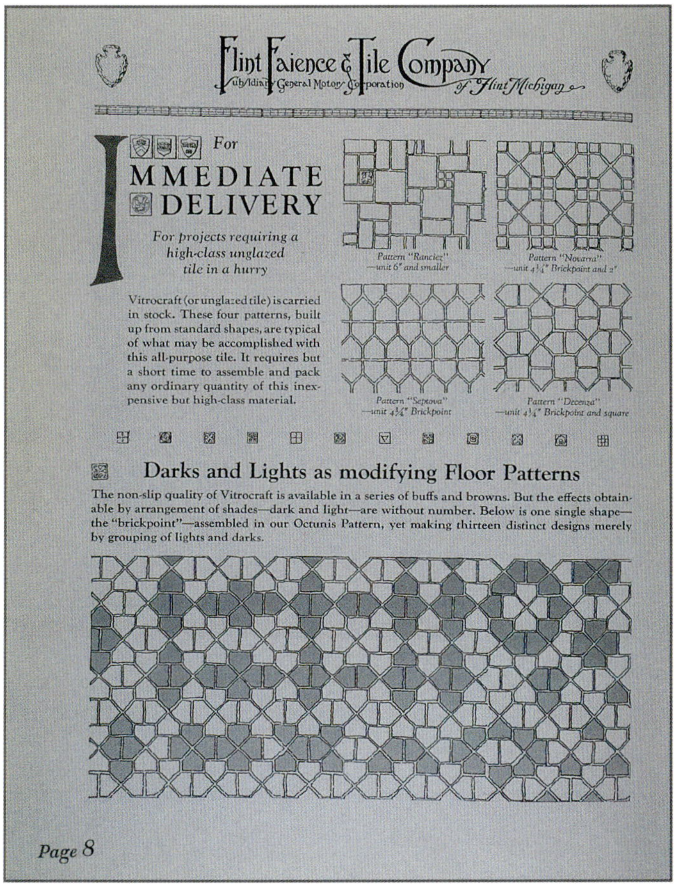
Flint Faience & Tile Company
Subsidiary General Motors Corporation of Flint Michigan

For
IMMEDIATE
DELIVERY

For projects requiring a high-class unglazed tile in a hurry

Vitrocraft (or unglazed tile) is carried in stock. These four patterns, built up from standard shapes, are typical of what may be accomplished with this all-purpose tile. It requires but a short time to assemble and pack any ordinary quantity of this inexpensive but high-class material.

Pattern "Ranciez" —unit 6" and smaller

Pattern "Novarra" —unit 4¼" Brickpoint and 2"

Pattern "Septova" —unit 4¼" Brickpoint

Pattern "Decenza" —unit 4¼" Brickpoint and square

Darks and Lights as modifying Floor Patterns

The non-slip quality of Vitrocraft is available in a series of buffs and browns. But the effects obtainable by arrangement of shades—dark and light—are without number. Below is one single shape—the "brickpoint"—assembled in our Octunis Pattern, yet making thirteen distinct designs merely by grouping of lights and darks.

Page 8

Descriptions and illustrations of Vitrocraft floor and wall tiles from page 8 of *Architectural Faience: An Introduction. Courtesy of Jim Graham.*

Warwick Masonic Lodge

see Masonic Temples

Waves

Wave motifs were also a stock design available from the Flint Faience Tile Company, as illustrated on page 15 of *Catalog "G,"* nos. 6625 A and B and no. 6675, all 6" x 3" border designs created with the raised line process. Additional raised line wave motif decorated tiles in size 6" x 2" border tiles can be seen illustrated on page 16, featuring nos. 6620 and 6673, as well as another wave pattern, no. 6599, a 6" x 3" available as a decorative strip for floors and walls. Shown on page 17 of *Catalog "G"* is an even narrower decorative strip with wave motifs in raised line decoration, which was advertised to "add a pleasing touch of color to a plain white bathroom wall." Illustrated was no. 6687, 6" x 1.5".

Detail from page 15 of *Catalog "G,"* showing stock design wave patterns.

Detail from page 15 of *Catalog "G,"* showing stock design wave patterns.

Detail from page 17 of *Catalog "G,"* showing stock design wave border patterns.

Wave motif tiles are one of the attractive features of the Flint Faience swimming pool area at the Park Gables Apartments/Condominiums located in North Chicago. Another attractive example is the wave border tiles in pinkish-lavender and green in an upstairs bathroom of the former Prosper Champion home in Flint, Michigan. These bathroom border tiles measure 2.75" x 6".

Wave border in raised line design in the pool area of the Park Gables Apartments in Chicago, Illinois, c. 1927.

Wave border in the bathroom of the former Prosper Champion home, Flint, Michigan. *Courtesy of Jim Fitzell and Jessica Higgins.*

Other examples of 2" x 6" border tiles with wave motifs can be found in the collection of Ken Galvas in amber and pink as well as sky (or water) blue. The former is *Catalog "G"* stock design no. 6687, while the latter is stock design no. 6626.

Raised line border tile, stock design no. 6687, measuring 6" x 2". $30-50.

Wave tile and checkerboard border tile, stock design nos. 6620 and 6626, each measuring 6" x 2". $30-50 each.

Wheatsworth Factory

The exterior walls of the original Old Stone Mill dating to 1808 still comprise a portion of the Wheatsworth Factory, which stands today on the banks of the Wallkill River near Hamburg, New Jersey. While the milling site changed hands a number of times over the years, it was not acquired by the F.H. Bennett Co. until 1921; that company later incorporated the trademark "Wheatsworth Company." (Fischer, 2003, 12) In greatly expanded facilities, Wheatsworth Mills, as it was later known, produced products such as stone ground crackers and other cereal-related products familiar to most contemporary consumers today.

Postcard of the Old Stone Mill in Hamburg, New Jersey. *Courtesy of Margaret Carney.*

In 1928, Bennett, the owner of Wheatsworth Mills, hired the famous set designer Joseph Urban to design an imaginative Gingerbread Castle next to the factory for the amusement of area children. Although there is no evidence of Flint Faience tile in this surrealist dream castle, at least one article published in 1930, when the Gingerbread Castle opened, noted that these tiles were utilized. An article in Vol. II, No. 10, October 1930 of *Keramic Tile Journal* photographed the castle and Old Mill with the entranceway columns clearly visible. While the Castle has no discernible tile, the stone entranceway columns have inset panels of Flint Faience tiles.

Entrance to the Old Mill at the Wheatsworth Factory, Hamburg, New Jersey. *Courtesy of Joseph G. Catullo.*

Gingerbread Castle at the Wheatsworth Factory, Hamburg, New Jersey. *Courtesy of Joseph G. Catullo.*

A series of twenty allegorical panels in Flint Faience featuring the theme of agriculture were created by Flint Faience and Tile Company Art Director Howard B. Burton prior to April 1929, when an announcement about them was published in the *AC Sparks* issue. Sixteen of the panels are set into stone pillars at the entrance to the mill's courtyard and on either side of the road at the edge of the mill property. Each is comprised of fifteen tiles surrounded by border tiles depicting sheaves of wheat. All most closely resemble the Arts & Crafts style of design in terms of the treatment of trees, landscape, buildings, and flowers. All of the sixteen panels relate to agriculture and specifically to the history of Wheatsworth and their products. For example, one panel is titled "Wheatsworth Mills Entrance," another "Wheatsworth Mills Cereal A Natural Food 100% Whole Wheat." One panel illustrates a stack of steaming pancakes and is titled "Wheatsworth Mills Flour Whole Wheat Self-Rising Flour." The Old Stone Mill is represented more than once as the raised line design on the tile panels.

Entrance panel at the Wheatsworth Factory, Hamburg, New Jersey. *Courtesy of Joseph G. Catullo.*

"Old Stone Mill" panel at the Wheatsworth Factory, Hamburg, New Jersey. *Courtesy of Joseph G. Catullo.*

"Flour" panel at the Wheatsworth Factory, Hamburg, New Jersey. *Courtesy of Joseph G. Catullo.*

"Cereal" panel at the Wheatsworth Factory, Hamburg, New Jersey. *Courtesy of Joseph G. Catullo.*

One of numerous allegorical tiled murals with the theme of agriculture, located at the Wheatsworth Factory, Hamburg, New Jersey. *Courtesy of Joseph G. Catullo.*

The Wheatsworth Factory site is remarkable in scope as it additionally contains four more larger outdoor tiled murals, each containing from twenty to thirty-three tiles. One magnificent panel consists of six large tiles with a design of the blazing sun in raised line process shining down on a wheat field, surrounded by border and corner tiles depicting wheat sheaves and mill stones. This is inset into a stone wall between the Gingerbread Castle and the Wheatsworth Factory, and nearby is a long tiled mural depicting fields being plowed, sown, and harvested. Equally impressive are the two identical tiled panels titled *Agriculture – Egypt*, one set into the exterior wall of the nearby restaurant, the Castle Grill, and the other in front of the Gingerbread Castle, set into another free standing stone wall. At least one other identical version of these two twin panels exists outside of Hamburg, New Jersey, with one in the AC/Delphi Plant in Flint, Michigan. Why two identical panels were installed at this one site is unknown. One has the border of wheat sheaves (near the castle) and the other does not (Castle Grill). For additional information on the other versions of *Agriculture — Egypt,* see that individual entry in this book.

"Sun" panel at the Wheatsworth Factory, Hamburg, New Jersey. *Courtesy of Joseph G. Catullo.*

Large "Wheat Cycle" allegorical panel depicting the plowing, sowing, and harvesting of wheat at the Wheatsworth Factory, Hamburg, New Jersey. *Courtesy of Joseph G. Catullo.*

Winter, Ezra

Ezra Winter, the muralist who collaborated with Flint Faience & Tile Company to create the Melville Shoe Corporation panel signage in Worcester, Massachusetts (see illustrations, page 211), was born in Manistee, Michigan on March 10, 1886. While educated at Olivet College, he was only twenty-two years old when he entered the Chicago Academy of Fine Arts. After graduation, he studied in Europe for five years, receiving the Prix de Rome. He was accordingly entitled to three years of study at the American Academy in Rome, where he was first interested in portraiture, and later he gravitated toward mural painting. His resulting successful career as a muralist in the United States included murals in the Library of Congress and the United States Chamber of Commerce Building in Washington, D.C., plus Rockefeller Center and the Guaranty Trust Buildings in New York City. He died April 6, 1949 at the age of sixty-three.

Y.M.C.A.'s

see Swimming Pools

Zodiac

It appears that one either loves or hates these cartoonish zodiac figure tiles created by Howard B. Burton (1881-1950), Art Director and Architect for the Flint Faience and Tile Company. In the April 1929 issue of *AC Sparks*, it was noted that the zodiacs "were treated in satyrical spirit instead of the conventional hackneyed figures found in the patent medicine almanacs of grandmother's day." (AC Spark Plug Company, 1929, 4) One set was exhibited in 1928 at the Metropolitan Museum of Art along with the American Federation of Arts traveling exhibition. Private collectors have avidly sought these small, strange figural tiles decorated with the twelve symbols of the zodiac.

A complete set of zodiac tiles can be seen in a circa 1926-30 black and white photograph of the fireplace facing in the Mount Vernon, New York, home of their designer, Howard B. Burton.

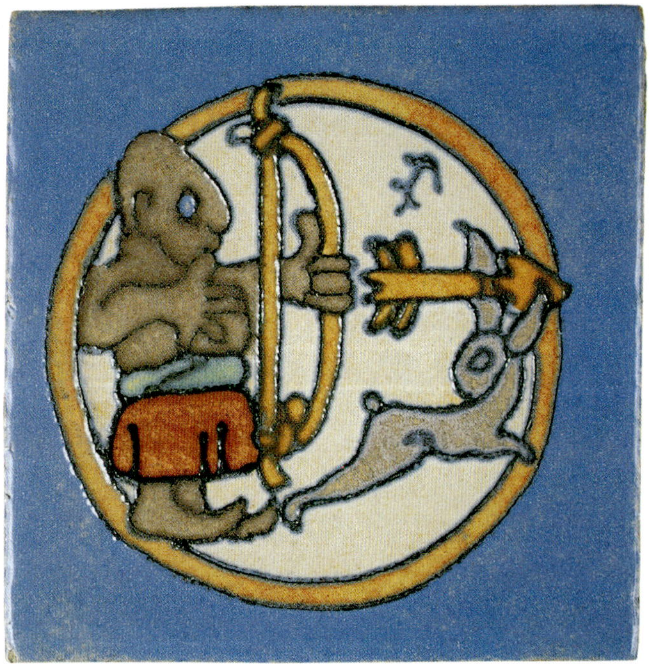

Sagittarius zodiac tile, measuring 4.25" x 4.25". $450-550.

Aries zodiac tile, measuring 4.25" x 4.25". $450-550. *Courtesy of Roger Ellingsworth.*

Aquarius zodiac tile, measuring 4.25" x 4.25". $450-550.

Fireplace in the home of Howard Burton, Art Director at Flint Faience, showing a complete set of zodiac tiles. *Courtesy of Kristine Burton, granddaughter of Howard Burton.*

Other stock designs featuring zodiac symbols can be found on page 24 in *Catalog "G."* These were intended to be used as decorative inserts for walls and floors. They were advertised as 2.75" square, a special size for random field designs in sun rooms. All featured inlay process decoration. Stock design numbers included nos. 6564-6575 and nos. 6409 and 6410.

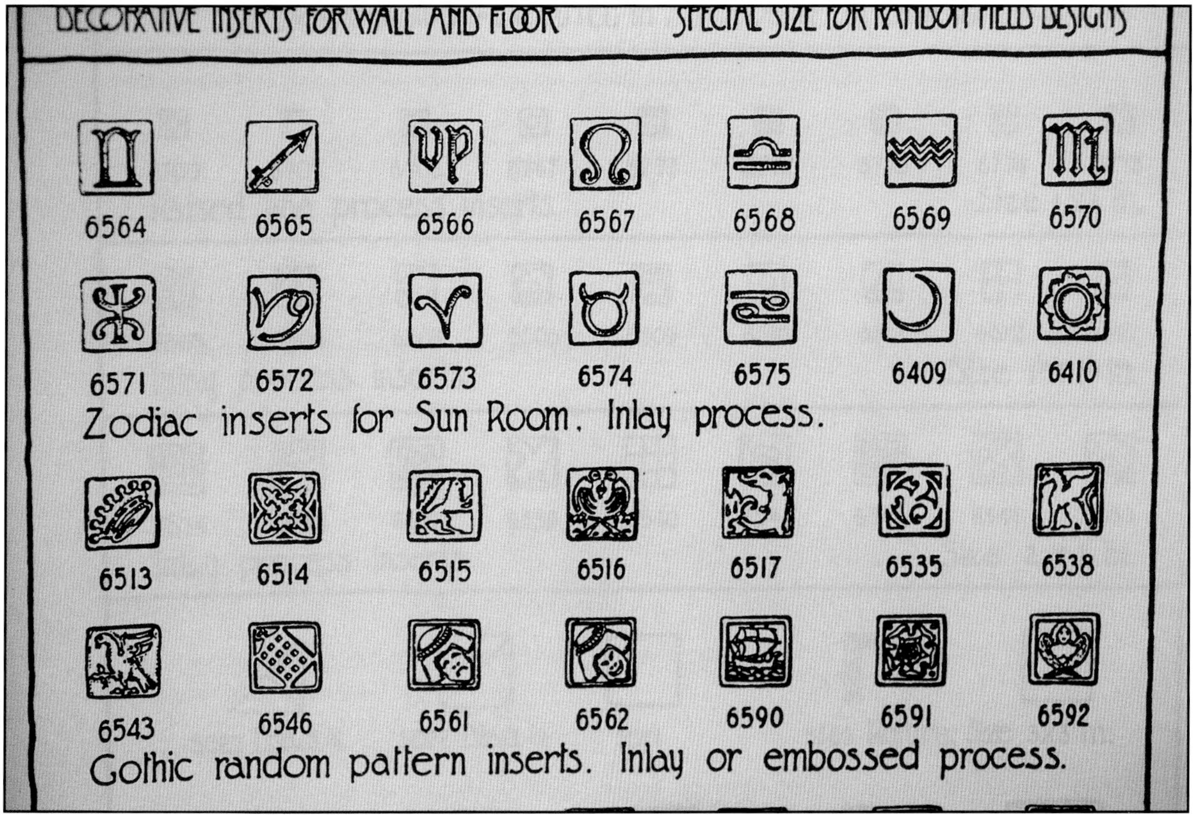

DECORATIVE INSERTS FOR WALL AND FLOOR SPECIAL SIZE FOR RANDOM FIELD DESIGNS

6564 6565 6566 6567 6568 6569 6570

6571 6572 6573 6574 6575 6409 6410

Zodiac inserts for Sun Room. Inlay process.

6513 6514 6515 6516 6517 6535 6538

6543 6546 6561 6562 6590 6591 6592

Gothic random pattern inserts. Inlay or embossed process.

Page 24 of *Catalog "G,"* showing a set of zodiac tiles.

The former Taine McDougal home, now owned by Linda and Joe Katrinic, Jr., located in Flint, Michigan, contains a small but exquisitely tiled entrance foyer featuring a central 18" diameter tiled compass comprised of nine pieces (see illustrations and description under separate entry for Compass) and the twelve 4.25" square zodiac figural tile inserts installed amongst a dark brownish black glazed tiled background. Taine McDougal was a ceramic engineer, graduating from the Ohio State University in 1911. He briefly conducted ceramic research for the United States government before beginning his career as a ceramic engineer at AC Spark Plug in 1914. He retired from AC in 1954 as director of spark plug engineering. Other notable achievements include his work on the atomic bomb and his ability to obtain an endorsement of AC plugs after Charles Lindbergh's famed flight in the Spirit of St. Louis.

Cluster of three zodiac tiles as installed in the former Taine McDougal home in Flint, Michigan. *Courtesy of Linda and Joseph Katrinic Jr.*

Foyer in the former home of Taine McDougal in Flint, Michigan, showing a complete set of zodiac tiles around a large center compass. *Courtesy of Linda and Joseph Katrinic Jr.*

Cluster of three zodiac tiles as installed in the former Taine McDougal home in Flint, Michigan. *Courtesy of Linda and Joseph Katrinic Jr.*

Cluster of three zodiac tiles as installed in the former Taine McDougal home in Flint, Michigan. *Courtesy of Linda and Joseph Katrinic Jr.*

The Sloan Museum in Flint, Michigan, has a set of 4" x 6" index cards with watercolor pattern illustrations of the zodiac figure tiles created by Howard B. Burton, and containing the Flint Faience glaze numbers that correspond with the appropriate hues for each tile. These are identical to those installed in the former Taine McDougal home in Flint, Michigan.

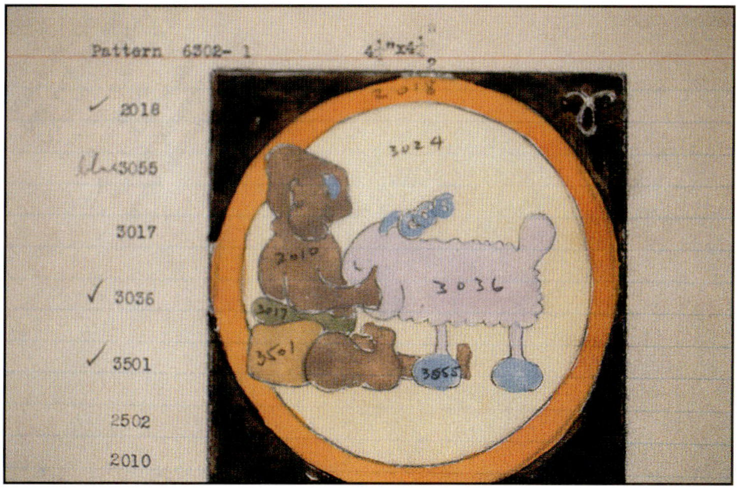

Aries zodiac watercolor sketch on an index card. *Courtesy of the Alfred P. Sloan Museum.*

Cluster of three zodiac tiles as installed in the foyer of the former Taine McDougal home in Flint, Michigan. *Courtesy of Linda and Joseph Katrinic Jr.*

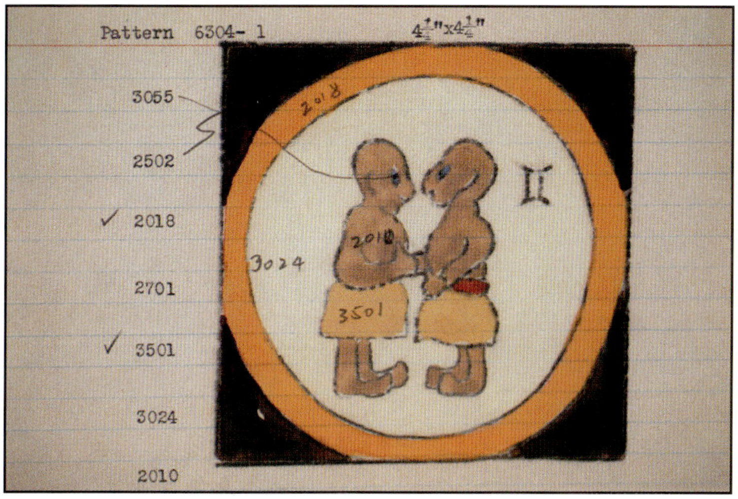

Gemini zodiac watercolor sketch on an index card. *Courtesy of the Alfred P. Sloan Museum.*

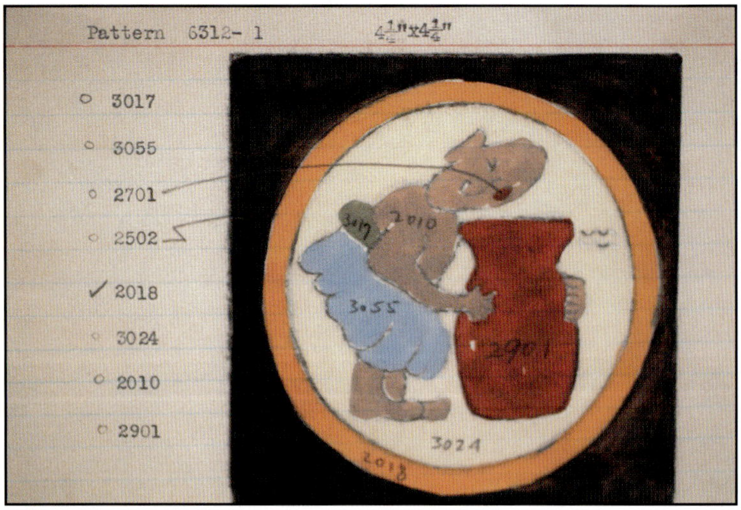

Aquarius zodiac watercolor sketch on an index card. *Courtesy of the Alfred P. Sloan Museum.*

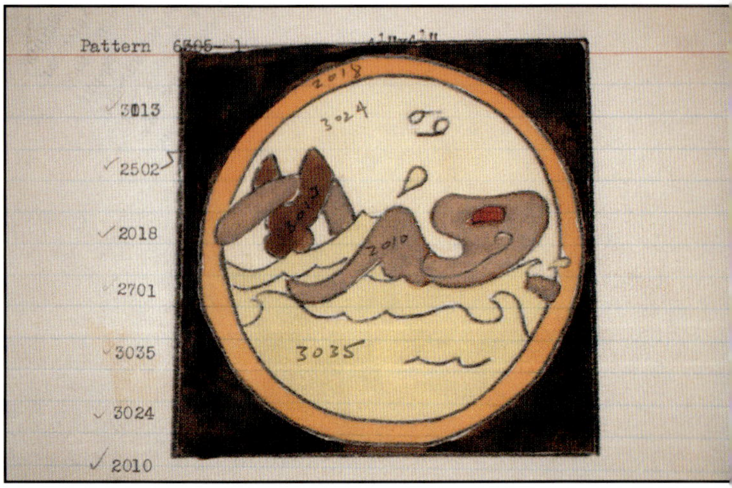

Cancer zodiac watercolor sketch on an index card. *Courtesy of the Alfred P. Sloan Museum.*

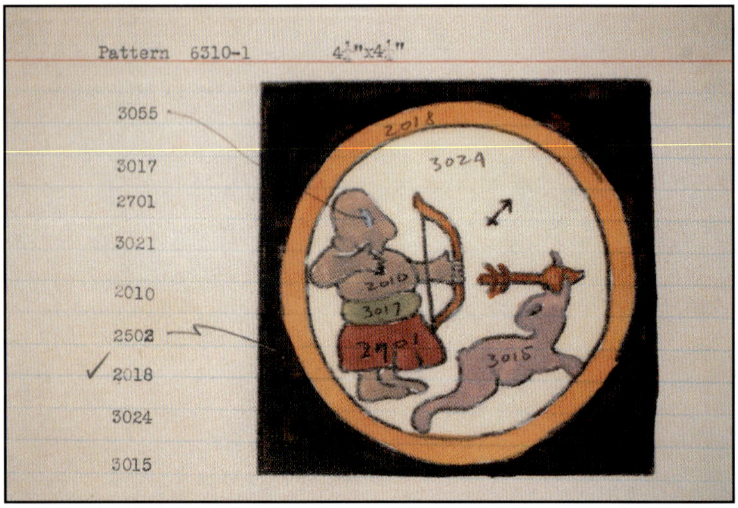

Sagittarius zodiac watercolor sketch on an index card. *Courtesy of the Alfred P. Sloan Museum.*

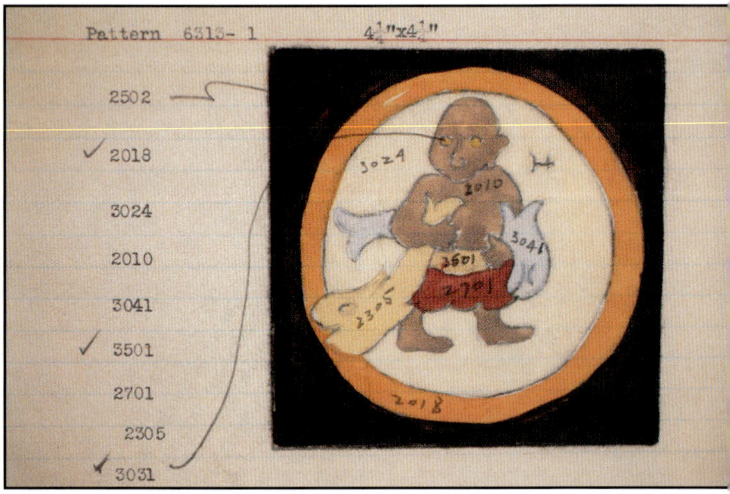

Pisces zodiac watercolor sketch on an index card. *Courtesy of the Alfred P. Sloan Museum.*

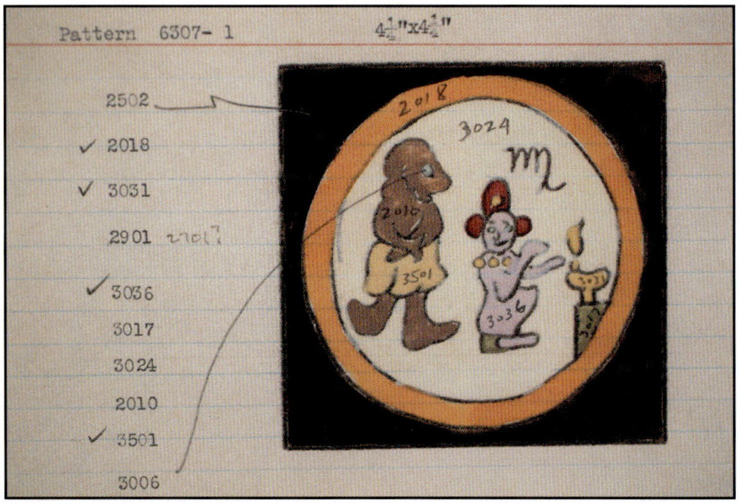

Virgo zodiac watercolor sketch on an index card. *Courtesy of the Alfred P. Sloan Museum.*

Leo zodiac watercolor sketch on an index card. *Courtesy of the Alfred P. Sloan Museum.*

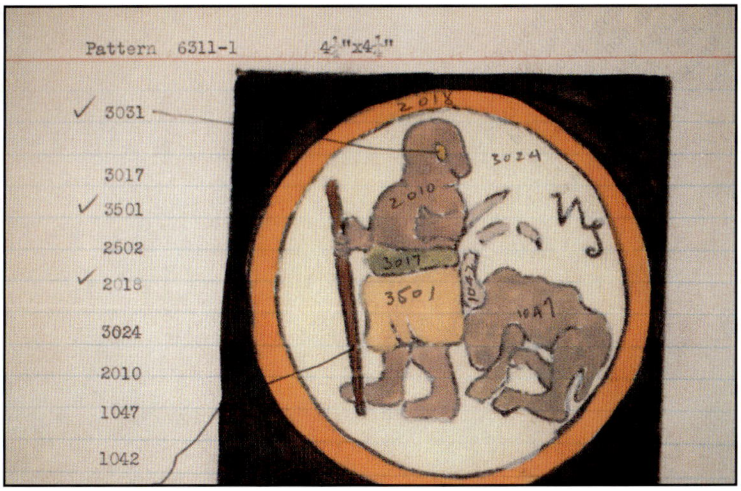

Capricorn zodiac watercolor sketch on an index card. *Courtesy of the Alfred P. Sloan Museum.*

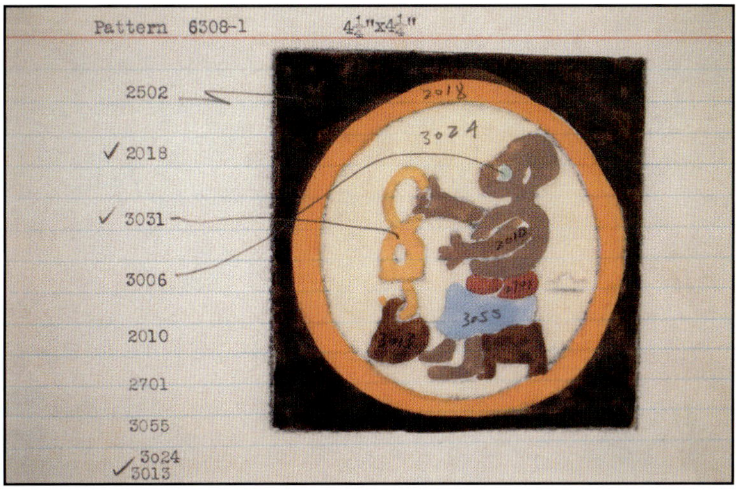

Libra zodiac watercolor sketch on an index card. *Courtesy of the Alfred P. Sloan Museum.*

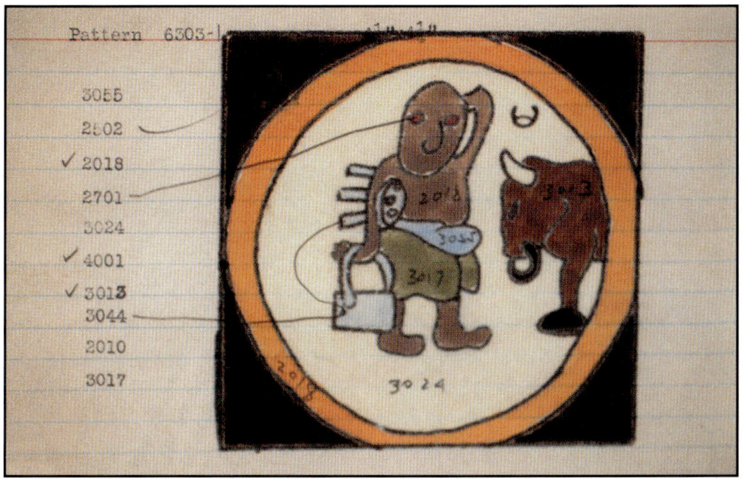

Taurus zodiac watercolor sketch on an index card. *Courtesy of the Alfred P. Sloan Museum.*

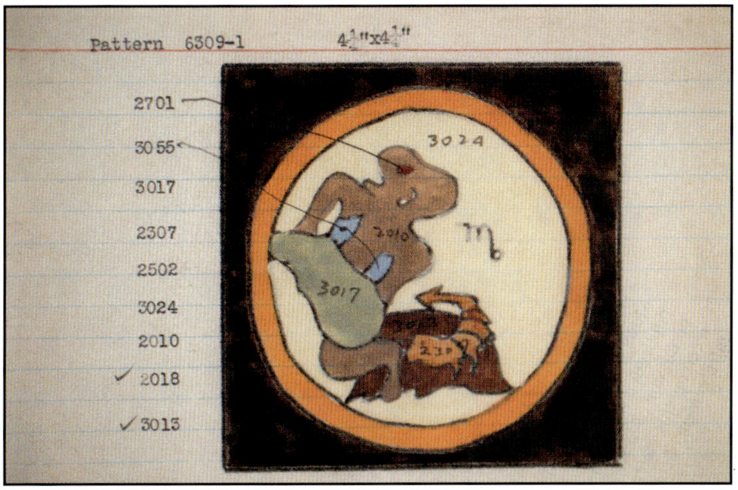

Scorpio zodiac watercolor sketch on an index card. *Courtesy of the Alfred P. Sloan Museum.*

Another complete set of twelve 4.25" square figural zodiac tiles is in the collection of Bill Shesko. Each decorated tile has a dark brown glazed background. The same style decoration can be seen on a large 13.25" diameter zodiac table top, also in the collection of Bill Shesko. The large central panel is encircled by smaller marine blue tiles. Another round zodiac tile, measuring 10.5" diameter, with Aquarius as the theme, is in the collection of the Everson Museum of Art in Syracuse, New York (acc. no. 90.250.115, gift of Mary and Paul Brandwein).

Twelve zodiac tiles in the collection of Bill Shesko, each measuring 4.25" x 4.25". *Courtesy of www.BungalowBill.com.*

Zodiac table top, diameter13.25". *Courtesy of www.BungalowBill.com.*

Probably the most stunning installation of zodiac tiles is that at the present day Villa St. Elizabeth owned by Evergreen Elder Care, Inc. in Reading, Pennsylvania. Constructed in 1926, it is the former Gustav Oberlander home located at 1201 Museum Road. Gustav Oberlander was a major force in the textile industry in America. The fabulous Flint Faience tile installation at the Villa St. Elizabeth is a 6' diameter panel featuring a central tile symbolizing the universe and encircled by flame designs, with twelve large zodiac roundels on the outer realm. Earlier, this installation had been identified as being from the Enfield Pottery and Tile Works, though the existence of watercolor sketches and numerous similar zodiac tile installations clearly created by Flint Faience lead one to believe that this installation, also, is from Flint Faience and not Enfield. The true confirmation of this piece being created at Flint Faience is the discovery that the centermost design pattern is the conjoined HBB signature of Howard B. Burton, art director and architect for the company. This signature is consistent with the one on the title page of the 1929 publication *Architectural Faience: An Introduction.*

Overview of a zodiac tile installation in the former Gustav Oberlander home in Reading, Pennsylvania. *Courtesy of Villa St. Elizabeth. Photos by Dave Zerbe Studios.*

Taurus the Bull zodiac tile, part of the installation in the former home of Gustav Oberlander, Reading, Pennsylvania. *Courtesy of Villa St. Elizabeth. Photos by Dave Zerbe Studios.*

Aquarius zodiac tile, part of the installation in the former home of Gustav Oberlander, Reading, Pennsylvania. *Courtesy of Villa St. Elizabeth. Photo by Dave Zerbe Studios.*

Gemini zodiac tile, part of the installation in the former home of Gustav Oberlander, Reading, Pennsylvania. *Courtesy of Villa St. Elizabeth. Photo by Dave Zerbe Studios.*

Universe Symbol in the center of the zodiac installation in the former Gustav Oberlander home in Reading, Pennsylvania. Note monogram of Howard B. Burton, zodiac designer, in the center. *Courtesy of Villa St. Elizabeth. Photo by Dave Zerbe Studios.*

Pricing

Antique tiles have become one of the fastest growing areas of interest in the field of pottery collecting. No more are they to be considered the poor cousin to the traditional forms of collecting. As more books are published, giving collectors a greater sense of buying confidence, the future will grow even brighter for the tile fan. However, for those that are new to this area of collecting, a few points may need to be discussed.

The first of these would be that tiles were meant to be functional. Unlike a vase that would get occasionally filled with flowers then be set aside in a cabinet, tiles were taking daily abuse in the shower, swimming pool, fireplace, fountain, or foyer. Many tiles have survived more than a hundred years in the heat of the summer sun or the in the icy blasts of winter. These pieces of clay have earned their place in the hearts of collectors. Because tiles have been exposed to harsh conditions during their lifetime it is normal to find flaws on some tiles. These minor flaws, such as craze lines, minor scratches, and light wear to high points, will not destroy the value of a tile as much as a minor flaw would devalue an art pottery vase. This not to say that collectors do not make adjustments in the amount of money they are willing to pay for a tile, it simply means that tile collectors realize it is not always possible to wait for a factory mint piece. Factory mint or pristine tiles are those that have survived the years without damage, and have never been installed. They usually come from the leftover stock of businesses that have folded, or after having found their way into the homes or collections of company employees. Factory mint tiles command the highest prices in the marketplace. An exception to this rule, and there are a few, would be if someone purchased a reclaimed or salvaged tile for sentimental reasons – there is no price guide for sentimental value. Tiles purchased for sentimental reasons or other personal interests generally carry prices that are hard to justify in the minds of other collectors. When these types of sales are reported in the public arena we are left to wonder "why did that piece go so high?" These spikes in prices complicate the problem of setting a reasonable range of values for a book such as this. Many people who have become accustomed to buying only pristine condition pottery may pass up some wonderful items before they realize that they may never find a piece like the one they just let slip though their fingers. The Flint Faience and Tile Company produced a multitude of one-of-a-kind designs and if we wait for a mint item of a particular design we may regret it. The collector must decide for himself how many imperfections he could live with and whether a particular piece could be reasonably restored.

Deinstalled tiles will be a major source of inventory for future collectors. Many of the great buildings that we have today will fall to the wrecking ball of tomorrow. When this happens, we must hope that legitimate contractors or salvagers will save these tile treasures for future generations. Salvaged tile will come with some mortar on the backs and sides and generally some chipping on the perimeter of the tiles. With careful cleaning and the addition of frames these tiles will regain most of their former glory. Once these pieces of art are back on the wall, few collectors make apologies for them.

Tile pricing is complicated by factors other than condition. We have to determine how we want to use or display a tile to help us determine how much we will pay for it. Shapes also play a strong role in setting the price of any tile. A large tile with an uncommon shape will find fewer collectors than a similarly designed tile with a more common shape. Similarly, tiles that have a bullnose edge (i.e., one that is curved to finish against a wall) or base tiles designed to finish against a floor will carry smaller price tags than one that is square on all sides. Architectural panels several inches thick with odd shapes will also find a smaller core of collectors. This is due to the problem of finding creative ways to display such tiles without expensive framing. We can use only so many bookends and doorstops. Large tiles will still manage to bring strong prices if they bear great art.

Subject matter will also play a role in the pricing of tiles. Presently, collectors are willing to pay premium prices for tiles with strong Arts & Crafts styling. Children, ships, nursery rhymes, animals, and tiles with an Art Deco flavor are also in vogue. These would generally garner more interest than a tile with a simple geometric design. The fact is that tile collectors collect tiles for as many varied reasons as there are tiles. No price guide will be accurate in all instances. We should collect what we like and pay whatever we feel comfortable paying. Some tiles will jump up in price while others will level off or may even drop some in price if large quantities of a particular pattern suddenly flood the marketplace. From time to time forgotten boxes of leftover stock do find their way into flea markets and shows. An overabundance of a pattern will affect prices of that pattern. This sort of occurrence happens rarely though. Our level of buying comfort will be determined by how much we understand the tile we seek.

The prices quoted with the captions in this book reflect prices most often seen paid by collectors. The author has gathered sales information from dealers, collectors, hobbyists, auction houses, and Internet auctions in an attempt to give the user the best reflection of what is happening in the marketplace. In the past, the prices of Flint Faience tiles were victims of the company's reluctance to advertise in the popular magazines and newspapers of the day. This decision not to advertise in the popular printed media left the collector of today with little written material to adequately assess the quality and scope of this artistic endeavor. Up till now, it has been the savvy collector who has realized that the hand built gems created by Flint Faience were undervalued in the marketplace. Serious collectors have quietly been buying up as many of these treasures as they can find, before the rest of the world discovers them. With the release of this book, new tile collectors will now have information to make knowledgeable purchasing decisions about the tile produced at Flint Faience. This should lead to more competition for the better tiles and an appreciable increase of prices in coming years.

Installations or Public Collections

Listed Alphabetically by Location

The following is a listing of documented Flint Faience installations or public collections, with notations if the site is known to have been demolished.

California

Los Angeles
Mrs. Oakley Thorne; residence

Connecticut

New Canann
New Canann High School

Delaware

Wilmington
Mrs. Dupont Laird; residence

Florida

Miami
Oakland-Pontiac; automobile showroom

St. Petersburg
Vinoy Park Hotel; promenade

Georgia

Atlanta
Fox Theatre in the Yaarab Temple; fountain, wall installations

Illinois

Chicago
Park Gables Apartments; swimming pool
Wharton residence; living room

Massachusetts

Belmont
McLean Hospital; hydrotherapy suite, demolished

South Dartmouth
Col. E.H.R. Green residence; tile compass with nautical motifs, set in center of tile-paved terrace

Worcester
Melville Shoe Corporation; exterior tile sign, designed by Ezra Winter, c. 1928

Michigan

Ann Arbor
Lorch Hall, University of Michigan; entranceway floor signage

Birmingham
Barnum School; kindergarten fireplace in old library

Bloomfield Hills
Brookside School; fountain

Dearborn
Henry Ford Elementary School; fireplace, drinking fountains

Detroit
Cadillac; showroom
Frank Couzen; residence
E&B Brewery; building exterior
Fisher Building; cafeteria, 1927-29
Fort Shelby Hotel; restaurant
General Motors Building; auto showroom, cafeteria
John Marshall School; kindergarten room sandbox, sink, drinking fountain, and exterior tiles
Koether residence; bathroom, 1923
Leland Hotel; demolished
Oldsmobile; showroom
Tam O'Shanter Club; removed during renovations
St. Paul's Church
University of Detroit Chapel, Faculty Building (Reilly Hall); altar arch, walls, chapel aisle floor, and Commerce Building
University of Detroit High School
Walker's Lunch
Webster Hall
Y.M.C.A.
Y.W.C.A.; swimming pool

Flint
AC Plant, Dort Highway and Davison Roads; exterior signage "Flint Faience Tiles – A General Motors Product" and old tiled employees entrance, Plant 2 West
George A. Barnes; residence, destroyed by a fire in 1955

Cadillac-LaSalle Sales; gas station and garage floor
Prosper Champion residence; exterior heraldic shields, fireplace, sunroom, bathrooms
Cody Elementary School; field tile accents and iridescent 3" x 3" tiles above the entrances
George C. Conn; residence
Crapo Farm; sign/plaque of head of Hereford cattle, now at University of Michigan, Flint campus
H.H. Curtice; residence
Delphi, Plant 2 West; stairwell to second floor, "Agriculture...Egypt" mural, also Administration Building "B" lobby, and Ceramics Research Lab
E.A. DeWater; residence
First National Bank Building; upper floor hallways, removed during renovations
Arthur Freeman; residence
Leonard Freeman; residence
Garfield Elementary School; exterior tiles and signage
Halo Burger, formerly site of Vernor's Headquarters, built c. 1928-30; interior and exterior tile work
IMA (Industrial Mutual Association) Auditorium; demolished, two plaques salvaged (depicting basketball and boxing gloves), now in the collection of the Sloan Museum; etc.
Robert T. Longway residence; three bathrooms
Taine McDougal home; zodiac and large compass
Martin Elementary School; field tile accents on the exterior, 4x4 tiles in a 4-tile pattern diamond shape
John Pierce residence
Pierson Elementary School; tiles similar to those at Garfield Elementary School, large open book murals
Sacred Heart Catholic Church; raised line design accent tiles
A.H. Sarvis; residence
J.C. Shaw; residence
Sloan Museum, collection: "AC" mural, formerly on exterior of crosswalk between factory buildings straddling Industrial Avenue, currently on exhibition; "Body By Fisher" sign; Flint-shaped sign; "Ceramics" and "Architecture" round tiles; "Tree of Life" 24-tile mural, each tile 8" square, mural size 23-3/4" x 63", currently in storage at the Alfred Sloan Museum, Flint, Michigan, donated by Dick Pohrt to the Genesee County Historical Society in 1955 and subsequently donated by the Historical Society in 1965, acc. No. 65.40.69; IMA plaques (listed above under IMA Auditorium); tile from Winchester Hospital, acc. No. 2000.741; etc.
St. Matthews Catholic Church; floors, sanctuary area
St. Paul's Episcopal Church; field tile and raised line tile
Edwin Sterner Company; display room, demolished
Edward T. Strong residence, President of Buick Motor Company; conservatory, sunroom, hallways, bathrooms, kitchen
Dr. Alvin Thompson; residence
Winchester Hospital (tile now in collection of Sloan Museum – see above listing); demolished by Burnash Wrecking of Flint
Y.M.C.A.; lobby floor, demolished
Y.W.C.A.; demolished
Zimmerman Elementary School; field tile accents on the exterior, 4x4 tiles in a 4-tile pattern diamond shape

Grosse Pointe
Grosse Pointe Memorial Church; floor aisles and sanctuary
Alvan Maccauley residence; built 1931, demolished
St. Paul's Church; fireplace

Grosse Pointe Shores
Edsel B. and Eleanor Ford residence; twelve tiled bathrooms, plus kitchen, butler's pantry, and basement floor, c. 1927

Jackson
H.H. Bassett Mausoleum; moved physically from Flint to Jackson, Michigan

Monroe
Motherhouse, Sisters, Servants of the Immaculate Heart of Mary; recently renovated

St. Clair
Lake Shore High School, built 1928; drinking fountain tiles, moved in early 1928 to Violet Elementary, Rodgers Elementary, and Masonic Heights Elementary schools.
South Lake, built 1927; nursery rhyme tiles in fireplace and sandbox, demolished

Wyandotte
Washington School; kindergarten sandbox and fountain, two fireplaces
Garfield School; kindergarten sandbox, fountain and fireplace

Missouri

St. Louis
Vesper Buick; automobile showroom

New Jersey

Atlantic City
Childs Restaurant
Jefferson Hotel; lunette with ship motifs

Hamburg
Wheatsworth Factory and Gingerbread House; allegorical panels

Rumson
Dalton Residence; Flintcraft mural, Apelles "Anadyomene"

New York

Alfred
Schein-Joseph International Museum of Ceramic Art; collection, six of eight custom tiles originally from Merrill Hall, Alfred University, circa 1929-32

Flushing
Gugenheim; residence

New Rochelle
Mr. Francis Hunter residence; fountain

New York
Brokaw; residence
Central Savings Bank
Dryden Apartment Hotel; tiled loggia, lobby renovated, status unknown except for a few in the basement area
Helena Rubenstein; showroom
Hotel Murray
Molla Mallory; residence
Alice Foot McDougall; restaurant
Park Avenue bathroom
San Carlos Hotel; renovated without saving the tiles
S.P.C.A. Building
Woolworth stores
Eugene Zukor residence; bathroom

Poncantico Hills
John D. Rockefeller residence; Kykuit Playhouse, swimming pool, 1925-27

Ronkonkoma
Cenacle Convent

Syracuse
Everson Museum of Art; collection, fourteen tiles
Howard Yates, architect; residence, mid-1920s, fireplace and riser tiles

Warwick
Warwick Masonic Lodge; entranceways and window sills

Ohio

Cleveland
Juvenile Court Building; collection of twenty-five tiles now on loan to the Western Reserve Historical Society
Mr. W.S. Ferguson; residence

Columbus
Baggs Memorial Library Collection, Art Department, Hopkins Hall, the Ohio State University; three tiles

Shaker Heights
Shaker Heights First Baptist Church, circa 1928; presentation drawings

Westerville
Ross C. Purdy Museum of Ceramics at American Ceramic Society; collection, five tiles

Oklahoma

Tulsa
Minck Hotel; section of lunch counter

Pennsylvania

Erie
Warner Theatre; fireplace facings

Philadelphia
Roberts-Nash; showroom
Cadillac; showroom
Packard; showroom

Reading
Gustav Oberlander residence, 1926; 6' diameter zodiac panel set in terrace pavement (now the Villa St. Elizabeth)

Peru

Presidential palace; bathroom

Puerto Rico

San Juan
United States Custom House; four lunettes, bathrooms, stairwells

Washington, D.C.

Mayflower Hotel

Wisconsin

Sheboygan
Kohler Company; Italian style bathroom

Bibliography

AC Spark Plug Company. *AC Sparks*. Flint, Michigan, August 1928.

_____. *AC Sparks Flint Faience Tile Number,* 3, no. 4 (April 1929).

_____. Unpublished transcript, *Report on Survey of Tile Plant,* received by McDougal in Paris, August 27, 1928.

AC Spark Plug Division. Unpublished typescript, *Chronological Story of the AC Spark Plug Division*, c. 1967.

AC Spark Plug Division of General Motors. *AC 25-Year Club, First Annual Dinner*. Hotel Durant, December 15, 1947, brochure including "A Brief History of AC."

_____. "Factory Art: Flint Faience Lives On." *ACtion* (March/April/May 1981): n.p.

_____. *1908-1984, A History of AC Spark Plug Division*. Flint, Michigan: General Motors Corp., 1984.

American Architect. "Interior Architecture: Nineteen Twenty-Eight Contributes to A Modern American Style." (January 5, 1929): 32-33, 37, 44-45.

American Ceramic Society Bulletin. "Who's Where in the American Ceramic Society?" 2, nos. 1, 2 (February 1923): 10.

_____. "Activities of the Society (Samuel J. McDowell)." 5, no. 1 (January 1926): 75.

_____. "Report of the Chairman of the Exhibition Committee (Art Division)." 6, no. 4 (April 1927): 109.

_____. "Notes and News – Obituary – Albert Champion." 6, no. 12 (December 1927): 373-375.

_____. "Personal News From Members of the Society." 7, no. 4 (April 1928): 96.

_____. "News From Members of the Society." 7, no. 11 (November 1928): 329.

_____. "American Ceramic Society Headquarters." 9, no. 3 (March 1930): 63.

_____. "Lamme Medal Presented to Taine Gilbert McDougal." 24, no. 8 (August 15, 1945): 289.

American Federation of Arts. *International Exhibition of Ceramic Art: Catalogue 1928, 1929*. Portland, Maine: The Southworth Press, 1928.

Andrews, Wayne. *Architecture in Michigan*. Detroit, Michigan: Wayne State University Press, 1982.

Bergmans, Carl. "Modern Ceramics of Art." *American Ceramic Society Bulletin*, 5, no. 2 (February 1926): 161-163.

Bridenstine, James A. *Edsel & Eleanor Ford House*. Woodlawn, Maryland: Wolk Press, Inc., 1988.

Burton, Howard B. "You've Got to Know Your Product." *Keramic Tile Journal*, 2, no. 4 (April 1930): 27-29.

_____. "Has Old Man Tile Been Too Busy Bailing Out To Notice What Is Passing?" *Keramic Tile Journal*, 4, no. 1 (January 1932): 21-23, 30.

Carney, Margaret. *Charles Fergus Binns: The Father of American Studio Ceramics*. New York, New York: Hudson Hills Press, 1998.

_____. "Flint Faience Sparks Interest." *Style 1900*, 16, no. 2 (Spring/Summer/May 2003): 60-67.

Ceramic Industry. "Boom for Faience Seen." 6, no. 1 (January 1926): 500.

_____."Form Flint (Mich.) Faience & Tile Co." 7, no. 2 (August 1926): 158.

_____. "What The Other Fellow Is Doing – Notes Culled From Glass, Enamel, Pottery, Refractories and Terra Cotta Fields." 10, no. 2 (February 1928): 212.

_____. "What The Other Fellow Is Doing – Notes Culled From Glass, Enamel, Pottery, Refractories and Terra Cotta Fields." 10, no. 3 (March 1928): 322.

_____. "Water Cooled Tunnel Kiln Burning Tile." 13, no. 1 (July 1929): 48-52.

_____. "Flint Tile Adopts Trademark." 3, no. 2 (August 1929): 194.

_____. "Flint Has Fine Catalog on Tile Work." 13, no. 6 (December 1929): 612.

_____. "New Building for Ceramic Department of Alfred University." 17, no. 6 (December 1931): 498.

_____. "Touring a Century of Progress for the Ceramist." 21, no. 1 (July 1933): 40.

Commission on Chicago Landmarks and the Chicago Department of Planning and Development. *Chicago Historical Resources Survey*. Chicago, Illinois: 1996.

Cox, George J. *Pottery – For Artists Craftsmen & Teachers*. New York, New York: The MacMillan Company, 1930.

Crawford, Kim. "Mexican émigré helped AC mold artistic past in clay." *Flint Journal*, September 19, 1982.

Curry, Ralph B. "AC Takes Over Plant on Dort." *Flint Journal*, April 4, 1936.

Derwich and Latos. *Dictionary Guide to U.S. Pottery and Porcelain*. "Flint Faience Tile Company, Flint, Michigan," n.d.: 91.

Eckert, Kathryn Bishop. *Buildings of Michigan*. New York and Oxford: Oxford University Press, 1993.

Emmons, Ann C. "Sw. Creek hopes to buy an identity." *Flint Journal*, March 20, 1973.

Fehr, Beulah B. "Arts & Crafts Tiles in Berks County, PA." *Tile Heritage* 4, no. 1 (Summer 1997): 20-21.

Fischer, Suzanne and Cultural Resource Consulting Group. *Intensive-Level Architectural Survey Report, Bridge H9-01 Replacement, Gingerbread Castle Road Over Wallkill River, Borough of Hamburg, Sussex County, New Jersey, CRCG #02-73-01*. Prepared for Maser Consulting, June 2, 2003.

Flint Daily News/Flint Journal. "Flint Faience Tile in Merger." March 2, 1932.

Flint Faience Tile Company. *Flint Faience Tile Company – Plastic Hand-Made Tiles in Glazed Faience and Unglazed Vitreous Grès for Wall and Floor, Catalog "G."* Flint, Michigan: Flint Faience Tile Company, Division of AC Sparkplug Company, 1926.

_____. *Flint Faience Tile Company Tile Contractors' Price Schedule G-1*. Flint, Michigan, effective April 15, 1926.

_____. *Flint Faience Tile Company List Price Schedule G-2*. Flint, Michigan, effective April 15, 1926.

Flint Faience & Tile Company. *The AC Line*. Brochure for Flint Faience & Tile Co., c. late 1920s.

_____."Suggested Sales Plan & Policy for the Flint Faience & Tile Company." unpublished report, 1928.

_____. *Architectural Faience: An Introduction*. Flint, Michigan, 1929.

_____. *Bathroom Flyer A-303*. Flint, Michigan, 1929.

_____. *Floor Flyer A-304*. Flint, Michigan, 1929.

_____. "Faience – The Ideal Floor for the Automobile Salesroom." *Tile Industry Manual*, 1929.

Flint Journal. "A New Industry – said to be assured to the City of Flint – Champion Ignition Company to locate here as an accessory to automobile business." (September 29, 1908).

_____. "Albert Champion, Head of AC, Dies in Paris Hotel." (October 28, 1927).

_____. "New Flint Factory of the Flint Faience and Tile Co., Dort Highway at Davison Road." (January 1, 1929).

_____. "New Flint Plant Built to Meet National Demand for Flint Faience and Tile Products." (January 1, 1929).

_____. "Product of Flint Plant." (July 13, 1930).
_____. "From Flint Plant to New York." (July 20, 1930).
_____. "In a Little Spanish Bath." (July 27, 1930).
_____. "Modeling is New Institute Course." (September 28, 1930).
_____. Flint Institute of Arts exhibition. (March 29, 1931).
_____. "Tile Panel by Flint Artist." (November 15, 1931).
_____. "Tile Pool for Steamer Manufactured in Flint." (April 17, 1932).
_____. "AC's Pension Setup Headed By Morrissey." (October 4, 1953).
_____. "Historical Group to Hear Engineer." (March 15, 1955).
_____. "E.L. Morrissey, AC Retiree, Dies." (February 5, 1965).
_____. "Walkway to nowhere." (June 1, 1976).
_____. "St. Matthew Catholic Parish to celebrate 75th anniversary." (November 8, 1986): A9.

Flint Saturday Night. "Formal opening of the new quarters of the First National Bank and Trust Company was held this week." (March 29, 1930): 10.
_____. "Exhibition of the Flint Faience & Tile Company at the recent international tile convention in New Orleans." 3, no. 52 (May 3, 1930): 13.
_____. "The 'Ginger Bread House' at Hamburg, N.J." (September 13, 1930): 10.

Frisone, Mrs. "Some historical notes on Barnum Junior High School." Unpublished, typed manuscript, dated October 30, 1975.

Fuller, Lee N. "Large Flint Industry, Manufacture of Decorative Tile, Reaches Wide Field, Is Given Recognition In Art Centers." *Flint Journal*, (May 5, 1929).

Journal of the Tile and Mantel Contractors Association of America. "Something New in Tile." 2, no. 3 (August 1928): 2-33.

Karlson, Norman. *American Art Tile 1876-1941*. New York: Rizzoli, 1998.
_____. *American Art Tile Price Guide for Collectors*. New York: Rizzoli, August, 1998.

Keramic Tile Journal, 1, no. 7 (June 1929): 48.
_____, 1, no. 10 (September 1929): 19, 35.
_____, 2, no. 2 (February 1930): 3.
_____, 2, no. 3 (March 1930): 3.
_____, 2, no. 4 (April 1930): 3.
_____, 2, no. 5 (May 1930): 3, 33, 35.
_____, 2, no. 6 (June 1930): 3.
_____, 2, no. 7 (July 1930): 3.
_____, 2, no. 8 (August 1930): 3.
_____, 2, no. 9 (September 1930): 3.
_____, 2, no. 10 (October 1930): 3, 12-13.
_____, 2, no. 11 (November 1930): 3.
_____, 2, no. 12 (December 1930): 3.
_____, 3, no. 1 (January 1931): 3.
_____, 3, no. 2 (February 1931): 3.
_____, 3, no. 3 (March 1931): 3.
_____, 3, no. 4 (April 1931): 3, 41.
_____, 3, no. 5 (May 1931): 3.
_____, 3, no. 6 (June 1931): 3.
_____, 3, no. 7 (July 1931): 5.
_____, 3, no. 8 (August 1931): 5.
_____, 3, no. 9 (September 1931): 5.
_____, 3, no. 10 (October 1931): 5.
_____, 3, no. 11 (November 1931): 5.
_____, 3, no. 12 (December 1931): 5.
_____, 4, no. 1 (January 1932): 9, 34.
_____, 4, no. 2 (February, 1932): 6, 16.
_____, 4, no. 3 (March 1932): 27.
_____, 4, no. 4 (April 1932): 4-5.
_____, 4, no. 5 (May 1932): 5, 23.
_____, 4, no. 6 (June 1932): inside cover, 4, hospital booklet insert.
_____, 4, no. 8 (August 1932): inside cover, 24.
_____, 4, no. 10 (October 1932): 7.
_____, 4, no. 11 (November 1932): 4, 14.
_____, 5, no. 3 (March 1933): 22.

Koehler, Vance. "The Arts and Crafts Tile." *Flash Point 6*, no. 4 (October-December 1993): 3-8.
_____. "American Decorative Tiles 1880-1950." *American Art Tile 1880-1950*. Lambertville, NJ: David Rago Arts & Crafts Movement Gallery, June 25-July 17, 1994.
_____. "Handmade *Looking* Tiles." *Tile Heritage*, 3, no. 2 (Winter, 1996/97): 21-30.

Lakeside Directory of Chicago, 3, 1928.

Lethbridge, Alice. "Bill Thomas' Halo Burger, Inc." *Through the Years in Genesee*. Northridge, California: Windsor Publications, Inc., 1985.

McDougal, T.G. "History of AC Spark Plug, General Motors Corporation." *American Ceramic Society Bulletin*, Vol. 28, No. 11, November 15, 1949.

McDowell, Samuel J. and Perry D. Helser. "Data on the Operation of the Continuous Tunnel Kiln at the Plant of the A.C. Sparkplug Company." *American Ceramic Society Bulletin*, 5, no. 6 (June 1922): 267-275.

McGinnis, Mack. "A Little History of Faience Tile." *Keramic Tile Journal*, 2, no. 7 (July 1930): 26-27.

Morrissey, Edward L. "Salesmanship." *Keramic Tile Journal*, 3, no. 3 (March 1931): 27-29.

Muller, Herman J. *The University of Detroit 1877-1977: A Centennial History*. Detroit, Michigan: The University of Detroit, 1976.

New York Times. "Prescribes Rainbow Tiles Only for Bathrooms of Rich." Business Section (November 1, 1925): 1.

Pederson, Jay P. *CVS Corporation, 45*. Detroit, New York, San Francisco: James Press, n.d.

Purviance, Evan and Louise. *Zanesville Art Tile in Color*. Des Moines, Iowa: Wallace-Homestead Book Co., 1972.

Rago, David. *American Art Pottery*. New York, New York: Knickerbocker Press, 1997.

Reed, Cleota. "The Smoker." *Tile Heritage*, 1, no. 2: 18-20.

Rhead, Frederick H. "American Ceramic Society Exhibition – The First American Ceramic Society Ceramic Display." *American Ceramic Society Bulletin*, 1, no. 1 (May 1922): 10-17.

Roberts, Ann Rockefeller. *The Rockefeller Family Home, Kykuit*. New York, New York: Abbeville Press, 1998.

Sekora, John J. *Ceramic Tile in 20th Century America*. Bay Head, New Jersey: Tile Contractors' Association of America, 2003.

Sims, Michael S. "Working in American Tile Factories, 1875-1945." *Tile Heritage*, Vol. V, No. 1, Summer, 1998.

Sinkevitch, Alice, Editor. *AIA Guide to Chicago*. New York, San Diego, London: Harcourt Brace & Co., 1993.

St. Matthew Church. *St. Matthew Church History 1911-1986*. Flint, Michigan, c. 1986.

Sweet's Architectural Catalogue, 1926.
_____, Twenty-Second Annual Edition, 1927-1928, Section B, F.W. Dodge Corporation, 1927: B1434-1435.
_____, 1930 Edition, Volume B, F.W. Dodge Corporation, 1929: B2025.
_____, 1931, Volume B, F.W. Dodge Corporation, 1930: B3081.

Tile Heritage Foundation. "A Celebration of American Tile Traditions." *Flash Point*, 12, nos. 1, 2 (January-June 1999): 1, 8-9.

Townsend, Everett. "Development of the Tile Industry in the United States." *American Ceramic Society Bulletin*, Vol. 22, No. 5, May 15, 1943.

Uncatalogued glaze recipes from Flint Faience and Tile Company, donated by Taine G. McDougal to the Sloan Museum in 1972.

Underwood, Barbara D. "From Barnum to Beaumont: The History of a School."

Unpublished, typed manuscript dated May, 1991.

Wires, E. Stanley, Norris F. Schneider, and Moses Mesre. *Zanesville Decorative Tiles*. Zanesville, Ohio, 1972.

www.cr.nps.gov/NR/travel/atlanta/fox.htm (Fox Theatre/Yaarab Temple, Atlanta, GA) 8/18/03

www.terrellhertiagesociety.org/texas%20midland%20railway%car.htm (Col. E. Green) 4/5/02

www.virtualvermont.com/history/hgreen.html (Hetty Green) 5/10/03

Index